WOMAN
and
NATURE

Literary
Reconceptualizations

by
MAUREEN DEVINE

The Scarecrow Press, Inc.
Metuchen, N.J., & London
1992

British Library Cataloguing-in-Publication data available

Library of Congress Cataloging-in-Publication Data

Devine, Maureen.
   Woman and nature : literary reconceptualizations / by Maureen
Devine.
      p.   cm.
   Includes bibliographical references and index.
   ISBN 0-8108-2612-7 (acid-free paper)
   1. American fiction--Women authors--History and criticism.
2. Women and literature--United States--History--20th century.
3. Canadian fiction--Women authors--History and criticism.
4. American fiction--20th century--History and criticism. 5. Women
and literature--Canada--History--20th century. 6. Feminism and
literature. 7. Nature in literature. I. Title.
PS374.W6D48 1992
813'5099287--dc20   92-33985

for Ryan and Luke, especially

Contents

Contents

Acknowledgements

Among those who have contributed to the ultimate shape of this book, I would especially like to mention Heinz Tschachler, Franz Kuna, and Peter V. Zima for their valuable recommendations, and Walter Hölbling and Kathy Cullen, who were both exemplary readers of the manuscript in its entirety, for their many suggestions, and to Hans Köberl for his technological know-how. The obvious absence of many female names here is due simply to the fact that there were hardly any women in Austria working in this field at the time I was writing; more recently, the situation has minimally improved. A stronger feminist input of ideas would have been welcome, and undoubtedly would have positively influenced the final result. In view of this, all the more appreciation is due to my supportive male colleagues, and to the strong women in my family.

Acknowledgement is also due for the poems of Emily Dickinson, "To Make a Prairie" and "Who Robbed the Woods", and the lines from "Tell all the Truth", reprinted by permission of the Belknap Press of Harvard University. Parts of this book have been previously published in slightly different form in *Utopian Thought in America: Untersuchungen zur literarischen Utopie und Dystopie in den USA*, ed. Arno Heller *et al.* Tübingen: Gunter Narr, 1988; and in *Women in Search of Literary Space*, ed. Gudrun Grabher and Maureen Devine. Tübingen: Gunter Narr, 1991.

Preface

The focus of this study is the relationships portrayed between woman and nature in some contemporary feminist novels, for feminist authors are looking at each of these concepts in ways that point to a reconceptualization that attempts to move away from the traditional dualistic patterns that define woman and nature only in opposition to man and culture. Very much part of the contemporary ecology and feminist movements, which have in turn appropriated contemporary academic trends in philosophy, linguistics, and psychoanalysis, the fictional texts embody dynamic elements of interaction with all of these disciplines.

The seminal ideas for this study have been germinating over the last several years, gaining some substance with each new feminist text I have studied, and gaining urgency with each new ecological disaster reported in the news media. Often enough there seem to be points at which feminist political agendas and ecological political agendas coincide, and for both groups, feminists and ecologists, there is a concern with "defining" the concepts central to them, namely woman and nature.

While this study is more modest in its endeavors than offering solutions for ecological or feminist political agendas, there seems to be a point, or a space, where the issue of the relationship between woman and nature emerges. It is here that the necessity of "defining" or clarifying the concepts of woman and nature appears to be clearest and most difficult. (I use the term "define" in this study sparingly, to avoid the impression of reductionist and essentialist meanings for woman and nature.) Both the feminist and ecology movements are shaking the foundations of these concepts, which are deeply embedded in our Western dualistic mode of thinking. Are there any ways of "defining" or conceptualizing woman other than by her dualistic counterpart man, and nature other than by its dualistic counterpart culture?

While these are some of the underlying considerations of this study that lie outside of traditional literary criticism, the questions I raise and answers I propose lie within the realm of feminist fictional

ix

texts, for the boundaries of "reality" and experience can be disregarded in fiction, and the fictional contexts can provide new possibilities for focusing on the concepts of woman and nature. This study, then, treats fictional texts by seven contemporary feminist writers of Canada and the USA who I believe have made stimulating statements in their texts on the concepts of woman and nature. These include: Margaret Atwood, *Surfacing*; Margaret Laurence, *The Diviners*; Marge Piercy, *Woman On The Edge of Time*; Sally Miller Gearhart, *The Wanderground*; Marilynne Robinson, *Housekeeping*; Alice Walker, *The Color Purple*; and Gloria Naylor, *The Women of Brewster Place*. The texts were published in the seventies and early eighties, a period in which feminist literature made great strides in both the publishing world and academia; a decade that saw an increasing awareness of the importance of ecology and ecological issues.

The difficulties inherent in such a study center on the complexities of the levels of language and gender analysis, the theories of language and gender that have become prominent in the last two decades, and the all-too-obvious role of dualism critique within those levels of analysis. For what has crystallized out of the preliminary investigation are the two major critical discourses that name the two parts of this study: ecofeminism and gynocriticism. Each discourse raises the issues of language and gender, ecofeminism from the ideology of feminist environmental criticism, and gynocriticism from the ideology of feminist literary criticism.

In each of the two parts of this study, then, chapters on nature, gender and language attempt to analyze the body of fictional texts in light of current theoretical considerations, and to consider how these discourses have influenced and been influenced by these texts. In part one, "Ecofeminism", the initial chapter discusses issues of ecofeminism as they are incorporated in the fictional texts, issues like the "other", the domination of woman in patriarchal society, the parallel domination of nature, and the views and attitudes toward nature. These issues tend to be paradoxical — on the one hand they seem to support the presumed relationship between woman and nature, and on the other hand critically undermine it. The following chapter turns to the issue of gender, for just as the concept of nature has been culturally determined, so has gender. Gender and gender roles have been treated with a great deal of complexity in the fictional texts. Because feminist interpretations of Freudian theories of gender offer a particularly rich field for discussion, this chapter considers the contributions of Juliet Mitchell, Nancy Chodorow, and Luce Irigaray to a feminist interpretation of Freud as it might interconnect with ecofeminist considerations of woman and nature in the fictional texts. In chapter 4, "Woman and Words" the issue of language is considered. Some contemporary feminist contributions to theories of language are taken up, particularly Julia Kristeva's; also the authors of the fictional texts are keenly aware of the implications language has for them as writers and for their protagonists.

In part two, "Gynocriticism" is concerned with a dialogue among gynocritics texts, the so-called "trans-Atlantic" critical circle, and the fictional texts on the issue of woman and nature. Thus, this section begins with an analysis of the author's uses of nature as the fictional elements of metaphor and theme. Following in chapter 6, "Literarity and Gender", three aspects of gender in fiction are discussed: "androgyny", with all its ensuing complications, as a possibility of reconstructing gender in literature, as primarily associated with Carolyn Heilbrun, as well as "the lesbian" alternative and "the mother" complex. And chapter 7, "Literarity and Words" concerns the strategies of written language the authors use in these feminist fictional texts. The final chapter, "Intertextuality and Reconceptualization", includes a discourse critique of ecofeminism and gynocriticism based on Kristeva's concept of intertextuality, examining the ways in which these discourses have been influenced and changed by the textual-literary discourse, and also how the discourse has influenced the novels. As this study is arranged topically, most of the fictional texts are discussed in each chapter, a procedure that might have lead to some overlapping, but, I hope, not repetition.

The authors and texts discussed in this study portray a variety of views on the concepts of woman and nature, and as a body, typify the dynamic role of woman in text and context. On the narrative level, all of these works have a common general theme: they all concern the felt need of establishing a female identity and of coming to terms with what it means to be a woman in our society. All of these works were published in the seventies and early eighties during the ascendance of both the feminist and ecology movements, which have made tremendous impact on North American society. Because the writers are feminists, it seems they would consciously reflect the concern with concepts of woman and nature and issues relating to them, including that of dualism.

This study asks some specific questions of the fictional texts using the frame of reference of the two discourses, ecofeminism and gynocriticism. These can be arranged into the what and the how: what concepts of woman and nature do the authors create — one freed from the constraint of dualisms, i.e., woman not opposed to man, nature not opposed to culture? Or what contributions have they made to this possibility of reconceptualizing them? How do the contemporary theories on language and gender interplay with the fictional texts? How do the fictional texts affect the discourses, how do the discourses get transformed in the texts?

The questions I am suggesting have many implications for theoretical study in an area that, with precious few exceptions, has not been directly addressed. Ecofeminism enjoyed a fleeting recognition as a serious academic discourse, before being taken into the esoteric by some of its more overly enthusiastic proponents. Still, however, I feel it offers one of the most promising approaches for developing new concepts of woman and nature while retaining its academic credentials. Gynocriticism, in its interpretative approach to feminist fiction, must ultimately take into account the numerous faces of feminism and fiction that lead to developing new concepts of woman and nature. Indeed, in the fictional texts discussed in this study, there are clear tendencies in this direction. And finally, I do not claim these two discourses are the only ones able to elucidate the problem addressed in this study, but they are certainly essential ones.

Maureen Devine
University of Klagenfurt
Klagenfurt,
Austria

What is woman?

(Sigmund Freud)

There is no such thing as woman.

(Jacques Lacan)

...the symptom is there — women are writing, and the air is heavy with expectation: what will they write that is new?

(Julia Kristeva)

A woman's writing is always feminine; it cannot help being feminine; at its best it is most feminine; the only difficulty lies in defining what we mean by feminine.

(Virginia Woolf)

1

Preliminaries

Particularly in the last two decades there has been a proliferation of women's writing at the base of which lie some questions concerning the concepts of woman and nature. That female is associated with nature and male with culture, each in opposition to the other, is a long established assumption, one of the basic dualisms in Western thought.[1] But women now are taking issue with the validity of this assumption, seeing that it relegates them to a position of "otherness", inferiority, and powerlessness relative to culture and male.

Certainly this is a highly political and ideological arena; political in the sense of relating to power structures, particularly those structures comprising a dominant culture geared toward male-oriented goals and controlled by hierarchical structures whose very logic and design results in the suppression of non-dominant groups like women. Feminist writers, too, have concerned themselves with such feminist issues as woman's role in society/culture and her relationships to nature; they are part of a feminist movement that has as its axiom "the personal is the political". This axiom has been further refined for feminist literary criticism by Sandra Gilbert as "the aesthetic is political, the literary is political, the rhetorical is political", because "every text can be seen as in some sense a political gesture and more specifically as a gesture determined by a complex of assumptions about male-female relations."[2]

This study further rests on the assumptions that fictional texts work through ideological patterns depicting and interpreting experience, and that feminist authors write such texts through a feminist ideology.[3] Indeed, a definition of ideology as a "system of representations by which we imagine the world as it is"[4] seems particularly suited to fictional texts. Rachel Blau DuPlessis goes one step further to say that "narrative may function on a small scale the way ideology functions on a large scale",[5] that is, fictional texts (here synonymous for her with narrative) produce the ingredients that define (fictional) boundaries for experience. These boundaries for experience, indeed, the ingredients that define it, like plot, conflicts, patterns, characters, metaphors, etc., are crucial issues for feminist writers and critics, because they are charting new definitions and redefining the boundaries of experience from a feminist ideology. In this sense ecofeminism and gynocriticism operate as discourses[6] organized around such a feminist ideology.

Ecofeminism and Gynocriticism

Among the essential elements of feminist ideology are the concepts of woman and nature implicated in dualism, and thus there results an implicit dualism critique, which attempts to extricate these concepts from those of man and culture. For example, in the seventies women began to make connections between their exploitation in what is seen as a patriarchal socio-political system and the system of exploitation of the environment. During this time and since, writings by scientific historians, psychologists, theologians, anthropologists and others have attempted to explain the ways in which the power structures of Western society (in this study specifically North

American, as influenced by Western European) have bonded woman and nature through the centuries, and have begun to delve into this imposed relationship between woman and nature to expose and identify the workings of it, past and present.

   Ecofeminism as discourse evolved out of the ecology movement in the early seventies,[7] and is connected with such theoretical writings as Ynestra King's "The Eco-feminist Imperative" and "Toward an Ecological Feminism", Mary Daly's *Gyn/ecology*, Carolyn Merchant's *The Death of Nature*, and others.[8] While King and Merchant avoid valorizing the identification of woman and nature, concentrating on historical analyses of this phenomenon combined with a strong critique of dualistic thought, the valorization at the core of the Daly text and a number of non-fictional texts by literary artists like poets Susan Griffin and Adrienne Rich[9] emphasizes the virtuous, good, and thus the morally superior character of woman and nature in relation to the patriarchal culture that dominates them. Such valorization can become problematical to a deconstruction of dualism. These ecofeminists are all united, however, in identifying the patriarchy as responsible for the destruction of both nature and woman: The alienation of man from nature puts him in a position of control and dominance. Man no longer sees himself as part of nature and has put himself in the hierarchy above all, which gives him the implicit right to exploit those beneath him.

   While it might be tempting to accept this analysis, succumbing to such a valorization of woman, and by implication nature, it is dangerously close to casting woman and nature in the role of the helpless, but morally pure, victim. This is analogous to succumbing to the dualism that ecofeminism has, in many ways, set about to critique. For, writing in 1980, on the celebration of Earth Day, King, one of the founding organizers of the ecofeminist movement, clearly states,

> We believe that a culture against nature is a culture
> against women ... It is time to reconstitute our culture
> in the name of that nature. (11)

King's statement is an attempt to reconsider the duality of man/culture versus woman/nature, because she assumes that women regard themselves as part of the culture that needs reconstituting in the name of nature ("our culture"). This is also an implication that women have sufficient power to consider deconstructing the concept of culture associated primarily with the male, and more succinctly, an invitation to see nature as a dynamic cultural construct, but not from an anthropocentric perception. These issues, it seems to me, are the central ones of ecofeminist discourse that must not only explore the identification of woman and nature, but also question it, and then move through the process of paradox. For by removing the dualistic constructs that unite woman and nature in opposition to man and culture, one must move on to explore the separate entities of woman and nature in other relationships and differences beyond opposition. These other possible relationships might expose the ideological contributions of ecofeminism.

Some of those ecofeminists who tend to valorize the identification between woman and nature focus on historical and theological analyses of the development of this identification over centuries and millennia; others focus on current activities in which women are leaders in ecological, anti-nuclear, and peace issues; and still others focus on spiritual aspects like the celebrations of rituals meant to reaffirm connections to pre-patriarchal goddesses, and the like.[10] While all of these are ecofeminist groupings, the latter seems to have left an irrevocable image of ecofeminism as an esoteric discipline that has left many academic feminists dubious of its critical potential. The Marxist feminists are especially skeptical about these valorizations, for they quite rightly accuse these groups of sidestepping the central issues and see the results of these fringe activities as further separating woman from central issues. Nevertheless, ecofeminism in the seventies and early eighties, concurrent with the rise of the ecology movement, made an impressive impact on women's literature, both fiction and non-fiction.[11]

Besides being a movement that brings together branches of both the ecology and feminist movements, ecofeminism has spawned a literary outgrowth in that some novels and writers have been referred to as "ecofeminist". However, such labels on literary texts seem to limit the works to a narrow interpretation of woman's relationship to nature, whereas the fictional texts themselves offer broadening views on the subject, and even occasionally confront its central paradox — calling into question the very identification between woman and nature that is its premise. In order to work through the issues, a form is needed, as King suggests above, to break through the idea of woman and nature as object, as, for example, Margaret Atwood attempts in *Surfacing*, when at the end her protagonist feels the woods and its spirits as neither masculine nor feminine elements, but neutral ones. The extent to which the fictional texts discussed here treat the relationship between woman and nature, thematically, or metaphorically, freed of their dualistic constraints, is indicative of the extent to which the writers are participating in the process of reconceptualizing them.

The second discourse of this study, *gynocriticism*, on the other hand, concerned as it is with woman and fiction, developed out of a feminist literary criticism, which began as a criticism of misogyny in literature,[12] and later turned to women writers. Feminist critics discovered that, as Elaine Showalter writes, "women writers had a literature of their own, whose historical and thematic coherence, as well as artistic importance, had been obscured by the patriarchal values that dominate our culture".[13] What was discovered was a long, if largely isolated and canonically ignored woman's tradition in literature. Patricia Meyer Spacks' *The Female Imagination*, Tillie Olsen's *Silences*, Ellen Moers' *Literary Women*, Elaine Showalter's *A Literature of Their Own*, Sandra Gilbert and Susan Gubar's *A Mad Woman in the Attic*, concern the perception of women's writing in a feminist context and take a decidedly historical perspective, although each offers a different perceptual framework.[14] For example, the Gilbert and Gubar text looks to the nineteenth century female writer and the challenges she faced in breaking social barriers and rewriting literary constructs in her texts. As discourse, gynocriticism is strongly associated with Showalter, who defined the specific phenomenon of "gynocritics" in "Toward a Feminist Poetics":

> The second type of feminist criticism is concerned
> with *woman as writer* — with woman as the pro-
> ducer of textual meaning, with the history, themes,
> genres, and structures of literature by women. Its

subjects include the psychodynamics of female creativity; linguistics and the problem of a female language; the trajectory of the individual or collective female literary career; literary history; and, of course, studies of particular writers and works. No term exists in English for such a specialized discourse, and so I have adapted the French term *la gynocritique*: "gynocritics ..." (128-9)

Gynocritics, like ecofeminism, is not unproblematic. Showalter's and similar definitions by Annette Kolodny, Sandra Gilbert, Josephine Donovan, Rosalind Coward, Susan Gubar,[15] and numerous others would have been left unquestioned in the American critical world had not a small but significant "trans-Atlantic" group brought the writings of the French post-modern critics to America. To a great extent, the writings by the Anglo-American feminist critics mentioned above in the eighties have turned to a discussion of the so-called French feminist theories and critics (Julia Kristeva, Hélène Cixous, Luce Irigaray, as well as, mainly, Jacques Derrida, Jacques Lacan, Gilles Deleuze, and Roland Barthes) who in many complex ways are "anti-feminist".[16] So that now, in the nineties, feminist literary criticism as gynocritics is certainly not as simple as it was some fifteen years ago. Nevertheless, Alice Jardine, one of the prominent "trans-Atlantic" critics can claim,

The analysis of female literary traditions, of the intersections between texts by women and prevailing literary conventions, and of female revisions of literary movements has changed the face of American literary criticism. (53)

However, feminist literary criticism genderizes itself in order to free itself from being genderized by a mainstream (male) literary criticism; in other words, "defining" itself to avoid being defined by others. But as a process, it continually reviews, reconceptualizes, and develops itself. In this context, feminism could move itself out of the gender problem,[17] but to a certain extent it is still involved in a sort of "empirical categorizing of texts" along gender lines.[18] This stance is complicated by the influences of the contemporary French critics, who have gained considerable attention in the USA, and who tend to view gender as particularly suspect, and even would view feminists who think in the traditional categories of women in opposition to men as being "male" themselves. These critics have divorced gender from biology, but by using the term "feminine" to define oppositional aspects in the dominant language order have made the field intensely complex.

Thus, while Showalter is concerned with gynocritics as an attempt to "construct a female framework for the analysis of women's literature" (131), in part to free it from a male tradition that is inadequate to an understanding of the context of a female tradition, she is relying on a dualistic theoretical stance that is being questioned and deconstructed. While Showalter calls this phenomenon "gynocritics", the slight variation, "gynocriticism" I use here, is concerned more with a dialogue of the texts: the dialogue emanating from and between gynocritics texts, the "trans-Atlantic" critical circle developing from a French feminist post-modern critique, and the fictional texts.

Interdisciplinary Context

Such a textual dialogue, however, has its basis in an interdisciplinary context that encompasses common ground. Both ecofeminism and gynocriticism as discourses emerged out of a feminist movement that has itself evolved from an on-going questioning and analysis of the very concept of woman and her role in society. It is clear that both discourses must confront dualism in the form of coming to terms with the concept of woman, and in parallel form with the concept of nature. In dealing with such complex issues as woman and nature one comes across numerous contradictions and inconsistencies, most of which relate to changing viewpoints on the issues themselves as espoused by the main branches of feminism that have evolved since the sixties. Furthermore, a discussion of woman and nature in terms of their dualistic counterparts is hardly avoidable at this point in time. The following overview is to point out the various directions this controversy has taken in an interdisciplinary context before we turn to the literary texts.

In fact, contemporary feminism has been deeply concerned with the dualisms of male/culture verses female/nature, beginning with Simone de Beauvoir's now classic text *The Second Sex.* There she addresses the nature versus culture argument, made popular by Claude Levi-Strauss, to explain the inferior status of women everywhere, and she begins the significant part of her analysis of woman and nature with Levi-Strauss' *Les Structures élémentaires de la parenté*:

> Passage from the state of Nature to the state of Culture is marked by man's [sic] ability to view biological relations as a series of contrasts: duality, alternation, opposition, and symmetry, whether under definite or vague forms, constitute not so much phenomena to be explained as fundamental and immediately given data of social reality. (xx)

Using Hegelian logic, she then explains the importance of opposition:

> ...we find in consciousness itself a fundamental hostility toward every other consciousness: the subject can be posed only in being opposed — he sets himself up as the essential as opposed to the other, the inessential, the object. (xx)

From these seminal ideas, Beauvoir formulated her now famous passage on woman as the Other, which illuminates this very basic assumption about women:

> Man seeks in woman the Other as Nature and his fellow being. But we know what ambivalent feelings Nature inspires in man. He exploits her, but she crushes him, he is born of her and dies in her; she is the source of his being and the realm that he subjugates to his will; Nature is a vein of gross material, in which the soul is imprisoned, and she is the supreme reality; she is contingence and Idea, the finite and the whole; she is what opposes the Spirit,

and the Spirit itself. Now ally, now enemy, she appears as the dark chaos from whence life wells up, as
this life itself, and as the over-yonder toward which
life tends. Woman sums up Nature as Mother, Wife,
and Ideas: these forms now mingle and now conflict,
and each of them wears a double visage. (62-3)

Certainly, Beauvoir does not advocate this identification, but
uses it to describe man's ambivalence toward woman and nature. This,
however, becomes a crucial issue. Can woman in effect disentangle
herself from nature, or can man clarify his relationship to both woman
and nature outside of dualism? To do this, one would have to
undermine the dualistic system of thought inherent in these ideas. As
we will see in the following chapters, attempts in exactly this direction
are being made.

Examples in anthropology, psychology, and literary interpretation of myths and legends also point to this identification between
woman and nature, and clarify how women were accorded their
inferior status and their relationship to nature. As the concept of
culture took on connotations of controlling natural forces, the metaphor
extended to male and female, and, as these are considered opposites,
the metaphor reached backward again, so that nature and culture are
considered opposites.[19]

There are many myths and legends demonstrating these ideas,
some speculating on matriarchal societies, others relying on the earliest
deities, goddesses of fertility, etc.[20] Contemporary feminist writing
also offers new insights into ancient myths and literature. Annis Pratt,
relying on a psychoanalytical approach to criticism, discusses these
early myths and legends in her work *Archetypal Patterns in Women's
Fictions*. One of the patterns established in the early myths is the
conquest of a territory by a male god signified by the rape of its
goddess, whereby he assimilated or usurped her magical powers. The
rape pattern was thus depicted as a primary relationship between the
male god, his newly conquered territory (nature), and its previous
female deity. In these stories, the identification of the female with
nature is complete and the (male) god becomes the oppressor of both.

Similarly, Carolyn Heilbrun, again from a psychoanalytical perspective, uses these earliest literatures for an even deeper glance into a possible matriarchal past. Joan Rockwell suggests that early Greek dramas can be interpreted as a means used to stabilize the relatively new patriarchal society and to stamp out any remaining tendencies toward, or longing for, earlier matriarchies.[21]

These examples demonstrate alternative explanations for the inferior status of women and their imposed relationship to nature. Psychology and anthropology address the issue as well, primarily concerning themselves with the validity of the relationship between woman and nature. Their argument is basically that women, because of their childbearing and related domestic roles, are limited to an existence dictated by their biology. The determining factor of their role is biological, and the women's sphere includes all familial relationships. Thus women are defined as being more "natural" and less "cultural" than men. The conflict arises from the levels of authority based on private and public images. Because authority is public, and women's sphere is the private, authority is not available to women. This becomes the basis of the power struggle inherent in the nature/culture dichotomy that spills over into the ambivalent situation of contemporary women. In part, this ambivalence manifests itself on a psychological level as a loss of a sense of self because women perceive themselves (and are perceived) as powerless.[22] Equally important is the resulting mutual exclusivity of culture and nature that is also implied.

Clearly connected to this nature versus culture idea is the issue of oppression and misogyny. Conquest is implicit in the relationship, with nature and woman on one side, man and culture on the other. Evidence of this is also found in the early Judeo-Christian writings, in which man's conquest of nature was a central theme.[23] The material/ spiritual dichotomy of Biblical intention paved the way for the hierarchal system of our modern thinking, with a male god removed from the earth and bodily cares at the pinnacle. In the Christian tradition, god is personified as a man neither born of woman nor subject to other physical processes like bodily decay after death. Through the systematic removal of god from natural processes and external nature, animal and human hierarchy was legitimized. With nature, including human nature, no longer sacred and spiritual, domination and exploitation were readily justified by the existing patriarchal powers.[24]

Both Mary Daly, radical feminist theologian, and Susan Griffin, poet and writer, trace the long development of misogynistic violence and the relationship between woman and nature. Through the Roman Catholic Church, patriarchal society by the Middle Ages had defined and promoted roles for women they could most easily be controlled by physically and socially, namely, the virgin, the mother, and the whore. This resulted in the systematic exclusion of women from meaningful roles in both political and religious life, that even for the powerful classes, for example, meant the repression of women in monogamous marriage in order to control primogeniture laws, etc. With the rise of modern science, the power of the church began to wane, but by then philosophical and scientific justifications for the control of nature, metaphorically linked to woman, were well-established.[25]

The scientific historian and early ecofeminist, Carolyn Merchant in her work, *The Death of Nature*, traces the development of misogyny through the 15th and 16th centuries. While the means for the scientific and technological exploitation of nature were not highly developed until that time, the means for the exploitation of women were well-developed in androcentric and misogynistic customs and laws. In their violent extremes in Europe, this exploitation encouraged the infamous witch-burnings, and also paved the way for scientific medicine to take over the control of women's bodies in their most specific female function, birthing. As a long-term consequence, women were also excluded from effectively participating in the political processes that eventually shaped the development of modern science.[26] Even today there exists "a literal identification of the male with technology."[27] Thus women were relegated to the position related to nature, and men to culture. These positions are again very evident in the period of the settlement of North America.

In looking at America's early writings, as Annette Kolodny has done, there is a marked transfer of the earlier Biblical ideologies onto the New World. In *The Lay of the Land*, she analyzes the numerous metaphors the earliest explorers used to describe the Garden of Eden (i.e., the garden of plenty before man was corrupted by

woman), and more specifically explicit sexual images like "virgin
lands", and "unspoilt forests". But beneath these metaphors and images
is the concept of imposing civilization and culture on this wilderness.
Kolodny calls this metaphor "a psycho-historical element of importance
for understanding the dilemma toward and destruction of the environment" (iv). In *The Land Before Her*, she examines how women had a
different view of the pioneering ideas, especially this Garden of Eden
myth:

> The psycho-sexual dynamic of a virginal paradise
> meant, however, that flesh and blood women — at
> least metaphorically — were dispossessed of para-
> dise. From the early decades of the 17th century on-
> ward, therefore, the English-speaking women ...
> struggled to find some alternate set of images through
> which to make their own unique accommodation to
> this strange and sometimes forbidding New World
> landscape. (3)

So to a certain extent women did not (metaphorically)
participate in this essential American experience. Essential, because it
is assumed that the central experience of entering the wilderness and
being reborn is what has shaped the American (male?) mind.[28]
Woman could not emerge from the wilderness and be reborn in nature,
because she "was" nature. She was what man needed to civilize, and
that, too, is part of the American image. In re-thinking woman's
relationship to nature, however, contemporary writers are attempting
to create, or at least attempting to address the possibility of other
relationships (as will be taken up later).

The Canadian experience in the wilderness however was
slightly different, and there is a prevailing ambiguity in the relationship
of Canadian authors to their natural environment, as will be evident in
discussing the novels of Margaret Laurence and Margaret Atwood.
Atwood, in her early critical work, *Survival*, suggests that a recurring
theme in Canadian literature is nature as monster rather than as idyllic
pastoral landscape, active rather than passive, as bringer of death
through drowning, starvation, freezing or becoming lost in the bush

(55). It is also worth pointing out here the difference in the historical concepts of nature in the US and Canada. Whereas in the US the Garden of Eden/paradise ideology and the virgin-to-be-conquered metaphor were the prevailing views, in Canada a perception of nature that incorporated fear and danger developed combined with a more pragmatic use of the environment. The difference between the Canadian and US views is related to the Canadian ties to European concepts of nature in contrast to the American emphasis on breaking away from Europe and its influences — influences which included not only the later "typical" Romantic view of nature as soothing spirit, but also the development of a more complex view of nature.[29]

But in an American historical context, nature in the form of wilderness is an essential element of the American experience. Indeed, if we look at "mainstream" American literature, there are some clearly definable trends. Especially in the colonial period, woman is associated with nature, and throughout the nineteenth century, wilderness was seen as chaos, disorder, dangerous and immoral, as indeed was woman.

In the Puritan view, these same images prevailed, for wilderness was evil, and the Puritan settlements were holy islands blessed by God. But as Roderick Nash in *Wilderness and the American Mind* points out, in a curious way the wilderness was also their salvation from a "corrupting" European civilization (35). Similarly, Puritan attitudes toward woman contain the same images of evil and are best exemplified by the only large-scale New World witch trials in Salem, Massachusetts, in the 1690's.[30]

In the first half of the nineteenth century, the Romantic movement in the US had tried to make nature respectable for it was then possible to live in the US without ever coming into contact with the wilderness, but this was a movement of the gentility.[31] In general, the pioneer viewpoint was more popular and widespread, and texts like Cooper's *Leatherstocking Tales* romanticized the qualities of the wilderness (and woman), and his Natty Bumppo became the archetypal figure, remaining pre-adolescent and moving in a wilderness full of repressed female sexuality.[32]

By the end of the nineteenth century, however, once the American wilderness had been tamed and settled, woman was "redefined" and burdened with the negative and inhibiting role of civilizing agent, holding the American man back from adventure. This redefinition can be seen in novels like Mark Twain's *Huck Finn*, where the portrayal of Aunt Sally as representative of civilization is such that Huck, of course, runs away, and in the end, faced with the prospect of returning to her, has had enough of civilization and "lights out for the territories". In later variations, Sinclair Lewis's *Main Street*, and even Margaret Mitchell's *Gone With the Wind*, the female protagonists as civilizing agents have become decadent. This idea again coincides with the changing views on nature and the wilderness, for by 1890, the end of the frontier was at hand, and by 1920 the US had become a full-fledged urban country complete with all the urban ills.

Of course, the views of nature were not so unified and static in the nineteenth century. In a parallel development, Ralph Waldo Emerson, in his essay "On Nature", conveys his belief that the whole of nature is a metaphor of the human mind. But this view, while important, remained associated with the New England Transcendentalists. Its practical fruition, in the work of environmentalists like John Muir, was the creation of the national parks to preserve wilderness areas from exploitation by man, for it had become clear that the wilderness had so continuously and consistently been "civilized" that the phenomenon of wilderness had nearly vanished from the continent.

Twentieth century views on nature have also shifted and changed. Theodore Roosevelt, for example, at the turn of the century, found the wilderness "manly". Nash suggests that at that time, coinciding as it did with the end of the frontier and the changing of the US to an urban population, a cult of the wilderness developed that "had more to do with racism, Darwinism, and a tradition of the idealization of the noble savage in his wilderness setting" (94). Literary precursors of this cult, like Walt Whitman and Herman Melville, kindled an interest in savagery, but Nash suggests a more solid base for this cult: "a general feeling that the American male was suffering from over-civilization" (152) and, predictably, woman was left out of the picture. Shortly after the time when Twain was sarcastically at odds with civilization, and Melville was awakening interest in the primitive as an antidote to the over-civilization of the American male, notable exceptions to this shift in views appeared. Kate Chopin's *The Awakening* (1899), in which the female protagonist discovers her sensual sexuality in the power of the Gulf tides and, doomed by her family and New Orleans society, she chooses a watery death, is one such work. But the book was considered outrageous and quickly withdrawn. However, the imagery appears in Willa Cather's *My Antonia* (1918), in which the protagonist becomes a champion of the cultivated landscape infusing qualities of substance to the earth she tills.

Thus, as the North American view of nature has tended to change with historical and social contexts, new metaphors have also evolved. When nature was chaos and disorder and needed to be civilized, it was feminine; when civilization became too much, woman was seen as the civilizing agent, and wilderness became manly, acceptable, coveted; thus, the woman-as-metaphor remains always opposed to the male need, and the male need remains always the desirable end. This turn-of-the-century attitude however can be seen as a brief American detour from the main metaphor, for coinciding with the current ecology movement, the concept of a feminine nature has again become prevalent. Ernest Callenbach's *Ecotopia*, James Dickey's *Deliverance*, Ken Kesey's *One Flew Over the Cuckoo's Nest* and *Sometimes a Great Notion* are only a few of the numerous examples of "mainstream" American literature that return to nature and wilderness and infuse them with feminine elements.

It is clear that the concept of nature in this discussion goes beyond the North American wilderness idea, though in other forms of "nature" the feminine metaphor is disturbingly prevalent as well. In *The Domination of Nature*, William Leiss differentiates three types of nature: the wilderness, the garden (these two are the predominant pastoral images), and "human" nature. Following a Hegel-Marx-Marcusian argumentation, Leiss analyses all these as cultural constructs. If we consider the third aspect of nature, human nature, we confront some disturbing Freudian metaphors of the unconscious as "the feminine", most recently espoused by Derrida and Lacan, and even Kristeva. Deriving from Freud, they call the wild untamable unconscious — that psychological wilderness — the feminine, and psychoanalysis can then be seen as a science whose aim, in provocative terms, is to discover, invade, control and civilize the unconscious *because* it is outside the realm of the conscious and thus metaphysically feminine. As Leiss suggests, psychoanalysis is the most recent expression of the domination of nature, and again, this image of nature is associated with the domination of woman.[33]

The renewed interest in nature as wilderness and garden, the preservation of which is the object of the current ecology movements, began to focus on the previously used system of images in which woman and nature were cast as foils to man's needs. My primary interest is in seeing how the voices of feminist authors approach this association between woman and nature in light of this renewed interest in ecology, ecofeminism, feminist theory, and gynocriticism.

At this point, it is relevant to ask whether the identification of woman with nature reveals anything to us about woman's nature or helps to develop a new concept of woman. Historically, this identifying relationship has supported a system of conquest, abuse, and control that reveals similar attitudes toward woman and nature, but has not functioned to create concepts of woman or nature freed from the constraints of opposition to man and culture. On the other hand, in feminism today, there are those who celebrate the identification of woman and nature, and those who see a danger in this. Why should woman today be associated with nature, any more than man? Why should woman be identified primarily by her biological function, whereas man is not?[34] The problem of the nature versus culture debate in our present-day seems to be more complex. Why are these concepts considered opposites? Why the necessity of mutual exclusivity? These questions are often raised in the contemporary novels discussed here and lie at the core of many of the contemporary theories on gender and language. In essence then we are discussing the consequences and implications of dualism and the efforts and attitudes of feminist writers, as evidenced in their texts, which support a reconceptualization outside of dualistic constructs.

Since Nietzsche first questioned the validity of dualistic thought, deconstructing the "Big Dichotomies"[35] has increasingly become the concern of twentieth century philosophers and theorists. Women came rather late to the debate, probably due to the status of women in the academy, but since Simone de Beauvoir published *The Second Sex*, the issue has become a central concern of feminists and, later, feminist theory.

Drawing from other disciplines, especially history and anthropology from a feminist perspective, major critical figures like Sherry Ortner, Michelle Rosaldo, or Carolyn Merchant have suggested that significant questions are not being asked, that a tendency to search for or believe in universal facts overshadows or disrupts a variety of complexities that would impose conditions on such universal facts, that cause, effect, essence and excuse are often confused, and that in current academic disciplines, prescriptive declarations quickly follow from descriptive researches.

In her paper, "Is Female to Male as Nature Is to Culture?", for example, Ortner attempts to revise the nature/culture dichotomy slightly by putting woman in an intermediate position between nature and culture, still identified unambiguously with man. Rosaldo, in "The Use and Abuse of Anthropology: Reflections on Feminism and Cross-cultural Understanding", suggests that contemporary social science thinkers of both sexes are trapped in turn-of-the-century, Victorian theories "that cast the sexes in dichotomous and contrastive terms" (404). She also suggests that however convenient and sensible these oppositional modes of thought might be, they are "inherently problematic for those of us who hope to understand the lives that women lead within human societies" (407). Merchant's *The Death of Nature* is also a critique of the oversimplification of casting gender into oppositional roles. They are not alone in suggesting that the dualism of gender is a social construct, just as nature and culture are. Critics of culture and philosophy are also questioning the use of dualistic paradigms that have been in the natural sciences for centuries, and in metaphysics for perhaps millennia.

Returning to Beauvoir, certainly one of the earliest of the contemporary feminists of existentialist leanings, it is relevant to trace current analyses of her position. Especially among the French feminists, who have had greatest influence on American feminist critics, Beauvoir's views have been strongly criticized as too fixed in the Hegelian/Marxist/Sartrean/existentialist vein. From this viewpoint, her primary thesis, that man's oppression of woman is an expression of the universal imperialism of human consciousness, is based on conflict and opposition that would not allow for a less dualistic perspective. Then, too, Beauvoir considers the oppression of women as ahistorical, in that women have always been subordinated to man, and consequently she would reject any notion of a matriarchal society previous to recorded patriarchal ones. In this sense she does not treat women as an oppressed class or race whose oppression spans a certain time.[36] Younger Marxist critics and authors (as we will see with Marge Piercy later) refute this interpretation and tend to discuss woman's oppression in historical terms. At the same time, Marxist theory is being revised by feminists to encompass a wider variety of concepts of class that can be anchored in interpretations of feminist reality.[37] Beyond this, there is evidence of the beginning of a more general critique of the concept of dualism as implying oppositionality and excluding complementarity.[38] In a direct reference to Beauvoirian discourse, Ynestra King, one of the founding organizers of the ecofeminist movement, questions the usefulness of the idea of opposition when she suggests in "The Eco-feminist Imperative", that "Sexism, racism, class divisions, homophobia and the rape of nature depend on this process of objectification" (11) and are both a result of it and dependent on it. Merchant, too, suggests that the sense of opposition is giving way to a sense of holism in which each element and aspect is essential to the workings of the whole, and that "the parts themselves take their meaning from the whole" (293). Holism instead of dualism thus becomes a way of negating the opposition accepted by Beauvoir as an ontological given.

In Alice Jardine's analysis of Jean-Joseph Goux's *Les iconoclastes*, for example, she summarizes his suggestion that the two new sciences of the late nineteenth century, dialectical materialism and psychoanalysis, put forth three parallel phases:

> In the case of Marxism: 1) the separation of Man
> from Nature; 2) Man versus Nature; 3) the interaction
> of Man with *another* Nature (historical materialism).
> In the case of Freudianism: 1) separation from the
> Mother; 2) Man versus Woman; 3) reunion with
> *another* Woman. (33)

In this analysis, woman and nature are clearly the twin objects of

Hegelian dialectic analysis, the problems, so to speak, which Man must confront and resolve. Indeed,

> the end points in these systems are remarkably similar; they involve, respectively, a reuniting of form with matter — *mater*ialism (but only after a period of *pater*ialism) and a new relationship to the feminine. (33)

Current feminist theory, much caught up in discussions of the basis of Marxism and psychoanalysis, takes its place in a process of deconstructing dualism.[39]

In the preceding overview, the interdisciplinary issues to feminism were sketched in order to identify the points of emergence of both of the primary discourses of this study, ecofeminism and gynocriticism. In appropriating them as discourses through which one can analyze and interpret feminist fictional texts and the concepts of woman and nature in those texts, this study deals primarily with the issues of nature, gender, and language as they relate to both of the discourses, and the texts. The discourses are imbedded in the fictional texts, so that the process of looking at the fictional texts through ecofeminism and gynocriticism is complemented by looking at these discourses through the texts. How do the authors deal with the concept of woman, of nature? Do these concepts evolve out of a dualistic mode? What sort of dialogue emerges from these texts? And conversely, have these writers been able to make a contribution to the discourses, extend, modify, change, critique them in any way, or deviate from them? How do the discourses get transformed in the texts?

In each part of this study, ecofeminism and gynocriticism, there are "thematic" or topical chapters relating to woman and nature, and a third chapter relating to the process of discourse, or critique of language; the concluding chapter on intertextuality takes up these latter questions.

The fictional texts used in this study cross lines of nationality, race, and literary genre in order to show that the concepts of woman and nature are so essential to contemporary feminist thought that they are evident in all these "categories" of narrative. Margaret Atwood

(*Surfacing*, 1972) and Margaret Laurence (*The Diviners*, 1974) are Canadian writers; Alice Walker (*The Color Purple*, 1982) and Gloria Naylor (*The Women of Brewster Place*, 1982) are black-American writers; Marilynne Robinson (*Housekeeping*, 1981), Marge Piercy (*Woman on the Edge of Time*, 1976) and Sally Miller Gearhart (*The Wanderground*, 1979) are white American writers, the last two represented by their utopian works. By using such "categories", of course, I do not wish to separate, but instead to more thoroughly emphasize that which unites these diverse texts, namely, their attitudes and approaches to woman and nature and the general theme of reconceptualizing female identity.

Margaret Atwood's unnamed protagonist in *Surfacing* sets out on a quest in the wilds of Canada, and in the process makes some remarkable discoveries about herself. In Margaret Laurence's *Diviners*, Morag Gunn is struggling to define herself in relationship to her daughter, to her own writing, and to her past. In *Housekeeping*, Marilynne Robinson suggests unusual directions for woman's growth embodied in the narrator Ruth, raised completely free of male influence, and her aunt Sylvie, whose unusual "housekeeping" attracts the attention of the townspeople and provides the catalyst for escape from the imposed confines of society. Alice Walker's letter novel, *The Color Purple*, spans the early adolescence and adulthood of a poor black woman in the South, struggling to retain a sense of identity and self-respect in an atmosphere of racism, misogyny and physical violence. Gloria Naylor's *The Women of Brewster Place* concentrates on an urban slum setting in which various female characters come together and fight for physical, psychological and sexual survival. Marge Piercy's protagonist in *Woman on the Edge of Time*, Connie Ramos, is portrayed as the ultimate victim: poor, Hispanic, female, and labeled insane. Through her drug-induced hallucinations, she becomes a "Catcher" of a future utopian society, Mattapoisett of the year 2137, and slips in and out of her "present" to the "future", where the possibilities of a society based on ecological and social harmony and the dignity of woman and man is contrasted to Connie's "present". The second utopian work, Sally Gearhart's *The Wanderground*, explores an all-female society with a close relationship to its natural environment, which is contrasted to the dystopian "City". The four latter works also focus on woman's sexuality and the possibilities of lesbianism as functional aspects of woman's identity, as well as an antidote to heterosexual violence.

These diverse texts are further united by a sense of woman in the process of breaking out of narrative boundaries. The authors seem keenly aware of these boundaries that confine them to certain possibilities of writing about woman, certain possibilities for focusing on nature, and certain limitations in the use of language, their writer's tools. Atwood's line, "It was the language again, I couldn't use it, it wasn't mine", begins a multi-level search through complicity and contradiction, which continues even through the world of silence, expressed in words, by contemporary female protagonists and authors in order to create a space in discourse. Making this space for themselves is a sort of literary act of defiance against the boundaries of fiction that would keep them confined to limited possibilities. The overlapping boundaries, that spatial "no-man's land", between the discourses of gynocriticism and ecofeminism and the fictional texts is where this study takes place.

NOTES

1.cf. Claude Levi-Strauss, *Les Structures élémentaires de la parenté*, qtd. in Simone de Beauvoir; cf. Sigmund Freud, *Civilization and its Discontents*, SE (Standard Edition), 21, pp. 59-145, "A Special Type of Choice of Object Made by Men", SE, 11, pp. 164-175; "Female Sexuality", SE, 21, pp. 223-243. This concept lies at the base of many of his writings; Simone de Beauvoir, *The Second Sex*, trans H. M. Parshley, (N.Y.: Random House, 1974); These ideas are taken up in a feminist context by Luce Irigaray, *Speculum of the Other Woman*, trans. Gillian C. Gill (Ithaca: Cornell UP, 1985); Nancy Chodorow, *The Reproduction of Mothering: Psychoanalysis and the Sociology of Gender*, (Berkeley: Univ. of California Press, 1978); Juliet Mitchell, *Psychoanalysis and Feminism: Freud, Reich, Laing, and Women* (N.Y.:Random House, 1975); Alice Jardine, *Gynesis: Configurations of Woman and Modernity*, (Ithaca: Cornell UP, 1985).

2.Sandra Gilbert, "What Do Feminist Critics Want? Or a Postcard from the Volcano," *ADE Bulletin*, 66 (1980); rpt. in Elaine Showalter, (ed.), *The New Feminist Criticism: Essays on Women, Literature and Theory* (London: Virago Press, 1985), p. 31.

3.I do not intend to concentrate on the concept of ideology here, and rather use it in a broad sense. Among the more useful texts regarding ideology, see P.V. Zima (ed.), *Textsemiotik als Ideologiekritik*, (Frankfurt: Suhrkamp, 1977); Zima, *Ideologie und Theorie: Eine Diskurskritik*, (Tübingen: Francke, 1989); A. J. Greimas and J. Courtés, *Semiotics and Language: an Analytical Dictionary*, trans. Larry Crist, *et al.* (Bloomington: Indiana UP, 1982); G. Kress and R. Hodge, *Language as Ideology*, (London, Boston: Routledge & Kegan Paul, 1979); Rosalind Coward and John Ellis, *Language and Materialism: Developments in Semiology and the Theory of the Subject*, (London: Routledge and Kegan Paul, 1977).

4.Louis Althusser, *For Marx*, trans. Ben Brewster, (London: New Left Books, 1977), p. 233. qtd. also in DuPlessis.

5.Rachel Blau DuPlessis, *Writing Beyond the Ending: Narrative Strategies of Twentieth-Century Women Writers*, (Bloomington: Indiana Univ. Press, 1985), p. 9.

6.I use the term discourse here, because each uses special vocabulary, is connected with particular theorists, and works out of a certain ideology. Discourse as simply narrative text is too broad, for each of the fictional texts discussed here would then be a discourse. To avoid confusing levels of analysis then, ecofeminism and gynocriticism are the primary discourses used here. For defining the term, cf. Michael Stubbs, *Discourse Analysis: The Sociolinguistic Analysis of Natural Language*, (London: Basil Blackwell, 1983); T. A. Van Dijk, *Text and Context: Explorations in the Semantics and Pragmatics of Discourse*, (London: Longman, 1980); and Greimas and Courtés, *Semiotics and Language*.

7.Like many of the theoretical ideas discussed in this study, ecofeminism has a Franco-American connection, in this case Mary Daly attributes the word "eco-feminism" to Francoise d'Eaubonne in her book *Le Féminisme ou la mort*, (Paris: Pierre Horay, 1974), 213-52. cf. Daly, *Gyn/ecology*, (Boston: Beacon Press, 1978, and London: The Women's Press, 1979), p. 9.

8.Ynestra King, "The Eco-feminist Imperative", in Leonie Caldecott and Stephanie Leland (eds.), *Reclaim the Earth: Women Speak Out for Life on Earth*, (London: The Women's Press, 1983); "Toward an Ecological Feminism", in Joan Rothschild, (ed.), *Machina ex Dea: Feminist Perspectives on Technology*, (NY: Pergamon Press, 1983), pp. 118-129; Daly, *Gyn/ecology;* Carolyn Merchant, *The Death of Nature: Women, Ecology and the Scientific Revolution*, (San Francisco: Harper & Row, 1980); and others like Sherry B. Ortner, "Is Female to Male as Nature is to Culture?", in Michelle Zimbalist Rosaldo and Louise Lamphere (eds.), *Woman, Culture, and Society*, (Stanford, CA: Stanford UP, 1974), pp. 67-87; Annette Kolodny, *The Lay of the Land: Metaphor as Experience and History in American Life and Letters*, (Chapel Hill: Univ. of N. Carolina Press, 1975).

9.cf. Susan Griffin, *Woman and Nature: The Roaring Inside Her*, (San Francisco: Harper and Row, 1978); Adrienne Rich, *Of Woman Born: Motherhood as Experience and Institution*, (New York: W. W. Norton, 1977).

10.cf. Daly, *Gyn/ecology*; Starhawk, *Dreaming the Dark: Magic, Sex, and Politics*, (Boston: Beacon Press, 1982); Nor Hall, *The Moon and the Virgin: Reflections on the Archetypal Feminine*, (London: The Women's Press, 1980).

11.In the 1990's there is a welcome move on the part of the influential *MS. Magazine* to have a permanent feature entitled "Ecofeminism" that might very well seem to refocus the critical potential of ecofeminism.

12. Kate Millett's *Sexual Politics*, (N.Y., 1970, and London: Virago Press, 1977) being perhaps the first; noteworthy too is Mary Ellman's *Thinking About Women*, (London: Virago Press, 1979).

13.Elaine Showalter, "Introduction", in Showalter, (ed). *The New Feminist Criticism*, p. 6.

14.Patricia Meyer Spacks, *The Female Imagination* (N.Y.: Alfred A. Knopf, 1975); Ellen Moers, *Literary Women: The Great Writers* (London: The Women's Press, 1978); Elaine Showalter, *A Literature of Their Own: British Women Novelists from Brontë to Lessing*, (London: Virago Press, 1978); Tillie Olsen, *Silences*, (N.Y.: Delacourt Press, 1978); Sandra M. Gilbert and Susan Gubar, *The Madwoman in the Attic: The Woman Writer and the Nineteenth-Century Literary Imagination* (New Haven, CT.: Yale UP, 1979).

15.cf. Kolodny, "Some Notes on Defining a 'Feminist Literary Criticism'", *Critical Inquiry*, 2/1 (Fall 1975), 75-92; Kolodny, "Dancing through the Minefield: Some Observations on the Theory, Practice, and Politics of a Feminist Literary Criticism," *Feminist Studies* 6 (1980), (rpt. in Showalter (ed.), *The New Feminist Criticism*, pp. 144-167); Sandra Gilbert, "What Do Feminist Critics Want?" in Showalter (ed.), pp. 29-45); Susan Gubar, "'The Blank Page' and the Issues of Female Creativity" *Critical Inquiry*, 8 (Winter 1981); Rosalind Coward, "This Novel Changes Women's Lives: Are Women's Novels Feminist Novels?" *Feminist Review*, 5 (1980) (rpt. in Showalter (ed.), pp. 225-240); Josephine Donovan, ed. *Feminist Literary Criticism: Explorations in Theory*, (Lexington: Univ. Press of Kentucky, 1975).

16. See Chapter 4 for further discussion.

17.We are already seeing texts which particularize the concept of "male/man" out of the cultural code. cf. Harry Brod, (ed.) *The Making of Masculinities: The New Men's*

Studies, (Boston: Allen & Unwin, 1987); and Alice Jardine and Paul Smith, (eds.) *Men in Feminism*, (N.Y., London: Methuen, 1987).

18.cf. Jardine, p. 63.

19.cf. Ortner, pp. 67-87. See also Julia Kristeva, *About Chinese Women*, trans. Anita Barrows (N.Y.: Marion Bayius, 1977).

20.For an interesting discussion of the relationship of women writers to myth, cf. DuPlessis, pp. 106-108.

21.cf. Joan Rockwell, *Fact in Fiction: The Use of Literature in the Systematic Study of Society* (London: Routledge & Kegan Paul, 1974); and Carolyn Heilbrun, *Toward a Recognition of Androgyny* (N.Y.: Alfred A. Knopf, 1973), chpt. 1.

22.cf. Michelle Zimbalist Rosaldo, "Woman, Culture and Society: A Theoretical Overview", in Rosaldo and Lamphere (eds.), pp. 17-42; Ortner, pp. 67-87; Chodorow, "Family Structure and Feminine Personality", in Rosaldo and Lamphere (eds.), pp. 43-66; Chodorow, *The Reproduction of Mothering* pp. 13-30; Rosaldo, "The Use and Abuse of Anthropology: Reflections on Feminism and Cross-cultural Understanding," *Signs*, 5/3 (1980), 389-417.

23.cf. Daly, *Gyn/ecology* , Part I; Merchant, chpts. 1-2; Annis Pratt, *Archetypal Patterns in Women's Fiction*, (Bloomington: Indiana UP, 1981); and Heilbrun, *Towards a Recognition of Androgyny*.

24.cf. Starhawk, pp. 5-7.

25. cf. Daly, *Gyn/ecology*, Part 1; and Griffin, *Woman and Nature*; Merchant, chpts. 1-4.

26.cf. Merchant, chpts. 5 and 7.

27.Joan Rothschild, "Introduction", Rothschild, Ed., *Machina ex Dea: Feminist Perspectives on Technology*, (New York: Pergamon Press, 1983), xviii.

28.cf. Ursula Brumm, *Geschichte und Wildnis in der amerikanische Literature*, Grundlagen der Anglistik und Amerikanistik, 11 (Berlin: Erich Schmidt Verlag, 1980); Brumm, "Nature as Scene or Agent? Some Reflections on its Role in the American Novel", in Teut Andreas Riese (ed.), *Vistas of a Continent: Concepts of Nature in America*, (Heidelberg: Carl Winter Universitätsverlag, 1979); Hans Huth, *Nature and the American*, (Berkeley: U. of California Press, 1957); Roderick Nash,

Wilderness and the American Mind, 3rd ed. (New Haven: Yale UP, 1982); and Richard Slotkin, *Regeneration Through Violence: The Mythology of the American Frontier, 1600-1860.* (Middletown, CT: Wesleyan UP, 1973).

29.For an indepth analysis of these historical perspectives, see Brumm, *Geschichte und Wildnis*; Brumm "Nature as Scene or Agent?"; Kolodny, *The Lay of the Land*; and Margaret Atwood, *Survival: A Thematic Guide to Canadian Literature*, (Toronto: Anansi, 1972).

30.Daly writes authoritatively on the period of witch-crazes, and duly points out that the New World attitudes were indeed different from the European ones, and the witch trials were more or less only vaguely reminiscent of the European mentality. cf. *Gyn/ecology*, chpt. 6.

31.cf. Nash, p. 60.

32.cf. Kolodny, *The Lay of the Land*, pp. 5-6, 81; Nash, pp. 75-80.

33.As we will see in chapter 3, this is in part the basis of the feminist critique of Freudian theory and the subsequent use and abuse of psychoanalysis and woman.

34.cf. Chodorow, *Reproduction of Mothering*, pp. 13-45.

35.cf. Jardine, *Gynesis*, pp. 71ff.

36.cf. Dorothy Kaufmann McCall, "Simone de Beauvoir, *The Second Sex*, and Jean-Paul Sartre", *Signs*, 5/2 (Winter, 1979), 210-11; Judith Butler, "Variations on Sex and Gender: Beauvoir, Wittig, and Foucault", in Seyla Benhabib & Drucilla Cornell, (eds.), *Feminism as Critique: Essays on the Politics of Gender in Late-Capitalist Societies*, (Cambridge: Polity Press, 1987), pp. 128-142.

37.cf. Benhabib and Cornell, (eds.), *Feminism as Critique*; and Lydia Sargent (ed.), *Women and Revolution: A Discussion of the Unhappy Marriage of Marxism and Feminism*, (Boston: Southend Press, 1981).

38.cf. James M. Curtis, *Culture as Polyphony: An Essay on the Nature of Paradigms*, (Columbia: Univ. of Missouri Press, 1978), esp. chpt. 3.

39.This discussion of holism versus dualism in feminism is representative of similar controversies in other academic and scientific fields that are questioning and reevaluating theories basic to their disciplines. Such shifts of position on basic premises can similarly be seen in physics, mathematics, biology, linguistics, and philosophy.

PART I

Ecofeminism

Ecofeminism as discourse has particular theorists associated with it, uses a particular language to express its concepts, and works within a certain ideology. It focuses on an overriding concern about the relationship between woman and nature. This has developed out of a feminist ideology (as a set of ideas through which we "imagine the world as it is") that wants to first come to terms with the concept of woman. This is not the essentialist questions of what she is and how she is different, but rather, what has made her what she is, how she sees herself in relation to man and society, and why she sees herself so. Ecofeminism, then, must confront the contemporary construction of sexuality, and society's representation of man and woman, in order to assert political, social and economic power for women in a framework of equality, which has potentially far-reaching consequences for the organization of our present social system.

Given this as the ideological framework, ecofeminism begins with the assumption that from a historical perspective, woman has been associated with nature, and seeks to analyze the development of this association and how it has led to the domination and exploitation of woman and nature as resources in patriarchal society. A number of critics identified with ecofeminism have written extensively on the topic. From Carolyn Merchant, Sherry Ortner, Ynestra King, and Annette Kolodny[1], we have detailed accounts of parallel use and abuse of woman and nature through the centuries. The images are easily available to us: nature as nurturing mother, the mother earth, virgin woods, images associated with the premodern organic world. It would be simple enough to cast these in the role of the protagonists, with the antagonist (villain?) being modern patriarchal mechanistic society; the market economy, industrialization, technology, progress. In short, everything we identify with our present culture. For ecofeminism as discourse, the process continues beyond structuring this scenario with such obviously defined dualism. Ultimately, as Merchant suggests, such a discourse would seek to liberate both woman and nature "from the anthropomorphic and stereotypic labels that degrade the serious underlying issues" (xvii), and in doing so undermine the very idea of such dualisms.

To a certain extent, the vocabulary and language of ecofeminism is a critique of metaphors and images which have associated woman and nature in dualistic opposition to man and culture, images of oppression and domination. Susan Griffin's work *Woman and Nature* is the example *par excellence* of a critique of female metaphor and nature imagery. Mary Daly's *Gyn/ecology* is also a critique of language itself as a system of oppression and domination used against woman which identifies her through metaphors and images of nature. So, clearly, ecofeminism as discourse is aware of its relationship to language as a value system. As Merchant makes clear in her work, images of woman and nature have had different values associated with them over centuries. As discourse, ecofeminism also influences language as a changing historical system because it is aware of the language of metaphor that has dominated the frame of reference of both woman and nature. In other words, there is a certain deconstructive element at work here that would expose the self-perpetuating value system and language system that identify woman with nature. In doing so, it seemingly contradicts the feminist idea that language is ideological[2] by the very fact that it realizes this.[3] It is at this point that the dynamics of discourse is most clear, and a dialogue of the texts takes place. This dialogue, or intertextuality as Julia Kristeva refers to it, indicates an important process in which understanding the texts involves setting up relationship between, in this case, the theoretical discourse of ecofeminism and feminist fictional texts, in order to create meaning and a new context. With this interaction of discourse and text, the reconceptualization of woman and nature begins by first disconnecting these concepts from their dualistic counterparts, man and culture, and then questioning the larger framework of dualism.

Who robbed the woods,
The trusting woods?
The unsuspecting trees
Brought out their burrs and mosses
His fantasy to please;
He scanned their trinkets, curious,
He grasped, he bore away.
What will the solemn hemlock,
What will the fir-tree say?

(Emily Dickinson)

He says that woman speaks with nature. That she hears
voices from under the earth, that wind blows in her
ears.

(Susan Griffin,
Woman and Nature: The Roaring Inside Her)

To have risked so much in our efforts to mold nature to
our satisfaction and yet to have failed in achieving our
goal would indeed be the final irony. Yet this, it seems,
is our situation.

(Rachel Carson, *Silent Spring*)

"I turned into a tree."

(Alice Walker, *The Color Purple*)

2

Woman and Nature

Feminist authors of fictional texts have to deal in one way or
another with woman's relationship to nature, for the simple reason that
character and setting are integral elements of fiction. The development
of the concepts of woman and nature, as depicted primarily through
the interplay of these elements in the texts, is the focus in this chapter.

In these fictional texts, there is certainly an awareness of literary license and traditions that cast female characters in roles that in one way or another accept woman as the clear ally of nature, both seen in dualistic opposition to man and culture. This perspective is surely not new. Numerous feminist critics have focused on the ways women writers have managed to unobtrusively get around such literary conventions as characters and plot that traditionally enclose and entrap women.[4] Characterization, plot, and setting are one thing, but dealing with much more subtle relationships in language that determine the way we think, and with expressions and analogies that frame our images and metaphors, are quite another. The lines of development are not clearly drawn for the authors focus on the issues in various ways. But, there seem to be some productive areas in which ecofeminism and feminist fiction intersect, and begin to chart new perceptions and concepts that move in the direction of deconstructing this association between woman and nature. In this chapter I will focus on three of these areas: ambiguity and self-perception, domination and destruction, and nature as a cultural construct. The first, ambiguity and self-perception, concerns the extent to which ecofeminism as discourse and the fictional texts are aware of themselves and their paradoxes. In the fictional texts, this is the extent to which the authors develop a critical perspective which addresses dualism and involves the process of deconstruction. The second area, domination and deconstruction, involves the use of the process of victimization as part of a dualistic idiom. The final one, nature as a cultural construct, concerns the extent to which both ecofeminism and the fictional texts confront and depict nature as part of a cultural phenomenon that defines our perception of it.

Ambiguity and Self-perception

To enter the discussion on woman and nature, one needs to be aware of one's own relationship to woman, to nature, to man and to culture before one can begin questioning them. Ecofeminism initiates this process of questioning the traditionally dualistic constructs of woman-man, nature-culture, rather than only explaining their workings. But the concepts are so thoroughly embedded in our dualistic system of thought, which continually defines them and perceives them only in terms of their opposites, that the result is a paradoxical situation: To break through the dualism, ecofeminism begins by accepting the oppositionality of the concepts. In other words, the paradox necessitates arguing from the inside outward. Once woman and nature are not taken to be the dualistic counterparts of man and culture, then a variety of alternatives are possible. How the authors of the fictional texts approach this initial paradox (having to accepts one's oppositional part in the dualism before attempting to break through it) is an important factor, which contributes to a self-critical stance in their texts. That self-criticism is a necessary step for feminism is a concern voiced by feminist critics like Jean Elshtain, who in "Feminist Discourse and its Discontents" comments that "a feminism that cannot criticize itself cannot in the last analysis serve as the bearer of emancipatory possibilities that can never be fixed and defined, once and for all" (612). Ecofeminism, by entering the paradox of dualism critique, moves through self-perception and self-criticism by accepting the premises of dualism and woman's role in it, and prepares the way for "emancipatory possibilities" that could move woman out of the paradox. This process is reflected in the literary works. Indeed, how the authors handle this problem of self-criticism is evident primarily in the way they approach dualisms and also, in particular, in the way they address the problem of the "other". Some resolve the conflict by allowing their protagonists to break out of the boundaries of dualism and, by analogy, acquire a certain self-criticism that questions the basic assumption of a special relationship between nature and women. Only those texts in which the authors develop a critical perspective and work through the paradox to the outside avoid succumbing to the dualism implied in woman and nature and actually contribute to the reconceptualization of woman and nature. It is important to keep in mind here that a resolution of the dualisms is one possibility, albeit a complex and delicate one, and that the results might also reflect this state. Indeed, feminist critic Myra Jehlen's suggestion for handling contradictions seems especially pertinent here:

> There are many ways of dealing with contradictions,
> however, of which only one is to try to resolve them.

> Another way amounts to joining a contradiction —
> engaging it not so much for the purpose of over-
> coming it as to tap its energy.[5]

So, just as a critique of dualism would suggest getting away from either/or answers, or demand more than a negation of dualism, another strategy, along Jehlen's lines, would be to join it to tap its energy. Both Ynestra King, in demanding that women be able to speak in the name of culture, "our culture", and Sherry Ortner, who suggests that women take a role as mediator between nature and culture, are dealing with dualism in this way.[6]

Turning to the literary texts, the authors discussed in this chapter begin with the assumption that woman and nature enjoy an ontological relationship that is inherently in opposition to man and culture. We see themes here that initially support the nature/culture female/male dichotomy. In some of these texts, however, this relationship is set up only to be questioned and rejected, while other authors get hopelessly ensnared in the paradox, and it becomes a complex trap. In the utopian works, the authors focus on the use of technology and gender roles in the communities portrayed,[7] while other works take up other aspects, in which women, through their identification with their natural environment, develop new self-perceptions. In some cases this identification is ultimately rejected or put into another perspective, in other cases this identification is seen in mythical terms and turned inside out to expose its misogynistic basis.

Succumbing to this dualism is, however, a crucial point for developing self-criticism on a literary level. First of all, in most of the works to be discussed here, the protagonists are, at least initially, portrayed as powerless, insecure, dependent on the expectations of (a) man for their self-esteem. All move out of this situation through a process of defining themselves away from such dependencies, i.e., changing their self-perceptions. The paradox becomes evident when the authors allow their characters to remain comfortably in situations that cast their protagonists in the traditional association with nature, while attempting to redefine them as women. They thus become ensnared in the dualism; it plays back on them, thwarting their possibilities. The narratives move through events which the protagonists interpret as oppressive and must confront their own participation in this oppression. This process indicates the beginning of self-criticism and usually progresses until the women break out of the roles that have socially defined them as women. Not all of the authors attempt to break through this paradox; some stay caught up in their dualisms, failing to fully question the basic assumption of a special relationship between nature and woman, while others offer alternative possibilities. All of the fictional texts discussed here use the woman/nature association on a thematic level.

Margaret Atwood's *Surfacing*, the earliest of the novels to be discussed, initiates the feminist issues relevant here. It begins with an assumption about a close relationship between woman and nature, which involves a journey into the past that is concurrent with the journey into the primeval forest.[8] This assumption provides the important setting, in ecofeminist terms, but also forms a set of contradictions and ambiguities that begin to question that relationship. One of these is the contradiction between the protagonist's constructed version of her past and the truth she finally confronts. For example, what she describes as the birth of her child is actually an abortion, the wedding scene is actually a hospital scene. A further important contradiction is the depiction of the Canadian wilderness and Canadians as victims of imperialist American destruction that must be revised when a group of disruptive intruders turns out to be Canadian after all. Yet another contradiction involves the protagonist's use of language[9], which also circumscribes her ambiguous relationship to Joe.

The emergence of these contradictions indicates the necessity of creating a new reality, one which involves the process of exposing the valorization of the relationship between woman and nature. Then, freed of the conflicts, having resolved or rejected the contradictions, or tapped their energy, the protagonist creates a new reality, in this case "the natural woman" (190).

Margaret Laurence's text *The Diviners* enjoys numerous parallels to Atwood's, and I think in a similar, but less intense and less self-conscious way, Laurence moves her protagonist to a type of self-criticism, although she does not work through the oppositional dualisms she uses. To a certain extent, her style of narrative is a form of self-criticism for the protagonist. Morag, a writer, is recalling memories of her past from photo albums, trying to work through the contradictions, continuities, and truths in her life so that she might be able to pass them on to her teenaged daughter. This narrative form allows Laurence to stay outside the paradoxes that Atwood takes on from the inside.

There are similar patterns in the two texts — that of discarding one's past and trying to put on the dress of urbanity and culture only to find that it does not fit, and finally of discovering that the essence of oneself as woman lies in a return to that rural setting of the past to confront the images of nature and culture. Also for both protagonists pregnancy is a means of affirming their femininity and rejecting a masculine culture that wants to negate this aspect of their being (see chapter 6). Morag's husband wants no children to interfere with his career, and, in *Surfacing*, the protagonist's lover insists she has an abortion. Both women ultimately defy this denial of themselves. Morag chooses Jules, a childhood friend, an Indian from her hometown Manawaka, to father her child, as a means of getting in touch with her alienated past, her rural environment, and her situation as outcast. The novel begins and ends with the river that flows both backwards and forwards, Morag's link to the past and the future.

Laurence views the woman/nature, man/culture dualities very subtly, but from the outside. On the level of the individual, her protagonist, Morag, realizes that her daughter must confront the very same problems, the very same sets of paradoxes. In this text it is undoubtedly the contrast to the urban scenes of Toronto, Vancouver, London that emphasizes the rural setting as one in which Morag finds her lifeline. Certainly also it is the dominant culture rather than man in general that is restrictive, stultifying, and negating, for Morag's lover Jules, an Indian, has suffered as she has. At the end, Pique, their daughter, sets off to discover her sense of self in the mountains among her Indian relatives. Morag's thoughtful reminiscences bring her to a conclusion that signifies a spiritual joining with her daughter rather than a geographical separation from her.

The contradictions and ambiguities Morag had worked through concerning her past lead her to a deeper understanding of her relationship to her daughter, and to herself. These include her rejection of her Manawaka surroundings and her step-parents because of their low social standing, but also her later rejection of her social standing through marriage; the clashing of societal expectations with her roles as woman, mother, artist; her sexuality and her relationship with the men in her life. Her self-searching does not, however, extend outward to a more thorough comprehension of the paradoxes at work within her. Instead, her realization that her gift is only temporarily granted ("The gift, a portion of grace, or whatever it was, was finally withdrawn to be given to someone else" [369]) is the final recognition of the ephemeral, and provides a holistic understanding of her place. Unlike Atwood, in staying outside the paradoxes she introduces, Laurence keeps them intact rather than displacing them. So that while the protagonist Morag arrives at a level of critique of herself and her past in relationship to her daughter, it is not within the same dimensions that Atwood has used. To a certain extent, Laurence keeps the woman/nature relationship intact, in that Morag finds her best inspiration in her isolated rural setting and makes much of the natural elements, and in her reveries has only negative connotations associated with the urban settings and her relationships to men. In this instance, Laurence succumbs to an implied association between woman and nature, and would have difficulty in restructuring this relationship. However, in the narrative text there is the implication of passing the unsolved problems of the mother on to the daughter, as if there is a recognition of things left undone.

Different elements are addressed in the two utopian texts, Marge Piercy's *Woman on the Edge of Time* and Sally Miller Gearhart's *The Wanderground*. In *Woman on the Edge of Time*, Piercy has created a protagonist, Connie, who is trapped in a dualistic pattern in which man symbolizes brutality, dominance, fear and hate, arrogance, and power, while woman in every aspect of life is seen as a victim. Connie is a poor Chicana committed to a mental hospital, her daughter having been taken from her, and her lover killed; her oppressive situation — she is continually drugged and eventually chosen for an experimental mind-control operation in which radio-controlled electrodes are to be inserted into her brain — is interrupted by visits from Luciente, a native of a future society of ecological and social harmony.

Through the utopian society of Mattapoisett of the year 2137, which manifests a relationship with nonhuman nature through its village-centered, rural atmosphere, Connie begins to question the universality of the oppositional stance of gender. From the future she can see that gender is culturally determined in her "present" society. Once she breaks through the universal level, it is only a short time before she questions the oppositional stance of gender on her individual level, which leads her to her climactic action against the doctors.

Piercy chooses to stay at the descriptive level, more or less demonstrating how dualism works and, in true utopian fashion, suggesting how a society based on organic principles operates.[10] Connie as a "catcher" does become a sort of mediator moving between the two societies, not unlike Ortner's description of woman's role as mediator between nature and culture. She is, however, too much the victim to be successful. Piercy stays outside, questioning duality from without and thus keeps her protagonist in those dualistic paradigms, rather than allowing her to move to self-criticism and self-perception, as Atwood might have done.

In Sally Miller Gearhart's *The Wanderground* there is a strong dualistic paradigm, and the author also uses violence and repression to emphasize it. She then offers a more positive resolution. There is no single protagonist; rather the text is composed of a series of stories concerning an all-female society, the hill women, in a completely natural wilderness environment and its troubled relationship to the dystopian "City", from which the women or their ancestors escaped. Again, the initial conflict situation depicts the two poles, women and nature in opposition to man and culture. The hill women live in complete harmony with their environment, and have developed powers and skills in order to live out of touch with the culture of the City. The City on the other hand is totally mechanistic, hierarchal and misogynistic.

The mediators between these two societies are not women (as Ortner might like), but men, a group called the Gentles. Gearhart creates a situation in her text, in which the women of the Wanderground are in a sense dependent on the Gentles in the City. A central issue of the text concerns the future relationship between the women and the Gentles, who are developing their innate powers similar to those of the women. There is a sense of inevitability that the women will have to accept the Gentles on a much more equal basis, a situation that the women initially see as threatening. This acceptance is a challenge to the purity of their feminist stance, for most of the women of the Wanderground accept the mutually exclusive oppositional dualism that completely separates woman and nature from man and culture. The representatives of the women warily overcome their opposition and reluctance in the course of the meeting and end it with a pledge of mutual respect.

This approach certainly represents an attempt by Gearhart to offer a mediating plane between the two extremes, the misogynist men of the City and the women of the Wanderground. The struggle for power in this chapter belies its ending, although there is a development which suggests that the women have become strong enough to accept this challenge to their autonomy. This autonomy marks an initial step toward a self-critical stance. By creating the role of the Gentles, Gearhart holds out a possibility of overcoming the dualism between woman/nature and man/culture, but unfortunately this is not pursued further in the text.

In *The Color Purple*, Walker presents numerous examples of oppositional dualisms in the form of thematic issues, i.e. black/white, rich/poor, victim/aggressor, dialect/standard, man/woman, culture/nature, most of which remain superficially addressed or completely unexplored. She does treat, however, the ones that concern ecofeminism very differently from the texts already discussed. The main text of the novel consists of letters written by Celie over a period of about 50 years. In her younger years they are addressed to God and later to her sister Nettie, a missionary in Africa, whose letters to Celie comprise a secondary text. As an adolescent and young adult, Celie, an uneducated Southern black, is subjected to physical and sexual abuse first from her step-father, then from her husband, Albert, whom she refers to as "Mr. ___". Through her growing love for the jazz singer Shug Avery, who is also her husband's lover, Celie learns what love and sexuality really are, learns to respect and love herself, leaves her oppressive home situation, and eventually becomes a successful seamstress and entrepreneur. The numerous secondary characters that move in and out of her letters create ample opportunities for her insightful comments on her own growth and maturity. Nettie's letters to Celie on the other hand, are concerned primarily with descriptions of Africa regarding colonial exploitation, and provide a counterpoint to Celie's own exploitation. The final harmonious happy ending is unusual for contemporary fictional texts, but nonetheless problematic, for too many issues are left unresolved in an aura of emotionally moving sentimentality. Crucial to this discussion of ecofeminism are, of course, the culture/nature, male/female and, as I will explore more thoroughly later, the aggressor/victim dichotomies she addresses. These dualisms Walker manages particularly well in letters to Nettie. Her approach differs from the previously discussed works, for initially Celie has no sense of identification with her natural surroundings. On the contrary, her rural environment symbolizes her poverty and her oppression, so emphatically so that she leaves her rural environment for the city, and there her happiness as well as her economic enterprise begins.

Walker carefully avoids the paradox others fall prey to, for her protagonist, having broken through the dualistic barrier to sexuality with Shug, becomes skeptical of anything that might stand in her way of self-fulfillment. Her lesbian relationship signifies, for her, a rejection of the oppositional character of heterosexuality,[11] just as leaving her rural environment signifies a rejection of the association between woman and nature. In the poignant chapter immediately following the block of Nettie's letters to her, Celie recounts a conversation with Shug on the validity of the concept of God, whom she views as a white man. Shug's views of God, which encompass the issue of nature as well, are much more sophisticated than Celie's. For example, Shug comments, "I think it pisses God off if you walk by the color purple in a field somewhere and don't notice it" (178), for she has already de-genderized God:

> Man corrupt everything, say Shug ... Soon as you
> think he everywhere, you think he God. But he ain't.
> Whenever you trying to pray, and man plop himself
> on the other end of it, tell him to git lost, say Shug.
> Conjure up flowers, wind, water, a big rock. (179)

But, Shug is attempting to ally woman and nature against man, as her suggestion to "conjure up" natural elements implies. Celie remains unconvinced, as she replies, "Every time I conjure up a rock, I throw it" (179). Using her protagonist as a commentator and critic, Walker can offer these themes that might be acceptable to others, and at the same time criticize them.

It is noteworthy here that both Walker and Gloria Naylor (*The Women of Brewster Place*) demonstrate a certain skepticism regarding the issue of woman and nature in their texts that is not apparent in the other texts. Both also see a very strong oppositional factor in the man/woman duality that is transcended through lesbian love.[12] Naylor uses setting to delineate the contrasts of the urban/rural landscapes, but neither are in alliance with woman. In *The Women of Brewster Place*, Naylor begins with setting, the city, depicted as dilapidated and oppressive. Like *The Wanderground*, it is a novel of stories with a collective protagonist, the women. Each story focuses on an individual woman and the circumstances which bring her to Brewster Place, a dead-end street, both literally and metaphorically, as it is cut off from the main parts of the city by a high wall. The women there

> were hard-edged, soft-centered, brutally demanding,
> and easily pleased, these women of Brewster Place.
> They came, they went, grew up, and grew old be-
> yond their years. Like an ebony phoenix, each in her
> own time and with her own season had a story. (5)

The protagonist, Mattie Michael, enters into most of the stories and the first story of the text is about her. She then becomes a central character and, with her story, the essential themes are established that are relevant to our discussion of ecofeminism.

Like Walker's Celie, Mattie understands women's love for each other as a means of transcending the dominance of heterosexual relationships, and consequently she defends Lorraine and Theresa, the lesbian couple who move in to Brewster Place, against the accusations of some of the other women. The wall is not only the scene of the brutal gang rape, but also the symbol of culture, the symbol of the ruling councilmen. It effectively cuts the women off from the life of the city, and it also blocks off natural life-giving elements in that Mattie notes that the wall is high enough to cut off the sunlight from her third story apartment. Naylor's handling of these initial oppositional stances shows she is neither easily deceived nor so simplistic. Ben, the kind old janitor, has been as victimized by society as the women. In his company Lorraine feels "no different from anyone else" despite Theresa's analysis of the world into "them and us." But the way to his basement room is Lorraine's downfall. After the vicious attack that leaves her demented and nearly dead, she kills Ben.

What Naylor is attempting here is a move out of the dualities she initially sets up. Of the women, only Mattie attains a level of self-perception and an understanding of what the women mean to each other. The forceful denouement, Mattie's dream of the women acting together, materializes as a triumphant block party, organized by the women in a show of political solidarity and creates the hope that the women might break out of the cycle of institutional victimization. However, the final chapter, "Dusk", tells of the death of the street brought about by bureaucratic decision-makers, not by the women.

One of the overriding issues is lesbian relationships, but Naylor does not work this through many possibilities. Rather she allows it to be destroyed by the brutality of the gang. Because of this, Naylor sets the most hopeful action in a dream, and the women go on as they always have. If Naylor gives Mattie certain insights regarding the transcendence of heterosexual opposition, she is certainly pessimistic about their possibilities. She falls short of developing a self-critical stance. Unlike Walker, then, she has in the end succumbed to the dualistic opposition she began with, after briefly suggesting it might be overcome.

Marilynne Robinson's *Housekeeping*, the last of our fictional texts, attempts a completely different vision that leads her through the paradoxes we initially began with, but, like Naylor, she stops short of a distinctly self-critical stance. The text concerns the personal narrative of a young girl, Ruthie, and her life with her sister, Lucille, and Sylvie, her aunt. Ruthie's grandfather, long dead, and her father she never knew are the absent males in the text. Mother and grandmother are dead, and the care of the two orphaned girls is left first to great-aunts, then to Sylvie. The setting is a remote village on the shores of a mountain lake. With Sylvie's arrival into their lives, the girls take on new dimensions, and eventually, Lucille goes the way of social expectations. Ruthie, however, under Sylvie's careful tutelage, comes to a greater understanding of what it means to be woman in a heterosexual society. In the text, there is a constant depiction of the masculine/feminine nature images that seem not so much opposed to each other but complementary: the mountains and the lakes, the house in the garden, etc. The dichotomy between nature and culture is played out on a broad plane, but that between man and woman is more discreetly handled. Having eliminated male influences on Ruthie and Lucille, Robinson then projects the development of the girls in an all-female group, but within a heterosexual cultural setting. They live together in the house near the woods above the lake, in benign neglect by societal standards, until Lucille decides to be like the other girls at school. Eventually, she leaves to live with another family in town, which draws the attention of some of the townspeople to their lifestyle. Sylvie and Ruthie, taking after her, are simply beyond gender restrictions. Threatened by the sheriff, they ultimately reject culture as well, because of its attempts to impose gender restrictions on them. After setting fire to their house, they escape across the train bridge and begin a life of tramping and riding boxcars. In other words, they have grown through and beyond the gender (and culture) dichotomies but as a result are outcasts, assumed dead.

Robinson does suggest a strong alliance between woman and nature. Having eliminated male/cultural influences on the family at the beginning, the women

> were cut free of the troublesome possibility of
> success, recognition, advancement. They had no
> reason to look forward, nothing to regret. Their lives
> spun off the tilting world like thread off a spindle,
> breakfast time, suppertime, lilac time, apple time.(13)

By the end of the text, Ruth and Sylvie, having let go of the last vestiges of propriety and cultural norms, become like the wind:

> If Lucille is there, Sylvie and I have stood outside

> her window a thousand times, and we have thrown
> the side door open when she was upstairs changing
> beds, and we have brought in leaves, and flung the
> curtains and tipped the bud vase, and somehow left
> the house again before she could run downstairs,
> leaving behind us a strong smell of lake water. She
> would sigh and think, "They never change." (218)

In creating the relationship between woman and nature as one of complete identification, Robinson leaves no room for self-criticism. Rather the subtle criticisms in the text are directed at Lucille for accepting the trappings of social expectations.

In all of these texts, then, similar patterns of dualism critique emerge. The authors have all approached the woman/nature aspect thematically beginning with an initial acceptance of the woman/nature association, through their portrayal of the female protagonist in relation to her environment. Then, through the course of the narrative, distinct changes in attitudes develop that reveal a variety of possibilities for dealing with dualism and paradox in these concepts of woman and nature — from a deconstruction as in Atwood's case to a symbiosis as in Robinson's.

Embedded in the issue of dualism is the concept of "the other". In dualism, one central division is the separation, through a process of objectification, of the self from everyone and everything else, perceived then as other. But as Simone de Beauvoir, Julia Kristeva, and numerous additional critics have pointed out, "the other" refers really to the "other" sex; encoded in our traditionally dualistic male-dominated culture, the other sex is woman. Woman *is* "other", as Beauvoir convincingly argues in *The Second Sex*[13]. Once woman understands this perception of "the other", it also demands development of a critical stance by woman toward herself. In a critique of dualism, Ynestra King in "The Eco-feminist Imperative", using language echoing Simone de Beauvoir, writes that the process of objectification that poses woman as other is responsible for most of our social ills:

> ... no person should be made into an 'other' to

> despise, dehumanize, and exploit. As women we have
> been an 'other', but we are refusing to be the 'other'
> any longer and we will not make anyone else into an
> 'other'. Sexism, racism, class divisions, homophobia,
> and the rape of nature depend on this process of
> objectification (11).

While this clearly calls for unity in all social sectors, King has raised another problem or contradiction. In refusing to be man's "other", ecofeminists refuse to be cultural objects, and insist on their subjectification in man's culture. Similarly they work to deconstruct the process of objectification that results in sexism, racism, class division, etc. But the difference between refusing to be an object (like Atwood's protagonist refusing to be a victim) and acting as part of a culture is an enormous one. King overlooks this difference and seems to equate the refusal to be an object with being the subject. This is a crucial difference when looking at the authors' literary approach to ecofeminism, because it deals primarily with the perception of woman by woman and demands a critical stance toward the self, and a clear perception of self, in cultural roles.

While Atwood's approach is quite clear (she stops at the refusal of objectification and leaves the possibility of identification with the dominant culture ambiguously open), and Gearhart and Piercy in their utopias leave no doubt as to their viewpoint, Robinson in *Housekeeping*, Naylor in *The Women of Brewster Place*, and Walker in *The Color Purple* exhibit unique attitudes about "the other".

Aside from their narrative techniques in which these authors use either a first-person narration as symbol of subjectivity (the woman as "I") or a collective protagonist,[14] these three authors achieve at the end of their texts what I can only term "a unity of spirit" as a means of acting in the name of and part of a woman-oriented culture and in the process have attempted to reconceptualize "woman". In attaining this end, the authors are similar in their non-heterosexual approach to the concept of "woman" and their rejection of material possessions that symbolize their own complicity. In each case the protagonists leave a materially comfortable, or at least relatively stable, situation that demands their adherence to patriarchal role ideals. This situation indicates their lack of power, their "otherness". Once they realize that *not* leaving is tantamount to complicity and compromise, staying in their respective "homes" is no longer possible.

In *Housekeeping*, Ruth and her Aunt Sylvie defy standards of gender. Their household is a female one, males having shared only brief interludes in their lives, and consequently they thought they were "cut free" of masculine influences, demands and expectations. They see no divisions, have no sense of "otherness", until they are cast into this role of the "other". Under their aunt's care, Ruth and Lucille gradually grow apart. Lucille becomes burdened by their unconventionality and wants to become socially acceptable and to reattach herself to this "troublesome possibility of success", recognition and advancement. Ruth perceives in her aunt's care a gentleness and attachment to the natural elements which she can rely on, while Sylvie teaches Ruth about reality, the awkwardness of civilization, and its ephemeral materialism. "Housekeeping" is the translation of "ecology"; through Sylvie's housekeeping, Ruth comes to see herself as very much a part of her natural surroundings, experiences the mutual influences implicit in the interaction with the environment, and comes increasingly to reject the dominant standards of civilization that demand "otherness".[15] Sylvie's housekeeping is a way of getting to the essentials of living. Ruth comments that "Sylvie in a house was more or less like a mermaid in a ship's cabin. She preferred it sunk in the very element it was meant to exclude" (99); she is holistic in every sense. But it is Ruth, the narrator, who reaches an understanding of both the importance and irrelevance of housekeeping, and finally, threatened by a society bent on reforming them, "there was an end to housekeeping" (209).

As part of the "unity of spirit" Robinson creates, the two women also reach a physical unity with their natural surroundings. In time, after the flood and under Sylvie's housekeeping, their garden enters their parlor:

> Perhaps she sensed a Delphic niceness in the scat-
> tering of these leaves and paper, here and not else-
> where, thus and not otherwise. She had to have been
> aware of them because everytime a door was opened

anywhere in the house there was a sound from all the corners of lifting and alighting. I noticed that the leaves would be lifted up by something that came before the wind, they would tack against some impalpable movement of air several seconds before the wind was heard in the trees. Thus finely did our house become attuned to the orchard and to the particularities of weather even in the first days of Sylvie's housekeeping. Thus did she begin by littles and perhaps unawares to ready it for wasps and bats and barn swallows. (85)

In the end, after Ruth acquires a meaning for her femininity, the two head out for a life of drifting, after setting fire to their house in a final renunciation of all pretension to social conformity. As one critic remarked, this type of withdrawal has some escapist elements in it; however, Ruth "does not so much turn away from reality as from the inessentials that obscure [it]".[16] Sylvie has behaved similarly with the housekeeping that she considers inessential but that is highly regarded in social terms. The interference of masculine authority, in the form of the sheriff, represents false social norms and puts an end to their housekeeping. Their ensuing life of drifting is "the only true condition in a world of transience."[17]

Above all, Robinson has created a pair of characters in total harmony with each other and their environment. In their understanding of the transience of possessions and in their gentleness they afflict no one else with their values. They critically understand and fully accept Lucille and her need for social conformity but they leave her because she can define herself only within the realms of heterosexuality and material possessions. They place their concern primarily on their own spiritual values, which include neither heterosexuality nor material possessions, and thus are able to define themselves as woman outside of those realms. They are not the "other", but become everything and nothing.

The concept of "other" and the perception of woman taken up by Walker is different from Robinson's. For Walker there is not much holistic symbiosis between woman and her environment; the rural experience is one of violence for Walker's characters.

More fundamental to Walker's sense of "other" is Celie's development as a woman who initially sees herself as "other", as object, as part of a system governed by forces beyond her immediate control. Her belief in that system then begins to crumble as she learns to take control of herself. As her love for Shug grows, she rejects heterosexual love. Her belief in a Christian god diminishes as she develops a more sophisticated philosophy of herself as woman, the symbol of which becomes the title of the novel and her link back to nature:

> Well, us talk and talk bout God, but I'm still adrift.
> Trying to chase that old white man out of my head.
> I been so busy thinking bout him I never truly notice
> nothing God make. Not a blade of corn (how it do
> that?) not the color purple (where it come from?).
> Not the little wildflowers. Nothing. Now that my
> eyes opening, I feels like a fool. Next to any little
> scrub of a bush in my yard, Mr.____'s evils sort of
> shrink. But not altogether. Still, it is like Shug say,
> You have to git man off your eyeball, before you can
> see anything a'tall. (179)

Celie can begin to see herself as a separate person, rather than as one defined by her relationships to men. In other words, she begins to see herself as subject rather than object. She begins to "define" herself. Celie leaves her husband and home when she realizes how victimized she has been and decides that *not* leaving with Shug would affirm her own complicity. Through her own artistic endeavors and talents, she is eventually rewarded with financial success and independence. Walker sets very little of the novel in the city (Memphis) and the possibilities Celie finds there are due to Shug rather than the city as representative of a cultural identity of man. Walker carefully avoids a rural/urban split. Celie's return to the rural South and her ultimate success there imply not the conflict between urban "civilization" and the pastoral landscape, but the individual social triumph of a black woman against racism and misogyny. This is a necessary prerequisite for Walker's harmonious final scene, symbolizing Celie's "unity of spirit".

In *The Women of Brewster Place*, Naylor creates something similar to Walker's view of woman in the character of Mattie. Having given up on men early in life, Mattie becomes an asexual mother, and yet fully comprehends the love and understanding women share with each other. She does not equate love with sexual relations, nor does she condemn Lorraine and Theresa, the lesbian couple. She has some basic control over her own life and does not consider herself as object in a patriarchal sense. She identifies with the women around her. All her meager material possessions were taken from her, first by her father's total rejection and then by her son's chicanery, but in each case, she gave of herself freely and without regret. Living on Brewster Place signifies the lack of any pretense about the importance of material possessions.

In these respects, then, Naylor clearly sees the difference between refusing to be an object and acting as part of a cultural identity. The black women have to contend with their double marginality, as woman and as black. So while the "unity of spirit" Naylor achieves is within a dream sequence, it is nonetheless important to Mattie's idea of subjectivity. Her dream of the women acting collectively, tearing down the wall with their bare hands, represents for Mattie the supreme act of subjectivity for women who have gone beyond heterosexual and material barriers.

Naylor, Walker and Robinson approach the idea of "other", object and subject, from the perspective of woman unrestricted by heterosexuality and materialistic possessions. The unity of spirit all three achieve in their works results from the protagonists defining themselves as women, rather than being defined by social conventions. There is still the difficult bridge between refusing to be an object and acting in the name of and as part of a cultural identity as mentioned in King's manifesto on ecofeminism and the process of objectification. However, in these three texts, that bridge, if not crossed, is at least being built.

Through their approaches to the dualisms they bring into their texts, and through their use of "the other", these seven authors begin to develop a critical stance that would perceive their protagonists as breaking out of the bounds of dualistic structures, and that would clarify their ambiguities more precisely. They are not equally successful, but a tendency is there. This tendency is fundamental to the issues of ecofeminism; just as the domination and destruction of the environment as a parallel development to the domination and repression of woman, and a view of nature freed of humanistic and Romantic interpretations that distort environmental issues are essential to the issues of ecofeminism.

Domination and Destruction

The tendency to completely dominate objects considered as unequal and unworthy is one of the results of the process of objectification that has been much criticized by ecofeminists of the caliber of King, Daly, Griffin, Merchant, and Ortner. The development of this tendency is well-documented, and Merchant, in particular, draws lines of parallel development between the increasing social restrictions on women, the beginning of modern technology in farming and mining, and New World explorations.

The idea of imposing civilization and culture on this New World wilderness is closely bound with the discovery of the New World. To a certain extent, the idea of a "New World" existed long before the "discovery" of the Americas; the idea lived in the utopian tradition, in the myths of paradise, including the metaphors and images of the Garden of Eden.[18] Linking this on a literary plane to a later Romantic pastoral mode that is particularly seen in North American settings, Leo Marx in his work, *The Machine in the Garden*, traces a set of images throughout the several centuries of American writing, namely, a garden setting, tranquil and abundant, interrupted by machines. Relevant to this discussion is that Marx also identifies the pastoral setting with the feminine and the machines with the masculine. In the ecofeminism paradigm, Marx's "interruption" becomes destruction, and these images are symbols not of the machines themselves but of the patriarchal system of domination that uses them destructively. This system of domination, as the authors depict it, initiates a complex process of victimization involving woman combined with simpler technological and mechanical destruction of the environment. These two related aspects would certainly support Marx's descriptive analysis and strongly delineate an ecofeminist intertextuality.

The issue of the victimization of woman is fraught with dangers, and can easily be overemphasized. Inherent in identifying the roots of exploitation/victimization of both woman and nature is a danger of according identifications which would reinforce the duality of culture/man and nature/woman. It seems popular at present to cast the oppressor role as male and the victim role as female and many complex factors currently support this interpretation. The first that comes to mind on a socio-political level is the hard fought battle in the USA in the courts to view rapists as aggressors, rather than as the victims of female wiles. Historically, the attitude generally subscribed to in all patriarchal societies was that of blaming the victim, which suggested that women who were raped were actually themselves at fault by wearing "suggestive" (of what, for whom?) clothing, walking alone, or any number of various circumstances that feminists attribute to simply being a woman. Forcing a woman to testify in court in front of a male judge, male lawyers, and the accused rapist psychologically prevented most rape incidents from ever coming to court. In addition, rapists were generally given easy sentences or were acquitted on technicalities. Susan Brownmiller's *Against Our Will*, her classic study on rape,[19] initiated a feminist outcry that was heard in the legal domain. The feminists demanded that the legal blame be placed on the rapist and that the woman must be solely seen as a victim of male sexual aggression. I bring up this issue, not only because four of the texts actually deal with rape, but because of the sensitive role the concept of the victim plays in feminism. While I obviously do not wish in any way to imply complicity between the victim and rape, there is a dilemma evident in the fictional texts that allows the role of victim to be cast too easily. Feminist critic Jean Elshtain takes issue with just this situation, when she comments,

> What is distressing is the repeated evocation in feminist discourse of images of female helplessness and victimization. The presumption is that the victim speaks in a pure voice: I suffer therefore I have

> moral purity and none can question what I say. But
> the belief in such moral purity may itself be one of
> the effects of powerlessness, and that belief, con-
> gealed in language, is endlessly self-confirming.
> (612)

Elshtain's view is pertinent to our fictional texts, because the tendency
of some authors is to assert this "moral purity" of the victim role. This
in turn reinforces the duality phenomenon, rather than attempting to
deconstruct it. Obviously, while this is not always the case, the tendency is there.

  If we consider the depiction of the victim role in these novels,
the two utopian novels and the black novels manage to portray
complex victimization processes and/or absolute victims. In *Woman on
the Edge of Time*, Piercy's protagonist, Connie, is Mexican, poor, and
female, and is consequently diagnosed as mentally ill. These are four
characteristics that push one out of the mainstream of American life.
All of the male characters in New York are considered moneyed,
"normal" and at least pretend to be white. What Piercy does most
assuredly here is depict a woman who is herself convinced she is the
absolute victim, not only of individual men, but of patriarchal power
structures. It is such power structures that treat women and the environment as objects and within these power structures both become
victims. Piercy reinforces such images by depicting alternating
passages of the gardener with a special license to use destructive
poisons on his plants, and the doctors experimenting with mind control
on the "uncooperative" women in the hospital. Piercy's means of
moving Connie out of this victim status is created in Connie's
connection with the Mattapoisett utopian community. But it is not
Connie's self-direction which helps her to develop a sense of her own
power, but rather the Mattapoisettian character Bee who tells her she
can free herself:

> There's always a thing you can deny an oppressor, if
> only your allegiance. Your belief. Your co-oping.
> Even with vastly unequal power, you can find or
> force an opening to fight back. (328)

Both Connie and the Mattapoisettians have the aura of "moral purity" Elshtain criticizes above. The Mattapoisettians have struggled to make the perfect society, gender-fair and ecologically sound, whereas Connie believes in herself as victim. Both seem morally pure. Only late in the novel does Connie realize that the Mattapoisettians are also willing to fight for their society, and do so collectively. Connie, as an individual, learns then that fighting back is necessary and can be successful. When she finds the opening to fight back, and kills all the doctors in charge of the brain experiments, her moment of victory is short-lived. Indeed, the final chapter of the text are hospital reports indicating that while she was briefly "at war" as she says, she ultimately lost. She remains the victim of the system.

The moral purity syndrome, one can argue, is the whole point of utopian novels which create a morally superior society that by inference or direct parallels shows the reader's society to be lacking. To a certain extent, both Piercy's work and Gearhart's *Wanderground* do play on this theme. The oppressors in both texts are clearly patriarchal urban cultures. Gearhart, however, gives her women of the Wanderground an uncompromising status, for the stories are about a society that was formed when the extremely oppressed and victimized women of the City began to fight back and escaped from the men, forming their own groups. Mother Nature plays an active role, too; gradually having had enough of the invasive, mechanized urban demands on her, she allows her energy fields to interfere with the functioning of all machinery and communication lines outside the City. Still, the women are so convinced of their moral purity that they do not want to allow any closer contact with the Gentles. In other words, the women's victimization ends when they actively fight back, which seems to be a continuing process. In both utopian works, however, woman's liberation is aligned with environmentally sound societies.

The most victimized women are to be found in the black novels, and in Piercy's novel representing Chicano culture, for the authors are dealing with multi-marginalized characters. Alice Walker in *The Color Purple*, in particular, takes meticulous care that the exploitation/victimization of woman and nature follows a parallel development, that of woman in Celie's case, that of nature in the case of the African tribe, the Olinkas. Celie's direct and personal victimization is "only" through the men in her life.[20]

With Nettie's letters, Walker, in Steinbeck-like fashion, attempts to fit Celie's situation of racist and misogynistic violence into a more general, even global, pattern. Although better educated than Celie, Nettie, in an almost naive fashion, expresses her sympathy for and identification with the Olinka people and their village life, which is totally dependent on their natural environment. The primary symbol of colonial exploitation is the road being built to the Olinka village and the destruction of their revered roofleaf trees, which leads directly to the destruction of the entire village and their native culture. Here the obvious oppressor is the white man, but Walker does not leave the analogy so simple, for the women of the village are also oppressed within their culture. To oppose the colonial whites, by demonstrably embracing previously forgotten tribal rituals and joining a sort of underground, Tashi, a young native woman, undergoes ritual genital mutilation, considered to be the most misogynistic of native rituals. In this way, Walker extends the male/female, culture/nature dualism to a system of violence across four cultural and racial bands: her step-father and Albert vs. Celie, the white sheriff vs. Sofia, the white colonial powers vs. the Olinka tribe, native rituals vs. Tashi. Furthermore, she manages to relate personal forms of violence to larger institutional forms of violence, but in both types, women are the ultimate victims. Through Nettie's letters we see associations that relate the violence directed at woman and at nature. Celie comes to understand the process of victimization through Nettie's letters, the sets of relationships mentioned above, and her understanding of her own victimization and that of her daughter-in-law, Sofia's. When Harpo unsuccessfully tries to beat Sofia, as his father beat Celie, it is Celie who tells him, Sofia cannot be beaten because she loves him and he cannot beat her because he loves her (65). This process of violence underscores women's status as victim, as is evident in Sofia's case who learned to physically protect herself through violence, because "A girl child ain't safe in a family of men" (46). She then turned this mechanism on the sheriff (she punches him), and, as a result the whole brutality of Southern law is turned against her. The violence initially portrayed as man against woman now becomes white against black and the violence and exploitation goes beyond gender to race. Celie comes to believe that violence only breeds violence, and that racism is also a form of misogyny, even when Sofia experiences the most vicious and subtle forms of racism from the sheriff's wife. Parts of Celie's development are her realizations that her submission breeds, in a circular fashion, the very violence she submits to, and her realization that she can leave.

Like Walker's text, *The Women of Brewster Place* has a considerable amount of physical and sexual abuse aimed at the various women. Many come from the rural South and are so victimized there that they come to try their lives out in the city, and end up in Brewster Place. In Mattie Michael's story, the peaceful rural setting is interrupted by her seduction by the town rogue, her subsequent pregnancy, her brutal beating by her father and the beginning of her odyssey. The other stories are similar — a man is invariably the cause of the woman's downward spiral. In "The Two", when a lesbian couple move in on the block, some of the women turn viciously against them, until one, Lorraine is attacked by the local street gang, beaten and repeatedly raped at the wall.

The solutions to the issue of women's victimization offered in these four texts seems simplistic on the surface — say "NO"! — but if we look further into the mechanisms of suppression the texts portray, they are "utopian" solutions, and ultimately the women do not succeed beyond the personal level. Walker's happy ending is the exception and is happy because of all the escapes, rather than changes, the various characters have masterminded to be together at the end. The women of the Wanderground have to come down from their hill to cooperate more fully with the Gentles. The women of Brewster Place all go their own ways as the street deteriorates, their collective action was only Mattie's dream. Connie Ramos's victory is all too brief, as noted in the appended hospital reports. Nature fares little better: the question of Mattapoisett's existence is unanswered for the future; Mother Nature's protective energy shield weakens occasionally; the Olinka culture is destroyed; the wall still cuts off the sunlight from Brewster Place. But, in each case, the protagonist(s) have had to confront their concepts of themselves as victims, and demand of themselves, as individuals, the will to fight or escape. There is no change in this process of victimization and domination in these texts, a process which claims woman-as-victim by man-as-oppressor. The analogous situation in the ecofeminism paradigm is nature's destruction by technology.

The imagery of the machine in the garden as an interruption of the tranquility of nature, as suggested by Leo Marx, and the ecofeminist version of this image is clearly being reinvoked in the novels here. In *Surfacing*, the interruption comes in the form of motor-boats on the lake, the bullet holes in the heron; in *The Color Purple*, the men with their tools and machines building the road to the Olinka village; in *The Wanderground*, all the machines outside the City; in *Woman on the Edge of Time*, the war machines threatening Mattapoisett, and medical technology threatening woman. In using these sets of images and metaphors, the authors are "reinventing" a motif for ecofeminist purposes, but at the same time are harking back to a pastoral theme that is, and was, not always relevant for woman.

If, as Kolodny suggests, European women in North America "struggled to find some alternate set of images through which to make their own unique accommodation to this strange and sometimes forbidding New World landscape" (3), then this alternative view opposed the one of the natural environment as a virginal paradise on which culture and civilization must be imposed. However, we find in the texts discussed here a view of nature that is initially a paradise that must be saved from culture. There is a very strong connection just at this point which relates woman and nature in opposition to man and culture, or, in Marx's terms, the machine. The machine as a metaphor for civilization or culture comes to destroy or enslave the garden; culture uses the machine as a means of domination and destruction, and so cast in these terms, it is difficult for feminist authors to work through a self-critical element that admits participation in the metaphor. Instead, there is an initial implicit agreement that "the garden" should remain in its original form and that types of machines intruding upon the garden alienate it from its original life-giving role.

Like the authors of the seventeenth, eighteenth, and nine-teenth centuries Kolodny discusses in her work, the authors here seem also to be struggling to find a unique interpretation of woman and nature as a means of accommodating current reality. These con-temporary writers have been influenced both by non-literary factors like the current ecology movement, and literary influences such as the renewed interest in utopian fiction in the mid-seventies and early eighties.

As part of the ecology movement that demands an end to destructive use of technologies and the end of technological processes that are indirectly destructive to the environment, ecofeminism advocates a view of humanity that is part of, but not hierarchally above environmental nature. To this end, King writes,

> eco-feminism supports utopian visions of harmonious, diverse, decentralized communities, using only those technologies based on ecological principles, as the only practical solution for the continuation of life on earth. (125)

Certainly one aspect of the literary strain of ecofeminism that has increased dramatically in the seventies is the interest in a feminist utopia that concerns itself with ecological principles and tends to valorize the relationship between woman and nature, instead of deconstructing it. From the ecofeminist point of view, such utopias can easily cast technology, symbol of patriarchal power structures that rely on a system of hierarchy and domination, as the cause of all social demise.

Of the two utopian texts, Piercy's offers a more differentiated view of technology, taking a closer look at uses of technology rather than technology *per se* and thus taking issue with the patriarchal system's use of it as a weapon of misogynistic domination and destruction. Mattapoisett is a technologically efficient community, using only those technologies "beneficial" to itself. On the perception of nature, Gearhart, on the other hand, takes the view that our society has simply not been able to cope with the demands of our environment and has shown its increasing ignorance and lack of courage in taking effective protective measures. In addition, Gearhart claims that technology has always been used as a means of enforcing the ecosphere to adapt to the human species. The hill women reject technology and the culture that spawned it to make a new beginning. But that is utopia. Elsewhere she writes,

To be sure, some groups of human beings have related well to the earth, have developed a consciousness worthy of our intellectual gifts. But,
precisely because they refused technology, they
became vulnerable to those who didn't. Technology
leads to power, domination, control. Our failed
consciousness in our relationship to the planet will
inevitably alas, prevail. ... The earth seems now to be
giving unmistakable signals that it can no longer bear
the weight, either of our numbers or of our arrogance. Nor, apparently, can we change our consciousness or stop the pell-mell rush to planetary
destruction.[21]

Her alternative suggestion is species suicide through cessation of
reproduction, however improbable the execution of the plan or the
fulfillment of the wish. Furthermore, she explains,

... recent history does not document even the slightest
inclination on our part toward species preservation,
but, rather, records our determination to poison and
asphyxiate ourselves. The greater virtue in my
solution rests in the fact that when we go, we will
have the decency not to take the rest of the planet
with us. ... and that the earth can then restore itself
from its long and difficult relationship with the
human race. (180)

While she realizes this radical approach will not be embraced, she
insists that this in no way detracts from the simple beauty of the
proposal. While one might be tempted to call this a nihilistic approach,
it is so only for *homo sapiens*, not for the rest of the world. Still in
this most radical of approaches, Gearhart hides a false modesty behind
a certain nostalgia, for surely in the billions of years of the planet's
existence, it has adapted to dramatic changes and influences. *Homo
sapiens*, in demonstrating an unnecessarily sinister disregard of its own
habitat, is significant, but by comparison only a rude irritation. What

Gearhart's nostalgia indicates is a longing for a habitat suitable for archaic mankind, in other words, for nature as a harmonious cultural construct rather than a pre-cultural entity.

Marge Piercy's stand on the domination issue is not so definitive. There is a strong relationship created between domination and technology in Connie's "present" situation in the novel. Those privileged to be higher up in the hierarchy have access to the development and use of technology, and through it retain their superior position. The white male doctors have the privilege of education and dominant culture; Connie's brother, Luis/Lewis, has acquired membership in the dominant (white, Anglo, male) culture; and Geraldo, lacking both education and membership in the dominant culture, still has the privilege of simply being male. These are all forms of domination that bring violence upon Connie, violence that is inherent in the system of hierarchy rather than in the individuals.

But, in utopian Mattapoisett, these issues are dealt with much differently. The prevalent attitude is not one of wholesale rejection of technological innovations. In this egalitarian society, people have overcome the problem of misogyny and the domination of women and have a strong sense of the interdependence of all things: No form of technology can be applied to solve any problem without discussing its effects on a vast range of other relationships. The issue is not dominance but harmony, and nature is incorporated into their culture. Even in very early utopias, the hierarchal system was seen as one factor impeding harmony with nature. The concept of dominance is so built into hierarchy that the resulting society sees itself as outside of natural processes, and nature *per se* becomes one more object of domination, however occasionally benevolent.

Nonetheless, Mattapoisett is a highly technologized society. What perhaps separates Piercy's utopia from others is the lack of a strong hierarchal power structure controlling the uses of technology and the implication that women are equally active and equally heard. Patricino Schweickart comments that the Mattapoisettians spend a lot of time "drawing the line between legitimate use and exploitative abuse of natural resources" (206), which indicates the value judgements of an organic society with a holistic approach to its environment in which only ecologically sound technologies are used and actual relationships are regarded as interdependent. At the same time, its strong ideological atmosphere creates other dichotomies and oppositions that are not openly confronted, but rather are hidden under value judgements formed by consensus. That is the weak point of the work. Mattapoisett is a high-tech, but in many ways archaic, society. Nevertheless, for Connie, it represents a liberating system.

Until the conclusion of Piercy's novel, there seems to be some hope that the human race is capable of change in sufficient magnitude as to move toward an ecologically sound environment. Luciente seems to challenge Connie to show the courage necessary to take the initiative so that Mattapoisett could actually exist. But the individual is too over-powered by the culture she is fighting against, or is incapable of really effective action. Connie finally goes to war, as she says, and kills the doctors who head the project; but the system takes its revenge, and Connie is returned to oppressive mental hospitals. So, at first glance, Piercy does not seem to offer much hope. Connie's action is ultimately taken as an individual, rather than as a collective, action. But, the courage to take action has been established and passivity has been overcome. Ultimately, Connie realizes our future cannot be left in the hands of the Dr. Reddings of the world. Luciente has educated her to be responsible for the things that happen to her. If she is sent back to the repressive mental hospital, it is at least with her brain intact, and not as a radio-controlled robot.

In contrast to Gearhart, it is Piercy's sense of ambivalence and her Marxist stance that saves her from an outright condemnation of technology. Although the power structures of Connie's "present" are clearly in control of technology and use it to control others, in Mattapoissett technology has not been rejected. Indeed, technology has a liberating function that poses a set of complex issues. While a radical feminist like Shulamith Firestone in her work *The Dialectic of Sex* advocates the abolition of pregnancy and home child care as the only way to effectively ensure the equality of men and women, Piercy has given the Mattapoisettians a similar option with the effect that babies are made in "brooders", and home child care is accorded a team of three "comothers", male and female, and numerous "kid-binders".The net effect is of a harmoniously functioning organic group with benevolent use of technologies within the community. The high-tech warfare conducted at the perimeters is indeed a great contrast, but the technology is available also for defensive uses, and the Mattapoisettians are reluctant but responsible warriors. Piercy's stance here is in notable contrast to those other ecofeminist utopias whose community settings are pacifist and non-aggressive. However, the discovery of the defense system at the perimeters provides the impetus for the protagonist to come out of her own passivity and pacifism to strike a blow at the hierarchal system that has victimized her.

In *The Wanderground,* the relationship between science and technology on the one hand and misogyny and violence on the other is made perfectly clear. On this point Gearhart allows no compromise. In her text, there is a wholesale rejection of technology and that is why it is so immediately attractive in its simplicity. The decision to abandon technology is radical and uncompromising, as is the idea that we have been dependent on various forms of technology for so long that, as Schweickart claims, "as a result of the hegemony of scientific reasoning" (201), we have neglected to develop our own innate powers and our own individual natures.

Outside the City, machines stopped functioning, animals stopped working for man, communications between Cities ceased, and male sexual responses diminished. In hunting the women, their guns jammed, and they were unsuccessful rapists, and the hunting dogs sabotaged their efforts to find the women. Farm equipment wouldn't work, horses refused the plow, rural factors power units failed (175). Women were safe only outside the City, and the hill women in their isolation developed unique powers for coping with life outside technology and the City.

The issue of technology appears to be a major consideration in this type of utopian work. In these two novels, the two poles are represented — total rejection of all technology and benevolent use of highly sophisticated technological developments. The dystopian scenes in both works, as well as the "present" setting in Piercy's work, represent technology as male-controlled and used to victimize women on all levels of social interaction. The effective choices are radically represented in societies in which women share equally in all social, political and technological aspects of society or, failing to achieve that status, in separatist communities in which women develop their own equally effective powers. There is no suggestion that the continuation of present societal structures might approach ecological balance, which is the goal of both the use of, or the rejection of, technology in these works.

Gearhart and Piercy differ also in the form of action or retribution required. Piercy raises the issue of women and violence as Connie associates violence on many levels and sees violence as the only means of retribution. In doing so she steps out of the role expected of her, that of the passive female. Gearhart's hill women, however, enjoy the protection of the somewhat mystical earth shield which allows them to develop without resorting to the use of violence.

Leaving the utopian genre, the motif of the machine in the garden is handled differently, but, as in Atwood's *Surfacing*, with the same implications. The protagonist finds numerous parallels between the change, destruction and death she sees in the present and her memories of the past. She also equates the violence and destruction she finds in the woodlands with "the Americans" who are spreading North like a virus over the Canadian landscape. But, the group of fishers and hunters in their motorboat turns out to be Canadian, not unlike her Canadian companions who are essentially as destructive as the Americans (128, 154). In her critique of *Surfacing*, Barbara Rigney takes the ecofeminist view that "the violation of nature by society is paradigmatic of the violation of woman by man" (101). She sees only that the dichotomy is reaffirmed. But while there are numerous examples, incidents and reconstructions that might confirm Rigney's paradigm, Atwood ultimately goes beyond it, seeing also that its other extreme, the valorization of woman, is itself a male construct that robs woman of her subjectivity and maintains her status as object. For this interpretation, the death of the protagonist's father is essential; a death by drowning, while photographing ancient Indian rock drawings. The feminine triumphs over scientific technology, as it were, causing also his death and protecting the exploitation of her hidden secrets. His death also sets the protagonist free from all she equates with mas- culinity so that her woman nature, "the natural woman", can emerge, freed of masculine constructs. However, again Atwood draws an am- bivalent conclusion, for the protagonist chooses to return to (male) civilization. Unlike Piercy and Gearhart, Atwood considers the possibilities of the present as her protagonist begins to move out of the restrictions of dualism.

In *The Color Purple,* Walker's technique is to juxtapose the African scenes with those of the rural South and, using the form of correspondence, shows the destruction of a native culture by the colonial powers building a road. The primary symbol of this destruction is the roofleaf tree, the center of this native culture which is wantonly cut down by the road builders as they cut a swath directly through the village. This establishes the superficial connection between the violence Celie experiences at the hands of black men and the violence the Africans experience at the hands of the white colonial powers.

This connection however is too simplistic to hold in a feminist context. The youth of the native village, appalled by the destruction of their culture, reject their new Christianity and return to their old rituals, including the practice of genital mutilation of women, a form of misogynistic violence. Thus, the issue here becomes the connection between women and nature. While Celie escapes the violence directed against her through the love of Shug and her entrepreneurial talent, her sister and family escape the violence in Africa by returning to the South, and the African daughter-in-law escapes through the love of the son. While the issue of woman and nature is certainly deliberately raised, the solutions are suggested on an individualistic level. Unlike Piercy and Gearhart, Walker does not take on the power structures responsible for violence and destruction, but stays within the range of the superficial connection between woman and nature.

It is clear here that the authors who purposely valorize the relationship between woman and nature must then portray culture and its derivative, technology, in destructive opposition in ecofeminist terms. They have left out the idea that Ynestra King expresses in the term "our culture", and the self-criticism that this implies by embracing a culture that, in ecofeminist terms, has a negative impact on the environment and human life. Again, only Atwood, by having her protagonist decide to return to the city with Joe, finally accepts the duplicity of the term "our culture". In considering the texts here, the struggle to find adequate literary means of expressing the need for a complex accommodation of woman to a contemporary situation in which technology in service of a hierarchal power structure is over-powering the natural environment, is not yet over, and has probably just begun.

Nature as Cultural Construct

In ecofeminist writings that concentrate on ecological and environmental issues, there is still an age-old tendency to portray nature in images that are feminine, and the metaphors reverse back onto nature, casting not only woman as attuned to nature, but nature as helpless, as exploitable, and as victimized as traditional woman. But the occasional female character begins to move out of this "trap". Of course not all of the authors here pick up on this tendency, nor do all ecologists and environmentalists, but very few attempt to break out of this construct, which in every sense is a cultural one. An adequate literary expression is difficult to develop probably because the views of nature tend to be static, while those of women are slowly becoming more dynamic. If the concept of woman is culturally determined, then so too is nature.

Nature as a cultural construct is best seen in the numerous and varied perceptions of nature held by different groups at different times, even in the North American setting, a context in which one refers primarily to the wilderness as nature. Whether it was the Puritans of the seventeenth and eighteenth centuries who saw the wilderness as godless, but nevertheless a sanctuary from a corrupt European civilization, and therefore one of their major paradoxes, or the later Romantics who, from a gentleman's perspective, found god in the wilderness, the pioneer perspective was primarily the taming of the wilds. Indeed Roderick Nash in *Wilderness and the American Mind* comments that

> Romanticism, including deism and the aesthetics of the wild, had cleared away enough of the old as-sumptions to permit a favorable attitude toward wilderness without entirely eliminating the instinctive fear and hostility a wilderness condition had pro-duced. (66)

By 1900, the wilderness was becoming rare and the over-crowded cities came to be regarded with as much hostility as the wilderness had been a century or more earlier. Movements for the protection and preservation of wilderness areas became popular (although some had existed as long before as 1830), but there were conflicts between those who advocated wilderness untouched by man and the "wise use" school. Well into this century, writes Nash, Americans "detected the qualities of innocence, purity, cleanliness, and morality [in primitive nature] which seemed on the verge of succumbing to utilitarianism and the surge of progress" (157). This concern was "owed much more to a general feeling that the American male was suffering from over-civilization" (152), and "the idea that virile manliness and wilderness were closely linked" (151). Nash ignores the sexual implications here, as if woman had no perspective on the wilderness, and that the close link between "virile manliness" and the wilderness was one of psycho-sexual metaphors; virile manliness could be most intensely experienced in a "feminine" setting where it had the image of and feeling of recuperating his manliness with the nurturing mother, or the image of the dangerous and chaotic virgin that needed to be conquered. By the twentieth century, of course, the subjugation of the wilderness that had been a primary theme for pioneers was no longer relevant. Nash quotes a guidebook for pioneer settlers as exclaiming:

> "You look around and whisper, 'I vanquished the
> wilderness and made the chaos pregnant with order
> and civilization, alone I did it!'." (42)

Nash ignores the sexual metaphor here as well as in the Puritan attitudes toward wilderness that are reflected in their attitudes toward sexuality; both wilderness and sexuality are to be subjugated and repressed.

Nash suggests that these theories of nature are being superceded today by more non-anthropocentric ones: the idea that nature-as-wilderness is amoral, that wilderness exists independent of what humans fear or hope it would be, and that it has a right to exist for its own sake, independent of whether mankind values it or not (269-270).

This position does not always coincide with the European view that defines nature either as a "sphere of pure externality upon which man acts," or man is part of nature, "a sort of dynamic process". In both cases, man and nature are inseparable, and, as Leiss in *The Domination of Nature* writes, the domination of nature and the domination of man[kind] cannot be thoroughly differentiated (xiv). He refers to Georg Lukács and Herbert Marcuse who both see nature as a social category and feel that the domination of nature has as its real object the domination of man in a capitalistic class sense. Or, more simply, there is no such thing as nature *per se*, only perspectives on nature which are related to various types of human interests (137). This is, then, what is meant by nature as a cultural construct and, needless to say, these theories and arguments are all accorded to individual men. Feminists like Kolodny suggest that women did not partake of the various views on nature uncritically, and Merchant and Ortner suggest that the sexual metaphors linking man and nature are symptomatic of woman's exclusion from cultural processes from which emanate such views of nature.

The fictional texts come to no startling conclusions on this issue. Only Atwood's protagonist comes close to extricating the idea of nature-as-wilderness from an anthropocentric perception. Initially, we have the machine in the garden motif. Then, the protagonist attempts to become part of the wilderness, and in the end, in conjunction with her decision to return to "civilization", she comments that nature is neither for nor against her, neither accepts nor rejects her; it is neutral, in a sense amoral, and it will continue to exist without her. At the opposite end, we have Walker's text, in which African nature is irrevocably changed, dominated, and destroyed by progress, technology, racism, and capitalism. Then, however, she imbues nature with archaic primitivism and feminine associations. Her purpose seems to further reinforce the association of nature with woman, in order to demonstrate the cause of their domination and destruction in patriarchal capitalism. Naylor, by contrast, seems distrustful of nature in such a feminist context, for her only descriptive setting is of the levee and the wild herb patch as the sensual scene of Mattie's seduction. In fact, in both of these texts about black women, the protagonists leave for the cities to escape rural oppression at the hands of their men. For

Naylor, though, the urban setting is just as cruel, with the wall being the ultimate symbol of white male power over women.

In both utopian works, nature is depicted as the victim of technological abuse, but there the similarities end. In *Wanderground*, Gearhart focuses more on the power and force of "mother nature" with her mystical possibilities and allows this "mother nature" to offer the women protection and power. Nature is actively feminine and, to this extent, is part of a non-hierarchal symbiotic relationship directed against the man of the City. In other words, nature becomes a sort of alternative cultural construct that is the basis of the women's society. King's suggestion that our culture must be reconstituted in the name of nature would seem to be fulfilled in *The Wanderground*. But without mixing the metaphysical and literary levels too much, it appears that nature, as a cultural construct in the utopian context, limits the possibilities of the narrative. Nevertheless, Gearhart seems to take these possibilities further than the other authors by constituting Nature as an active character.[22]

Piercy, on the other hand, retreats to the Marcusian philosophy of nature, which might not be surprising given her political background as founding member of the Students for a Democratic Society (SDS), and envisions a practical use of nature. As such, nature exists as a resource to supply the communities with their livelihood and is not genderized. This is a far cry from Atwood's wilderness, in which her mother continuously fought to keep a little patch of cultivated garden, fenced in from encroachment by the forests. Mattapoisett is altogether a cultivated garden, carefully planned and executed for the benefit of the community. And, as such, it becomes monotonous and rigorously serviceable to the Mattapoisettians.

The portrayal of nature and the wilderness as unequivocally feminine, as in the *Wanderground*, is repeated only in *Housekeeping*. Robinson, like Gearhart, becomes somewhat trapped, for the only solution for Sylvie and Ruth is escape on the train which initially was the absolute masculine element. Rather paradoxically, the images of nature as purely feminine do not suffice for the resolution of the narrative.

The question arises then, for what purpose do these feminist texts pursue nature settings and images. In the framework of ecofeminism, these texts, as a body, seem to question the cultural representation of nature as feminine, even if one has to go "beyond the ending" (DuPlessis) of the narrative to do so. For example, the implication of Gearhart's women regarding the Gentles; Piercy's completely degenderized nature in Mattapoisett's uncertain future; Atwood's neutral nature and her protagonist's planned return to civilization; Naylor's ambivalence or even negative association of "nature" and its consequences for women beyond the end of the street. These issues are not resolved by the end of the narrative, but, at least, a direction is given that goes beyond the close. In a slightly larger context, they are contributing to a deconstruction of the dualism that would insist on the woman/nature versus male/culture dichotomy.

Ecofeminism as discourse, in which much of the literature concerns sifting through the identification of women and nature in its historical analyses, exhibits a tendency to valorize the woman/nature relationship, which results in supporting the very dichotomy it wants to overcome. This situation does not necessarily invalidate the argument, but demonstrates a paradoxical problem for feminist discourse. A necessary precondition for criticizing language and concepts, disentangled from deeply rooted opposition, is questioning that language and those concepts. This is a problem that will be discussed at length in chapter four, but is also pertinent to the problems of nature as a cultural construct because it emphasizes the difficulties in conceiving the possibility of a nature that might exist outside of man's perspective. Within the paradox of having to frame concepts in a language that might not be suitable for them, disentangling nature from its cultural construct is an exercise that evokes Jehlen's suggestion for dealing with paradox, that of tapping its energy. In this context, it seems that Gearhart, in spite of the ideological problems she encounters, is more successful than the other authors in deconstructing the nature/culture dyad. By suggesting the inadequacies of language in dealing with the society of *The Wanderground*, she addresses the underlying theme of going beyond language to envision the possibilities of nature, but the utopian mode seems to be the only narrative way of doing this. Atwood's recognition of the language problem, for example, brings her protagonist back to civilization.

There appears to be in these texts an acknowledgement by North American writers of the problematic relationship between language and the various ways of viewing and defining nature, whereas European philosophers have seen nature only as a cultural construct and indeed tend to draw a nebulous line between man and nature. Building on this problem, Leiss can comment that one of the last vestiges of the domination of nature is in fact psychoanalysis that attempts the domination of man's own nature (xiv). With this in mind, then, we turn to the problem of woman and gender, in particular, the intersection of Freudian theories on woman, feminist theory, and ecofeminism.

NOTES

1. see Note 8, Chpt.1.

2. Zima, *Ideologie und Theorie*, p. 45.

3. Greimas and Courtés in fact define ideology as "thus characterized by the actualized status of the values that it takes up. The realization of these values...abolishes, *ipso facto*, the ideology as ideology." in *Semiotics and Language*.

4. Among those that I take up in Part II are: Gilbert and Gubar, *The Mad Woman in the Attic*; DuPlessis, *Writing Beyond the Ending*; and Showalter, *A Literature of Their Own*.

5. Myra Jehlen, "Archimedes and the Paradox of Feminist Criticism", *Signs: Journal of Women in Culture and Society*, 6/4 (1981); rpt. in Elizabeth Abel and Emily Abel (eds.), *The Signs Reader: Women Gender and Scholarship*, (Chicago: Univ of Chicago Press, 1983), p. 80.

6. King, "The Eco-feminist Imperative", p. 11; and Ortner, p. 85.

7. Feminist utopias as a genre share some common characteristics that explore gender relationships and some characteristics that have been incorporated into ecofeminist issues, like the treatment of the environment. One of the earliest feminist utopias is Charlotte Perkins Gilman's *Herland*, published in 1915, that incorporated all of these characteristics. These include: equality of class and sex, a communal system of child

care and the sharing of parental responsibilities, elimination of family names and gender-specific work, protection from and the freedom from the fear of rape and violence, community provisions for all types of social services, communal property with personal rooms. cf. Lucy M. Freibert, "World Views in Utopian Novels by Women", *Journal of Popular Culture*, 17/1 (summer, 1983), pp. 49-60.

8.cf.Joseph Campbell, *The Hero with a Thousand Faces,* Bollingen Series, 17 (Princeton: Princeton UP, 1973), pp. 126-149; Josie P. Campbell, "The Woman as Hero in Margaret Atwood's *Surfacing*", *Mosaic*, 11(1978), pp. 17-28; and Arno Heller, "Literarischer Ökö-feminismus: Margaret Atwood's *Surfacing*", *Arbeiten aus Anglistik und Amerikanistik (AAA)*, 9/1 (1984),pp. 39-50.

9. See chapter 4.

10.In referring to organic societies, I use the term in the same sense as Carolyn Merchant when she defines an organic community as one "growing out of peasant experience and village culture, (...) based on the leveling of differences and stressing, instead, the primacy of community, the collective will of the people, the idea of internal self-regulation and consent" and further, that the laws of "nature dictated an original equality among the parts of the village community, cooperative land use, and communal sharing of tools and goods." (p. 76).

11.See also chapter 6 of this study.

12.Further discussed in chapter 6.

13.See pp. 8-9 above.

14.These narrative techniques are discussed in chapter 4.

15.cf. Katrina E. Bachinger, "The Tao of *Housekeeping*: Reconnoitering the Utopian Ecological Frontier in Marilynne Robinson's 'feminist' Novel", in Leo Truchlar, (ed.) *Für eine offene Literaturwissenschaft: Erkundungen und Erprobungen am Beispiel US-amerikanischer Texte/Opening Up Literary Criticism: Essays on American Prose and Poetry* (Salzburg: Verlag Wolfgang Neugebauer, 1986), p. 15.

16.Gunilla Florby, "Escaping This World: Marilynne R. Robinson's Variation on an Old American Theme", *Moderna Språk*, 78/3 (1984), p. 214.

17.Florby, p. 214.

18. In particular Kolodny discusses this theme in *The Lay of the Land.*

19.Susan Brownmiller, *Against Our Will: Men, Women and Rape*, (N.Y.: Simon and Schuster, 1978).

20.It is notable here that Walker has broken a literary taboo, in that she depicts the black man, who has generally enjoyed the status of the victim under racism and white oppression in American literature, as oppressor himself.

21.Gearhart, "An End to Technology: A Modest Proposal", in ed. Rothschild, p. 180.

22.See chapter 5 for further discussion.

One isn't born a woman, one becomes one.

(Simone de Beauvoir)

The woman's body is the terrain on which patriarchy is erected.

(Adrienne Rich)

The men have power and the women have pleasure in all the versions of this myth.

(Robert Scholes)

3

Woman and Gender

In ecofeminism woman's relation to gender often involves complex maneuvering around traditional patriarchal/cultural "norms" regarding gender. This is crucial to an ecofeminist discourse that re-evaluates the position of woman in relation to nature in a cultural construct, because it also allows gender to be considered as a cultural construct. The focus of this chapter is the way the authors represent woman in the texts and the way woman perceives herself against the backdrop of patriarchally defined gender. But, in the name of ecofeminism, the domination and suppression of sexuality as part of the domination of nature, coupled with the particular problem of the "feminine" unconscious, leads us back to Freudian theory of gender which has been much discussed among both feminist theorists and literary critics. Feminist critique of Freud is primarily attributed to Juliet Mitchell, Luce Irigaray and, slightly later, Nancy Chodorow.[1] Together they contribute relevant insight for an ecofeminism interested in deconstructing dualism. But before turning to these critiques of Freud, a brief look at some cultural-literary perceptions of gender might be helpful.

The ideals of femininity have typically been defined by the dominant culture, from which realm woman was generally excluded. But these ideals of femininity[2] (and masculinity) have changed dramatically over centuries, while the concepts of male and female have remained relatively constant. These distinctions might seem obvious or pedantic but are important because the oppression of woman is primarily achieved by "imposing certain social standards of femininity on all biological women", whereas feminism "insists that though women are undoubtedly *female*, this in no way guarantees that they will be *feminine*."[3] The changing ideals and stereotypes of femininity pose problems for determining which sets or mixes of such images are current at any time. In Showalter's *A Room of Their Own*, Gilbert and Gubar's *The Mad Woman in the Attic*, and even DuPlessis' text, *Writing Beyond the Ending*, address the way particular authors worked around and away from the nineteenth and early twentieth century British, American, and Canadian stereotypes and ideals of femininity. These authors create the impression that the cultural norms, the stereotypes mixed with the ideals of femininity, were rigid and restrictive. However, characterizing a decade or a century well in the past demands a type of generalization filtered through time that is less difficult to arrive at than characterizing a contemporary situation.

If one wishes to speak of contemporary ideals, norms, or stereotypes of femininity, then perhaps the post-World War II decades would be the place to begin the contemporary discussion. The "happy housewife syndrome" as the ideal image of womanhood is one that, despite Betty Friedan's *The Feminine Mystique*, and Kate Millet's *Sexual Politics*, is still with us and those who do not fit the pattern are still considered different, in spite of the many national statistics that reveal a life-style far removed from this "ideal". This femininity of the fifties also emanates from a period when in the US woman was particularly "voiceless", having little or no access to cultural input. What this image also reveals, by way of absence, is the marginality of women of color. The authors of the seventies and eighties discussed here experienced at least a decade of upheaval as a buffer zone, and during that buffer period numerous critical studies of cultural stereotypes of women in mainstream fiction appeared. Contemporary authors have subsequently reacted against this earlier "ideal" through the ideology of feminism. Thus, the portrayal of female protagonists in these works offer a varied representation and it is obvious that neither Robinson, Gearhart, Piercy nor, to a certain extent, Walker, are intent on creating "realistic" characters in "realistic" situations. It seems that feminism, in emphasizing the difference between woman and femininity as a cultural construct, has created new possibilities for the portrayal of female characters. In our ecofeminism discourse, this "problem" simply reconfirms the cultural construct of gender which, as nature, needs to be reconceptualized.

On the textual level, these authors create protagonists who defy what they see as femininity as a cultural code of gender, which they have had no part in formulating. In this sense, the texts each deal with an implied femininity in the form of cultural expectations juxtaposed against a woman-perceived womanhood, and there emerges a textual conflict around the perceptions of gender.

In Terms of Sexuality

In ecofeminism, the issue of gender has wide implications for the way one views culture and nature, for gender takes its dualistic part in the "Big Dichotomies"[4]. And, it is difficult to discuss aspects of gender without taking Freudian theory on gender and sexuality into consideration. A slight detour through some key feminist objections to and interpretations of gender and sexuality is necessary at this point, in order to clarify similar issues in the texts.

Feminism, all through its colorful spectrum, has had a troubled relationship with Freudian theory. Freud's writings on woman and femininity seem, in very general terms, to confirm woman's secondary and oppressed role in contemporary society, and are encased in decidedly misogynistic, patriarchal ideology. While any extensive feminist analysis of Freudian theory is of little relevance to the scope of this study, there are points of intersection between ecofeminism and three prominent, if very different, feminist Freudian critics, which will be explored here. Juliet Mitchell's rather orthodox defense of Freud from a feminist viewpoint, Luce Irigaray's massive critique based on her psycho-linguistic and philosophical background and Nancy Chodorow's alternative reading of Freud's oedipal theory and its social implications. All have in common the rejection of an essentialist view of woman, a rejection of biologism (which maintains that biological sexual differences determine gender as a social construct), and an awareness of paradoxical stances regarding the feminine and gender as a dualistic construct.

Initially, contemporary feminist criticism of Freud rejected the American practice of psychoanalysis that tended to keep woman in her place. Later, in the seventies, critiques involved a more careful reading of Freud's writing, but emerged with little difference in the opinions of the critics: Freud developed a devastating, misogynistic, narrow and contradictory theory of woman because he himself subscribed to a patriarchal logic that deemed woman inferior. Juliet Mitchell's orthodox-Freudian critique of feminist views of Freud forced feminists to read Freud more carefully. In her defense of Freud, she insists that his interest was in the unconscious and its development as a "collective mind", rather than prescriptive social behavior. Her analysis also addresses the accusations that Freud, as a product of his times, sought a theory of gender that fit the status quo and tended to be grounded in biological determinism: Lacking a penis, the girl child feels inferior and seldom makes a complete transfer during the proper oedipal phase. The question of gender, then, becomes a biological argument based on possession or lack of a penis.

At about the same time that Mitchell's work appeared, Luce Irigaray's *Speculum of the Other Woman* was published in Paris. A student of Lacan (and the Lacanian interpretation of Freud), her work was a ravaging critique of Freud's theories of femininity and sexuality.[5] Briefly, she argues that Freud based his theories of femininity and sexuality on the visibility of sex differences; one sees the penis and the lack of one. Looking at woman, Freud saw nothing, which leads Irigaray to term woman as a Freudian absence outside of man's perception, which cannot be represented. She shows, in a somewhat Beauvoirian manner, that woman is man's Other. Even Freud's opening question "What is woman?" is, for Irigaray, an essentialist trap, for to define woman would be to follow the logic of the "phallologos", language that sustains the hegemony of male culture through its very use.[6] Thus, she rejects the idea of equality of women and men, knowing that such an equality would be built upon male logic:

> They must not pretend to rival them by constructing a logic of the feminine that again would take as its model the onto-theological. They must rather try to disentangle this question from the economy of the logos. They must therefore not pose it in the form "What is woman?" They must, through repetition-interpretation of the way in which the feminine finds itself determined in discourse — as lack, default, or as mime and inverted reproduction of the subject — show that on the feminine side it is possible to *exceed* and *disturb* this logic.[7]

Her own tactic is to mimic master (male) discourses, to over-do them in order to undermine them, knowing that the feminine codes will be read between the lines. But, more relevant here is her alternative theory of sexuality, developed in *The Sex that is not One* and "When Our Lips Speak Together". In these works she claims that because women have several sex organs (breasts, clitoris, vulva, vagina), and thus several sources of pleasure, their sexuality is multiple and inclusive, not restricted to one or none and cannot be possessed. Man's view of sexuality is visual and dualistic, based on the visual proof of his possession (penis) and her lack; woman's sexuality is tactile rather than visual, which does not coincide with the dominant either/or, me/not-me dualistic view of sexuality and gender.

 While Irigaray is concerned with a feminist approach to Freud through language and perceptions of sexuality, Nancy Chodorow arrives at some similar conclusions from a sociological investigation of Freudian theory of sexuality. In Chodorow's *The Reproduction of Mothering* and, later, in "Gender, Relation, and Difference in Psycho-analytic Perspective", she develops an alternative scenario of the oedipal phase for girls that has far-reaching consequences for women's perceptions of self and sexuality. In brief, girls do not go through a traumatic break with their nurturing mother, but continue on in an identification phase:

> This process entails a relational complexity in feminine self-definition and personality which is not characteristic of masculine self-definition or personality. Relational capacities that are curtailed in boys as a result of the masculine oedipus complex are sustained in girls. (*Reproduction*, p. 93)

Thus developing gender relationships becomes more important for girls than developing gender difference. Chodorow is also interested in the converse situation for boys and suggests, in "Gender, Relation, and Difference", that the core gender identity in boys "is more conflictual and more problematic (13)." Because of their initial close association ("a primary oneness") to the mother figure, boys have as part of their core gender identity "an underlying sense of femaleness that continually, usually unnoticeably, but sometimes insistently challenges and undermines the sense of maleness"(13). Consequently, the perception of rigid gender boundaries becomes necessary for males. On the other hand, girls do not need to see themselves as "not-male" because of the sense of continuity and similarity they experience with their mothers. She concludes that

> This relational context contrasts profoundly for girls and boys in a way that makes difference, and gender difference, central for males — one of the earliest and most basic developmental issues — and not central for females. It gives men a psychological investment in difference that women do not have.[8]

This seems to coincide with Irigaray's suggestions that woman's sexuality relies on multiplicity, that either/or gender categories are not central, and that woman's perception of her sexuality does not coincide with Freud's perception. Chodorow departs from Irigaray with her analysis of woman as absence and beyond representation, for Irigaray ventures too close to essentialist definitions of woman, even though she says that to essentialize woman is not her intention.

Another point of intersection, between Chodorow and Mitchell, involves the symptomatic aspect of patriarchal ideology that constructs gender to fit its needs. Both Chodorow and Mitchell are concerned with the ideology of patriarchy that defines woman in her reproductive functions and keeps her "a second sex", an oppressed member of society. Both attack the nuclear family as one of the major symptoms of this ideology. But, they arrive at this point differently and offer differing solutions. Chodorow sees in the nuclear family a means of training children for their gender roles in the next generation of nuclear families. Breaking this cycle would sufficiently interrupt the process of the oedipal phase which demands from boys a traumatic transference of their identity from mother to father and demands from girls the later process of establishing autonomy and separateness. Hence, she advocates equal parenting with its resulting impact on the trauma of gender identification. If children of both sexes had intense primary attachments with persons of both sexes in the pre-oedipal stages, then the oedipal phase would play out much differently. There would be no need for boys to reject their mothers in order to identify with their fathers. For girls, there would be an early emotional attachment to a male model with whom she could also identify.

Mitchell, however, seems more interested in the workings of patriarchal ideology in society rather than its impact upon individuals. For her, the unconscious is where patriarchal law asserts itself in each individual, which assures this patriarchal ideology in each individual. She claims that the nuclear family was created "to give that law a last hearing" (413), for patriarchy is now a redundant ideology even though it continues through the unconscious. "...Its [the nuclear family's] importance lies not *within* it so much as *between* it and the patriarchal law it is supposed to express" (413). In keeping with this, she writes,

> Under patriarchal order women are oppressed in their
> very psychologies of femininity; once this order is
> retained only in a highly contradictory manner this
> oppression manifests itself. Women have to organize

> themselves as a group to effect a change in the basic
> ideology of human society. (414)

Her solution is to adopt a strategy that is not a "righteous challenge to
the simple domination of men (though this plays a tactical part), but
a struggle based on a theory of the social non-necessity at this stage
of development of the laws instituted by patriarchy" (414). And her
predictions are that once patriarchy and capitalism are overthrown, then
"new structures will gradually come to be represented in the unconscious" (415) — probably across a time span that brings us to utopias
and millennias.

In presenting the general ideas associated with each of these
feminist theorists, different aspects of the feminine and woman emerge
which correlate with ecofeminism's treatment of gender: one that
valorizes woman and one that sees gender as a cultural construct.
Chodorow argues, in "Gender, Relation and Difference", that these two
positions within feminism are clearly distinct: The first one sees gender
differences as innate and claims "women are intrinsically better than
men and their virtues are not available to men" (3). Therefore, society
should not be de-gendered but taken over by women. The second is
the "de-gendering" model that sees female characteristics and virtues
as also desirable and achievable for men and that social constructs,
ipso facto, are changeable.

But, in ecofeminism, these two are not as distinct as
Chodorow sees them. While there is a valorization of woman, it does
not necessarily imply an innateness, only a valorization of woman as
she stands *now* in male-female difference. It is the same logic that
casts woman as man's other, the logic of dualism, that ecofeminism
attempts to undermine, to "deconstruct". A valorization of the feminine
as innate reinforces the logic of dualism rather than deconstructing it.
The essentialist approach to woman defines her in opposing relationships to man, and undermines an ecofeminist goal of disentangling the
otherness of woman (and nature) as dualistic constructs. Such an approach circles back on itself and keeps man at the center of any
perception of woman. But, as we are considering a particular time
segment in the process of gender relations, then this tendency to
valorize woman *now* should be considered as part of such a process,

rather than an attempt to solidify and reinforce gender differences. This becomes particularly clear in the fictional texts, which we turn to now. In these texts, the "representations" of gender depict dynamic processes that deal with gender roles and difference. Like Mitchell, Chodorow and Irigaray, the authors move away from the implications of defining "woman", and instead turn toward problematizing dualism within gender constructs.

Fictional Femininity

In light of these gender constructs, the fictional texts offer some striking similarities on the plot level that stem from the authors' positions outside of the mainstream of patriarchal ideology. That is, they can see, feel, and are aware of the workings of patriarchal ideology on them. Therefore, as might be expected, their depictions of femininity are not representations of patriarchal ideals of gender identities. It is also noteworthy that nuclear families are either not portrayed at all or are depicted only as destructive influences. Equally important, there is no indication that the nuclear family is desirable or is a goal "beyond the ending", that is, either encoded as a subtext or implied as a continuation of the plot beyond the close of the narrative.

Problems of representation and narrative strategies in fiction are pertinent to gynocriticism and will be discussed in Part II; however, it is relevant to note here that the authors we are examining have developed and work through a number of oppositional possibilities for the depiction of gender and gender institutions in narrative. Collectively they exhibit, in DuPlessis' terms, "a critical sensibility — dissent from the culture by which women are partially nourished and to which women are connected" (39).

In basically all of the texts, the authors examine the conflict between the protagonist's own development and the social construct of gender. This conflict catapults the protagonist to a plane of self-awareness and invariably allows her to see the social construct of gender as victimizing her in one way or another. Feminist critic Ellen Morgan in "Humanbecoming" suggests that such a protagonist is in a process of transition in which "her task is the integration of all her parts, disconnected as they have been by the socialization which has prepared her to play the feminine role" (272). It is clear in these texts that this socialization on the part of the protagonists comes also from the self, in the form of self-repression or self-censure. This internaliza-tion of the expectations of the dominant culture evident in these texts is, at the same time, used by the authors to suggest a new conscious-ness for their protagonists, one that moves toward feminist values. This movement has the effect of undermining a patriarchal system that demands a definition of woman which would confine her to narrowly constructed roles, limiting her development as a complete being. Taken together, the texts nevertheless avoid a vague humanistic holism as a response to gender depiction. Rather they suggest that woman can reject any number of roles defined by the dominant culture, without having to substitute others. This attitude reflects Ynestra King's idea of reconstituting culture in the name of nature in order to reverse the process of domination and destruction that is similar for both woman and nature. Indeed, in many of the texts, the women have created or developed a "culture" of their own within which they develop freely their own ideas of femininity. Needless to say, as we will see in the following discussions patriarchally-defined family roles and sexual roles are not part of that "culture".

The nuclear family, as a major symbol of patriarchal ideology that restricts and confines woman, finds its expression in these texts as well. Briefly, regarding this idea of the nuclear family, we see Laurence's Morag, separated from her parents by their death and subsequently raised by step-parents who do not fit the nuclear family pattern. Morag's attempt to re-create a family through her marriage to Brooke fails and she chooses motherhood without a partner. Atwood's protagonist, also feels only alienation from her original nuclear family and sees motherhood beyond the boundaries of a nuclear family as a necessity. That in the end she decides to return to civilization is a symbol of her resignation but not her commitment. Robinson's protag-onist, Ruthie, never knew her father, and her mother's suicide leaves her without such family ties. Even in the grandmother's generation, direct male influence in the family was eliminated which, of course, does not mean the girls grew up outside of the patriarchal order, for this is represented by the villagers. Sylvie fails to provide the framework of traditional family life (indeed she is an outsider in every way), and Lucille is lost to them when she makes a conscious decision to become part of the circle of village life, with its patriarchal implications.

The two Black novels, with their emphasis on communities of women, provide an alternative view of life outside of nuclear families. It is certainly necessary in this context to mention that the black experience in America has been anything but conducive to the development of the nuclear family as a symbol of the patriarchal order. With its history of family division through slavery and poverty, the black experience is a vivid example of the negative workings of patriarchal ideology. Still, the patriarchal *ideal* of the nuclear family has not been eliminated, even if it is largely removed from any reality. Motherhood has little to do with traditional family life in these two texts. Indeed, motherhood and the systems of childcare as depicted by Walker and Naylor are subversive to the patriarchal order because they undermine the idea of the nuclear family.

In Walker's *The Color Purple*, Celie's father is dead and she has already borne two children by her step-father who are being raised by step-parents and her sister Nettie. Her husband, Albert, has several children from a previous marriage. Shug already has three children by Albert. Albert's daughter-in-law, Sofia, has five children with Harpo and another with "the prizefighter". Mary Agnes takes care of Sofia's children while Sofia is in jail, and Sofia takes care of Mary Agnes's when Mary Agnes goes off to Memphis to sing. The men become more and more irrelevant as the women raise each other's children. Although this is not the main emphasis of the text, this non-nuclear situation provides the atmosphere in which the women offer mutual aid and comfort and love. Men are seen as ineffectual because they want to claim possession of their wives and are powerless against the women with their numerous relationships.

In *Brewster Place*, Naylor emphasizes the community of women that attempts to function outside of the male domain. As individuals, the women may have initially been part of nuclear families but, like Mattie, not having played by the rules, they become outcasts and take up life on Brewster Place. The characters, who are portrayed as narrow-minded and intolerant, are those who are involved in keeping the patriarchal order as intact as possible, i.e., those who see the lesbian couple as a threat to their heterosexual relationship with their own husbands, and consequently reaffirm patriarchal relationships. Naylor creates one scene in which such characters disrupt a neighborhood meeting organized to fight against the landlords. They become so involved in supporting all forms of the patriarchal order that they indirectly also support the atmosphere of hate which finally destroys Lorraine, whom they see as an outsider and a threat to their heterosexual values.

Finally, the utopian novels launch the most direct attack on the nuclear family as a vicious symbol of reductionist gender roles, almost as a prerequisite for utopia. The nuclear family has been eliminated as an institution altogether. In *Woman on the Edge of Time*, Piercy constructs her Mattapoisett society around multiple-parent family units with communal living quarters. This arrangement produces much looser parent-child ties and promotes independence in the children. The protagonist, Connie, saturated with patriarchal ideals, finds these community situations distasteful at first, because she regards them as threatening to the only positive aspect she sees in herself, the experience of motherhood and her intense relationship to her daughter. Eventually, she realizes that even this relationship is defined and controlled by the dominant male-oriented society, which has the power to take away her daughter. In Gearhart's *Wanderground*, no form or symbol of patriarchy is allowed to exist within the Wanderground. No familial structures are proscribed. Motherhood exists. Impregnation rituals and communal childcare are mentioned, but these are not problematized. It is as if to suggest that without male domination and control, these feminine functions are not "problems".

The absence of the nuclear family in these texts exemplifies a type of critique the authors use to undermine the depiction of gender institutions. The author's disregard for the convention of the nuclear family acts as a basic critique of the way gender constructs work against woman. In other words, without the burdens of nuclear families, the authors can depict other possibilities for character development.

The expression of sexuality the authors depict provides another dimension to woman and gender. Specific female experiences, like pregnancy, childbirth, motherhood, menstruation, and lesbianism, which historically have been denied fictional treatment, are treated creatively as positive core experiences for women. Motherhood, for example, is demonstrated through various possible arrangements that do not depend on the nuclear family. In addressing these experiences, the authors treat their characters more fully as woman-as-subject. The more these experiences are recognized and acknowledged as part of woman's sexuality, the less these protagonists allow the dominant culture to construct and limit their sexuality for them. The depiction of these experiences invariably coincides with a break in consciousness, or a reevaluation of the self, that marks the end of the old self-repressed state and signifies the beginning of a new sense of self. In Atwood's *Surfacing*, we see the point of coincidence between the protagonist and her pregnancy; in Walker's *The Color Purple*, Celie and her lesbian relationship to Shug; in Laurence's *Diviners*, Morag Gunn and her pregnancy; in Naylor's *Brewster Place*, Mattie and the lesbian couple; in Robinson's *Housekeeping*, Ruthie and the discovery of "mother"; and in Gearhart's *Wanderground* and in Piercy's *Woman on the Edge of Time*, all of these experiences are treated in the utopian scenarios of unencumbered sexual relations. In each of these texts the positive nature of these exclusively feminine experiences are indicative of the characters' femininity and selfhood.

These conceptions of female sexuality are supported by a number of more subtle literary conventions. The protagonist in *Surfacing* comes to realize that the gender contradictions victimizing her are manipulations that prevent her from seeing herself. She breaks the mirror Anna uses in applying her daily layers of makeup to please David, and in it she recognizes herself as a victim of a male ideology. But she also perceives the mirror as a distortion of man's vision of himself — which is why in the end she decides she could trust Joe because he is "only half-formed" (192). She must, however, come to a point of clear recognition. She sees her complicity in the inability to communicate, "mirrored" in Anna's and David's relationship, in which they spend a lot of time erecting barriers against each other's sexuality and mask their attitudes about uninhibited, unemotional copulation. The protagonist, in turn, ritualizes her copulation with Joe, which is equally deprived of emotion, in order to fulfil her desire for pregnancy. DuPlessis dismisses Joe as "the woodsy impregnator [who is] sent away when his job is done," (98) however, this ignores the fact that eventually she decides to return to him. As a reversal of her earlier abortion in which she felt she was a manipulated object, she now sees pregnancy and her imagined childbirth scene (161-2) as crucial to her idea of sexuality as part of female experience and subjectivity, and as indicative of her newly developing consciousness. Morag Gunn in *Diviners*, like Atwood's protagonist, refuses to become the woman that her husband Brooke expects her to be. From the beginning of her relationship with Brooke, she seems to question his values, but at the same time, she tries to hide anything that might displease him, and "She will do whatever he wants her to do" (196). She hides her past and the significance of Manawaka from her husband in order to be what he wants her to be for him. But it is Jules finally who accepts her as a complete entity, which allows her to accept herself as such. Equally important, she then accepts him as a complete entity. She sees Brooke as having been negatively influenced by his parents' restrictive view of gender, which he has carried over to their relationship. When she discovers other aspects of herself that cannot be related to Brooke, like her literary talent, she begins to subjectivize herself, i.e., she begins to see herself no longer as an object of Brooke's affection and to realize positive aspects of her sexuality. This marks the budding of her new consciousness as a woman. Her decision to have a child and her pregnancy are acts of rebellion against a husband who wants to deny her these aspects of her sexuality.

Similarly, in the utopian works, female experiences are viewed as catalysts for changing consciousness. Expressions of sexuality are the most obvious examples because they are intended to portray gender freed of repression, in contrast to their respective dystopias. The whole text of *Wanderground* is geared toward or centered around the rejection of the role of woman as evolved in the City, which creates room for alternative roles for women. Unfortunately, this leads to the valorization of many aspects of female experiences: the conception ritual with the seven sister-mothers in the Deep Cella (43-52), the ovulation and menstruation rituals (14), etc. References to lesbianism are not so much celebrated as taken for granted: "When sleep came it was no less sweet and deep than their loving" (17).

In Mattapoisett, Piercy confronts a dilemma in attempting to equalize sexuality. There remain no primarily female experiences like childbirth and pregnancy which can be personally experienced, and bi-sexual preferences become the norm. Piercy would probably agree with the statement that "there is an implicit and inescapable antifeminism in any insistence upon the difference between the sexes."[9] In Mattapoisett the sense of something missing might stem from the absence of individual sexual uniqueness, for in removing the implicit and inescapable misogyny of Connie's "present", Piercy eliminates implicit and inescapable difference.

Here we come upon another point of conflict with the French critical influences. Jardine cites this point, the differences between the sexes, as crucial. Paraphrasing Lyotard, she writes that "neutralization is the ultimate goal of capitalism — the erasing of differences to increase exchange value" (43) and thus part of another master discourse. Irigaray comments on this as well: "sexual indifference, sustaining the truth of all science, the logic of all discourse"[10] In other words, the striving for sexual equality should not be equated with the elimination of sexual difference, as writer/critics like Miles and Piercy would suggest. This is an important point, although only in the utopian texts is equality without difference taken to be a "goal", a direct result of eliminating the oppositional stances of sexual identity (man and woman). The other texts seem to be rather comfortable with the idea of woman as different, although this is not seen as a particularly easy way out of the dilemma, because it leaves the oppositional stances still in tact. Exceptions here are the lesbian experiences portrayed by Walker and Naylor, in which the oppositional aspects are de-emphasized and woman's sexual multiplicity becomes a core experience.

Before Celie of *The Color Purple* can reach an understanding of her sexuality, she must break through the cycle of violence surrounding her. The conception and birth of her two children were scenes of violence and sadness; sexual relations with her husband are demeaning and loveless. In her life of pain and abuse, she has had no time to think about herself as subject. Her subsequent relationship to Shug is the key to her discovery of sexuality and communication. Their lesbian relationship is one means of overthrowing absolutely the social construct of woman as envisaged by a patriarchal society and, for Celie, marks the end of her consciousness as object. While much has been made of this relationship between Shug and Celie, Shug does return to a heterosexual relationship which both hurts Celie and brings her to a greater acceptance of individual differences of sexual/political expression. Celie begins to "define" herself instead of internalizing man's definition of her. Initially, Shug's sense of sexuality becomes Celie's model. But eventually Celie grows beyond Shug. She sees that despite Shug's apparent independence, Shug actually sees herself in relation to man. Celie continues her growth as a self-defined woman.

Mattie of *Brewster Place* is a protagonist in between two levels of consciousness and represents double marginality. She has long defined herself apart from men, and sees the sexuality expressed in pregnancy and motherhood as something akin to what Walker, in her essay "In Search of Our Mothers' Gardens", explains as,

> we have asked for love, we have been given children.
> In short, even our plainer gifts, our labors of fidelity
> and love, have been knocked down our throats. (197)

But Mattie's sexuality is also part of the community of Brewster Place and she has unending sympathy for those who live there, including the lesbian couple Lorraine and Theresa. Unlike Walker's Celie, Mattie does not have a lesbian relationship herself. She does, however, question the reactions of the other women to Lorraine and Therese:

> "But I've loved some women deeper than I ever
> loved any man," Mattie was pondering. "And there
> been some women who loved me more and did more
> for me than any man ever did."..."Maybe it's not so
> different," Mattie said, almost to herself. "Maybe
> that's why some women get so riled up about it,
> 'cause they know deep down it's not so different
> after all." (141)

She also questions the brutal retribution the gang extracts from Lorraine for her lesbianism. Mattie has already seen the patriarchal system as one of victimization, but the jump from the institutional violence of the system to the personal violence in Lorraine's gang rape and the murder of Ben catapults her to a new level of awareness which precipitates action. For Mattie, this level of awareness does not include a more understanding view of man. For her, women alone are important. Consequently, the destruction of the wall, with the women using their bare hands till their fingers bleed mingling their blood with that of Lorraine's (and Ben's), can also be interpreted as tearing down the barriers erected against their sexuality.

A last example is *Housekeeping*, which is, on the one hand, devoid of sexuality in conventional terms because it is devoid of the men who define women, but, on the other hand, it is full of the sexuality of women who clearly conceptualize themselves. Lucille fails to put Sylvie in categories of conventional sexuality, and finally the village fails to put Ruthie in such categories. Sylvie expresses her femininity in her housekeeping, for example, or her gentleness, her preference for darkness, etc. In a key passage, in which Ruthie has left Lucille at the drugstore where Lucille intends to buy hair lotion, nail polish, fashion magazines etc., for her, Ruthie muses,

> And I was left alone, in the gentle afternoon, indifferent to my clothes and comfortable in my skin, unimproved and without the prospect of improvement. It seemed to me then that Lucille would busy herself forever, nudging, pushing, coaxing, as if she could supply the will I lacked, to pull myself into some seemly shape and slip across the wide frontiers into that other world, where it seemed to me then I could never wish to go. For it seemed to me that nothing I had lost, or might lose, could be found there, or, to put it another way, it seemed that something I had lost might be found in Sylvie's house. (123-4)

Her sense of self is too strong at this point to drift over to Lucille and "that other world" of conventional sexuality. She remains beyond the boundaries of cultural constructs that she finds limiting and confining.

At least at the plot level, these texts imply their conjunction with a general critique of conventional sexuality which defines, limits and constructs woman as existing only in relationship to man. Taken together, they celebrate woman's sexuality in its multiplicity and, in doing so, they take progressive steps to oust man from his central position in woman's lives. As Celie comments, "You have to git man off your eyeball, before you can see anything a'tall" (179) — which brings us back to dualism and its demise.

As I mentioned at the beginning of Part I, ecofeminism is to a certain extent a critique of means, such as gender constructs and language (as we will see in the following chapter), which have associated woman and nature in dualistic opposition to man and culture. Ecofeminism as discourse attempts to undermine the logic of dualism. Through feminist critiques of Freudian theory on femininity and gender, even from such diverse interpretations as Irigaray's, Chodorow's and Mitchell's, it becomes clear that woman possesses a great many more aspects than those Freud would attribute to her. In light of such critiques, Freud's theories on femininity and gender seem reductionist and essentialist, exactly because they view woman only in dualistic opposition to man. What these critics attempt (and in this endeavor are well supported by the authors) is to offer different scenarios and interpretations. In Irigaray's and Chodorow's views, woman is not tied to a me/not-me, either/or, subject/object orientation, but bases her orientations on multiplicity. In this context, woman is more capable of accepting nature as an all-encompassing principle that cannot be broken down into its controllable parts. The idea of nature as part of self, male or female, is based on such a holistic view. This has equal implications for culture, and, of course, for man as part of the duality principle that is being "deconstructed". From such a stance, for example, Ynestra King can say "our culture" in the name of ecofeminists and can suggest "reconstituting our culture in the name of nature." The authors have created fictional possibilities for the development of woman beyond an androcentric system, but they remain bound by the language they use. It is on another level, then, that we turn to language as it affects writing, fiction and ecofeminist discourse.

NOTES

1.Mitchell, *Psychoanalysis and Feminism*; Irigaray, *The Speculum of the Other Woman*; Chodorow, *The Reproduction of Mothering*; and "Gender, Relation and Difference in Psychoanalytic Perspective", in Hester Eisenstein and Alice Jardine (eds.), *The Future of Difference*, (Boston: G.K. Hall, 1980, rpt. 1986), pp. 4-19.

2.Basically, the accepted practice within feminism is to use 'male' and 'female' as biological designations, 'masculine' and 'feminine' as cultural and social ones. In adopting these forms, feminism can more easily eliminate the confusion of defining biological woman through cultural standards.

3.Toril Moi, *Sexual/Textual Politics*, (London: Methuen, 1985), p. 65.

4.cf. Cixous, "Sorties" in *La jeune née* (Paris: 10/18, 1975), 115-246, qtd. in Jardine, *Gynesis*, p. 72.

5. Although she does not otherwise reject Freud, she maintains — as do Chodorow and others — that Freud began developing his theories on woman and gender, and then, sensing his discoveries were too revolutionary even for himself, he backed away. Robert Scholes in "Decoding Mama" in *Semiotics and Interpretation*, (New Haven: Yale Univ. Press, 1982) offers an interesting semiotic interpretation of Freud's theory of the feminine.

6.See chapter 4 for a further discussion.

7.Irigaray, *Ce sexe qui n'en est pas un*, (Paris: Minuit, 1977), pp. 75-6. qtd. and trans. in Moi, *Sexual/Textual Politics*, p. 139; cf. Irigaray, *The Sex That Is Not One*, trs. Catherine Porter and Carolyn Burke, (Ithaca: Cornell UP, 1985).

8. Chodorow, "Gender", p. 14. See also Dale Spender, *Man-Made Language*, (London: Routledge & Kegan Paul, 1983).

9.Rosalind Miles, *The Fiction of Sex: Themes and Functions of Sex Difference in the Modern Novel*, (London: Vision Press, 1974), p. 110.

10.Irigaray, *The Sex Which Is Not One*, p. 67.

When we speak of the need for a special language for
women, what then do we mean?

(Mary Jacobus)

"... it's the fault of the pronouns ..."
(Samuel Beckett, *The Unnamable*)

"Look like to me only a fool would want you to talk in
a way that feel peculiar to your mind."
(Alice Walker, *The Color Purple*)

4

Woman and Words

Woman's relationship to language in ecofeminist discourse
revolves around the means and usages of metaphor that reinforce the
woman/nature, man/culture dualism on the lexical, semantic, and
narrative levels. Such reinforcement of dualism through language is
symptomatic of a "phallologocentrism" that sustains the hegemony of
male culture through its very use. This concept of "phallologocentrism", originated by Jacques Derrida, figures prominently in the works
of French feminist theorists and through their works has come into the
Anglo-American critical feminist discourse. "Phallologocentrism"
describes a signifying system organized around gender that maintains
the male-identified subject at the center of words.[1]

One can begin with the idea that language is power and
meaning, and that for many centuries women have been largely denied
access to and use of public language, the language of dominant discourse. They have therefore been unable to influence it, make it
responsive to them, or expressive of their needs. Focusing on this
"phallologocentrism" as a system of signification, feminist critics show
its negative impact on woman, and develop their interest in language
as a space that has been repressed by that phallologocentric discourse.

Current research on language is rooted in the nineteenth and early twentieth century, which experienced renewed interests in language as a mirror of power and language as social behavior that communicates cultural values as well as defines and maintains social roles. It has been given a great impetus by a group of influential voices from the French post-structural, deconstructionist, semiotic critics, acutely aware of the possibilities and pitfalls of woman in her relationship to the phallologos. While I do not intend to discuss these French theorists in depth, as a whole they have had enormous impact on the American feminist critical world. Their points of intersection are of interest in interpreting the way the feminist authors concerned here come to terms with language as both a limiting and a liberating factor in attempting to create new concepts of woman and nature outside the realm of dualism. In this way we return to the problem of language depicting nature, or nature as cultural construct.

In France, the now prominent feminist theorists and critics, with intellectual backgrounds in psychoanalysis, linguistics, and structuralism that differ dramatically from their English-speaking counterparts, have led the way in language research and are concerned with the structure of language and with language as narrative. Julia Kristeva, Luce Irigaray, and Hélène Cixous[2] have each approached these aspects of language. For Irigaray, the feminine is a signifying system, for Kristeva, the feminine is the semiotic, for Cixous, the unconscious. There is among these women an important emphasis on the feminine as pre-oedipal, the period of development before children acquire language. If language is masculine (the phallologos), then the pre-masculine logos must emanate from the relationship between mother and child previous to the child's language development. Thus in this pre-verbal time, communication is unconscious, semiotic, emotional, metaphorically "feminine". It is significant in our context of ecofeminism and the relationship between woman and nature that this pre-verbal unconscious is called "the feminine", for it is this unconscious that is being probed in psychoanalytical theory. And, it is this unconscious as the object of psychoanalytical theory which Leiss suggests is the latest expression of the domination of nature, that is, of his third category of nature, human nature (earlier expressions being the physical and social domination of human nature). Far from getting away from dualism, this terminology, the unconscious as "the feminine", seems to reinforce a metaphysical dichotomy. In fact, not all of these French critics would agree to the label "feminist" I use here precisely because it is generally couched in opposition, and feminists who consider themselves in opposition to the male, and thus who still work within oppositional dualism, would be rejected by these women as "male".[3] Much of the research emanating from these feminist theorists focuses on the sources and development of woman's linguistic context, and addresses the concern that women must express themselves in a system that is repressive.

But the problem remains of looking more closely at the linguistic terminology that seems to reinforce the dualistic aspects of language. On the one hand, we take the "phallologos", which denies woman access to language, on the other there is "the feminine" which refers to the pre-verbal, pre-oedipal unconscious, which can only be expressed through a submission to language (the phallologos). The two poles must have a point of intersection in the signifying process, and this point creates a potential for influence and change. For Kristeva, the language of literature, fiction and poetry, holds the possibilities of developing "a new position for the speaking subject."[4] Only when woman can claim subjectivity for herself can the intersecting point between the "phallologos" and the "feminine" become the dynamic of change for woman's relationship to language. But not even the concept of the subject is without its pitfalls, for in the context of the "phallologos", it is dualistic.

The feminist critique of language at this point in time is necessarily paradoxical, because it must use the phallologos to undermine it; this feeling of paradox is expressed in texts by Irigaray and Cixous. Both are concerned with the narrative level of language and how woman must find a language system expressive of herself. Irigaray begins her essay, "When Our Lips Speak Together":

> If we continue to speak this sameness, if we speak to
> each other as men have spoken for centuries, as they
> taught us to speak, we will fail each other. Again ...
> words will pass through our bodies, above our heads,
> disappear, make us disappear. Far. Above. Absent

> from ourselves, we become machines that are spoken,
> machines that speak. Clean skins envelop us, but they
> are not our own. (69)

She expresses a sense of distrust that language has betrayed woman
because it has been a vehicle of oppression. Cixous in "The Laugh of
the Medusa" also wants woman to invent a language that would not
deny her selfhood:

> It's not to be feared that language conceals an
> invincible adversary, because it's the language of
> men and their grammar. We mustn't leave them a
> single place that's any more theirs alone than we are.
> If woman has always functioned "within" the dis-
> course of man, a signifier that has always referred
> back to the opposite signifier which annihilates its
> specific energy and diminishes or stifles its very
> different sounds, it is time for her to dislocate this
> "within", to explode it, turn it around, and seize it; to
> make it hers, containing it, taking it in her own
> mouth, biting that tongue with her very own teeth to
> invent for herself a language to get inside of. And
> you'll see with what ease she will spring forth from
> that "within" ... (887)

Both Irigaray and Cixous it seems would advocate a woman's
language whose signifiers challenge the very concept of universality.
But this demand, while still vague, offers an image that I began with,
that of working from "within" a particular paradox through to the
outside. Such a process suggests again a self-critical stance and an
awareness of participation in or submission to phallologocentrism.

Nevertheless, this idea of a special language for woman is
very problematic in our context because of its dualistic implications.
However, numerous other feminist writers and theorists have spoken
of this need and have directed their attention to the lexical level
(mainly pronoun changes), the semantic level (for example, renaming
and redefining), as well as at the narrative level (often, woman as

subject).[5] Besides posing a practical problem, i.e., what actually is meant by a woman's language?, there is the additional danger that after deconstructing phallologocentrism, such a language could become yet another dominant discourse. Feminism in theory has to reject the replacement of one system by another, break through another aspect of dualism, and accept the heterogeneity, or multiplicity, it celebrates.

This concern with language recognizes the complex and pervasive factors surrounding the concepts of woman and nature, and acknowledges that attempting to reformulate these concepts outside of oppositional dualism demands breaking through the laws of language that maintain dualism. On the semantic level, writers and critics like Adrienne Rich and Mary Daly[6] are concerned with and committed to renaming and redefining concepts, recognizing that the power to name should be a significant characteristic of feminism. Daly's ponderous work, *Gyn/ecology*, is a trip through the labyrinth of language, which she explains as:

> Gynocentric writing means risking. Since the language and style of patriarchal writing simply cannot contain or carry the energy of women's exorcism and ecstasy, in this book I invent, dis-cover, re-member. At times I make up words (such as gynaesthesia for women's synaesthesia). Often I unmask deceptive words by dividing them and employing alternate meanings for prefixes (for example, *re-cover* actually says "cover again"). I also unmask their hidden reversals, often by using less known or "obsolete" meanings (for example, *glamour* as used to name a witch's power). Sometimes I simply invite the reader to listen to words in a different way (for example, *de-light*). When I play with words I do this attentively, deeply, paying attention to etymology, to varied dimensions of meaning, to deep background meanings and subliminal associations ... (24)

The result is an exercise in language deconstruction that occasionally resorts in a sort of overkill in "dis-spelling" or "dis-covering" woman's suppression and oppression in the phallologos. She is more cleverly descriptive than visionary, here, but she shares Gearhart's and Piercy's insistence that changing language will bring about social change, and that language must be restructured to allow for new vocabulary that will describe the resulting social changes. Daly attempts to appropriate language for woman by naming, re-naming, inventing and reinventing words in order to reveal the system of the phallologos and its impact on woman. Her approach takes over this same system for woman, uses its powers for woman to create another master discourse in her own name which is a result that critics like Irigaray and Cixous warn against. While Rich in her approach through poetry and lyrical prose is more visionary, she, too, finds that being "released into language ... is learning that it can be used as a means of changing reality".[7] Daly and Rich are both writers who acknowledge the limiting and liberating factors of language.

On the narrative level, the feminist writers discussed here are all concerned with woman's place in language that, to a certain extent, evolves from the semantic level. The creation of new semantic imagery allows authors to reconceptualize relationships and the self. In these fictional narratives, the emphasis on woman-as-subject with special attention to female first-person narrative, the problematization of foreign languages and dialects, and the female protagonists' more general critical stance toward language itself are important issues for these authors.

These critiques of language on various levels, however, intersect with and partially emanate from the theories associated with the French critics mentioned previously. The debt to these French critical theories becomes even clearer in the questions that the Anglo-American feminists are formulating that circumscribe the emphasis on woman and language: How do women cope with a logos which basically denies their existence? What is the nature of women's access to culture and their entry into literary discourse? To what extent must women submit to phallologocentricity as the price for this entry? How can the feminine break through the limitations of language in order to liberate it from its own boundaries?[8] Kristeva's theory of the "chora", as an articulation that precedes figuration, suggests that the chora is successfully repressed after entering into the Symbolic Order, i.e., acquiring language and thus submitting to the phallologos. But, she leaves open the possibility that the chora can be perceived as a disruption of language outside the realm of traditional linguistics — such as silences, absences, meaninglessness, contradictions, etc.[9] For feminist authors, the problem runs a parallel form in whether it is possible to disrupt the phallologos from within. They are keenly aware of their use of and entry into the literary plane through the phallologos and have begun to confront the problems this poses for them.[10]

Woman's relationship to language intersects with ecofeminism primarily on two levels: woman-as-subject on the narrative level, and, on the semantic level, the use of metaphor that reinforces the dualism it would like to deconstruct. Woman-as-subject becomes an attempt to consciously reject the object role of the phallologos, which, with man at its center, would deny the possibility of the feminine subject. Metaphor, with its subtle relationships to patriarchal order, poses some specific challenges for ecofeminism as a discourse. As an element of language, metaphor is a carrier of ideology, and as such influences woman and her relationship through language to nature. Ecofeminism, in critiquing dualistic patterns that reinforce this association, exposes the workings of metaphor and the ideology behind it.

Subjectivity

The problem of subjectivity in the texts is a complex one; the very concept of subjectivity is fraught with "dangers" of the ideological sort, emanating as it does from the idea of the "self" as a complex of structures and manifestations that inevitably are reductive as fixed sexual identities. It becomes a trap of "Western male humanism" (7), as Toril Moi suggests, that makes "subject" a central concept. On the other hand, if language is seen as depriving woman of subjectivity by conceptualizing her as object and depriving her of voice, on the fictional level at least, woman could be given back her voice, her sense of self as subject, her "I".

In our ecofeminist context, these fictional texts confront a dualism that denies woman subjectivity and language responsive to her needs. Bridging the gap between narrative strategies (discussed in Part II) and these authors' sensitivity to language and particular literary techniques is the particular phenomenon of the female "I", first-person narrator, woman-as-subject. Of the seven novels discussed here three are exclusively written in the first-person (*Surfacing, Housekeeping*, and *The Color Purple*), two are in a first-person mixed form (*Woman on the Edge of Time*, and *The Diviners*), and two have collective or "choral" protagonists (*The Wanderground*, and *The Women of Brewster Place*). In this period in which authors are interested in female possibilities, I think this phenomena is not coincidental. This female "I" is not that of the stream-of-consciousness writing which "with its tendency to equate reality and value with consciousness cannot sufficiently express her experience, which is political and social as well as personal and psychological".[11] The woman-as-subject that emerges from these works represents the conviction of the authors that language can be the key to liberation for woman, rendering her capable of interpreting and conceptualizing herself and her socio-political environment.

This stance is perhaps more difficult to maintain than one would like to hope because it enters the discourse on woman at precisely the point where the French theorists and critics are questioning the validity of subjectivity and identity, tied as these concepts are to the phallologos. Having considered subject and object in terms of dualism ("I" and the "Other"), Kristeva, for example, repeatedly insists that psychologically "the other" is the other sex. The difference between subject and object correlates then with sexual difference, and for the female subject, this implies a simple reversal still within the realm of language law and the phallologos. So again, the authors are caught up in a paradoxical stance in which creating a female "I" becomes "a position which is at once subversive and dependent on the law."[12]

The way out of this subject-object dyad might be the idea of the "anonymous neuter", which Jardine explores in relationship to theories by Barthes, Derrida, Todorov, Blanchot. However, significant to our consideration of the female subject, she asks, "Could it possibly be that the new philosophically valorized 'neuter anonymity' of the text or world — a valorization of singularities beyond sexual difference — is but a new attempt to escape the rising voices of women?" (117). In this way, Jardine points to the central paradox of feminism which does not want to ignore sexuality, yet wants to overcome the opposition to the masculine. Still the anonymity or neutrality as expressed by these critics, while transcending opposition, might also serve to deny woman's sexuality.

On the other hand, woman-as-subject might be the entry point to the phallologos that at the same time could change its points of reference, or even begin to deconstruct it. However, I don't think the texts here accrue the power, within the bounds of the narrative, to assert the woman-as-subject as a possibility for deconstructing the phallologos. Indeed, this may be impossible, if the boundaries of narrative, as circumscribed by the "Symbolic Order", are ones which deny woman's subjectivity. Woman might have to begin writing outside of the bounds of narrative, but that, too, may be future fictional material (or in Piercy's and Gearhart's sense, utopian). Nonetheless, the prevalence of woman's voice in these novels is striking. The authors here are purposefully and decisively attempting to create their female protagonists as subjects, or as women who work their way towards asserting their subjectivity. The texts encode three dilemmas for consideration of the female subject; these I refer to as the dilemma of reluctant subjects, the dilemma of "I", and the dilemma of "we".

The Dilemma of Reluctant Subjects

In the reluctant subject paradigm, there seems to be an open struggle between the protagonist and earlier versions of herself that the authors express through a mixed narrative, alternating between the first-person and omniscient points of view.

Piercy's *Woman on the Edge of Time* is of this kind. The narrative is entirely from Connie's point of view, but is not entirely in first-person, which indicates Connie's lack of subjectivity, at least in the beginning. The opening paragraph indicates this point of view: "Connie got up from her kitchen table and walked slowly to the door. 'Either I saw him or I didn't and I'm crazy for real this time', she thought." And later on, there is another indicator of Connie's socio-linguistic problem: "'We wear out so early,' she said to the mirror, not really sure who the 'we' was. Her life was thin in meaningful 'we's'" (35). Connie is even for herself an object.

If we understand Luciente as Connie's hallucinatory projection of herself, then Connie has so objectified herself as to make herself separate to herself. Through Luciente we see Connie's progression towards becoming a subject. It is this issue of subjectivity that is problematic for Piercy's character, Connie. By the end of the work, she is no longer able to call up Luciente, because she has come to see herself no longer as object, but can experience herself as a subject. In a passage at the end of the novel that parallels her comments to the mirror quoted above, a much changed Connie asserts, "'I just killed six people', she said to the mirror, but she washed her hands because she was terrified of the poison. 'I murdered them dead'" (375). When she asserts herself as an active subject, she no longer has need for Luciente as a projected objectification of herself:

> She thought of Luciente, but she could no longer reach over. She could no longer catch. She had annealed her mind and she was not a receptive woman. She had hardened. But she thought of Mattapoisett.
>   For Skip, for Alice, for Tina, for Captain Cream and Orville, for Claud, for you who will be born from my best hopes, to you I dedicate my act of war. At least once I fought and won. (375)

For Connie, gaining her subjectivity is synonymous with taking action against the Other. That the penultimate chapter is a collection of hospital reports about Connie shows that the system has taken its revenge, unable to accept such a woman-as-subject. This ending is indicative of Piercy's skepticism about the power of a woman-as-subject: on an individualistic level such a power cannot counteract a society determined to destroy this woman-as-subject.

Although she plays with much less dramatic themes in *The Diviners* Laurence uses a similar narrative technique. Her protagonist, Morag, is another reluctant subject. Laurence focuses on the protagonist's point of view without always using her first-person voice. This enables her to use a different sequential pattern in her text, one in which the narrative begins at the end, giving the mature Morag a point of view of herself that suggests she is already the primary actor, the woman-as-subject in the text. However, Laurence seems unsure of her protagonist, for she employs many traditional techniques that would serve to undermine the idea of Morag as woman-as-subject, such as using flashback techniques that serve to "objectify" the younger version of Morag. In this sort of Bildungs narrative, in which the protagonist moves herself through historical sequence, the plot normally takes over, pushing the "I" to the edge and focusing on the younger version of the "I" as a third person Other, until at the end, the character is reunited with the personal narrator. In other words, Morag sees herself in the past as object, particularly in the photo-album images of herself, and the scenes in the past are written in third-person narrative. But because there is a continual returning to the present between these forays into the past, Laurence maintains the focus of the text through the woman-as-subject, Morag. The net effect of all this is not so much the creation of a forceful woman-as-subject, but the evaluation of one capable of withstanding paradox and contradiction. Indeed, Laurence begins her text with this implication: "The river flowed both ways ... This apparently impossible contradiction, made apparent and possible, still fascinated Morag ..."

Through their protagonists as reluctant subjects, the authors do project the feminist dilemma: How finally can a woman perceive herself wholly as subject — much less assert herself as subject or retain her integrity as subject — in a patriarchal society? While Laurence puts Morag on the fringes of society as Morag's own choice, where she can function alone and isolated, Piercy puts her protagonist Connie on the fringes of society by fact of birth and social discrimination. The narrative mode reflects this dilemma: finding a space for oneself, safe but isolated at the fringes (one imposed by the patriarchy), or striking out from a fringe area alone only to be destroyed. In neither text do the protagonists positively throw off their reluctance to be the woman-as-subject. Connie reacts to dangerous situations in dangerous ways; Morag is content to live within her contradictions, hoping for solutions in her daughter's generation.

The Dilemma of I

The novels in which the protagonists act in the first-person pose a different dilemma. In this case, it is less a social problem of acceptance than one of projecting the female self, the woman-as-subject, through language. In these texts, the female "I" has already, in effect, become the woman-as-subject through the act of narration. Embodied in the female "I" is a character who projects herself, who breaks through a code of silence. In *Surfacing*, *The Color Purple*, and *Housekeeping*, "I" experiences development and change that unite the reader and protagonist. In *Surfacing*, this unity is heightened by the fact that the protagonist is never identified by name. Like the Invisible Man, she speaks in our name, too. Each text is unique but they are united by this use of the female "I" moving through a minefield of dominant culture codes that would deny the existence of a female subject-narrator.

DuPlessis would like to have the female "I" announce Virginia Woolf's "woman's sentence", one that has its basis, as DuPlessis phrases it, "in cultural fearlessness rather than in biology". It is a woman's sentence because of "its cultural situational function, a dissension stating that women's minds and concerns have been neither completely nor accurately produced in literature as we know it" (32). What Woolf wanted the "woman's sentence" to signify is a break from a dominant narrative tradition in which women are not subjects, and what she termed the "woman's sentence" has to a great extent become an assumption for the writers discussed here. Woolf's woman's sentence seems to be for these writers the point of beginning rather than the goal. In all of these three texts which utilize a first-person narrator, the first words of the text are in first-person, an "I" that firmly announces herself: "*I* can't believe I'm here" (*Surfacing*); "My name is Ruth" (*Housekeeping*); "I am fourteen years old" (*Color Purple*).

Atwood's female "I", nameless protagonist/narrator has a much more difficult function than the characters of the other texts. She moves through language as well as silence; one could say that she is becoming a woman-as-subject through the act of her own narration, but it is an incomplete process. If language can also be a liberating factor for woman, it can only be approached by a subject. The ambivalent ending, in which the protagonist remains skeptical about her relationship to language indicates that this process of analysis has not ended for her. Atwood's is a realization that language denies woman subjectivity and is combined with a sense of betrayal, a move toward completely rejecting language that ultimately fails, and a careful, wary approach to language as the only possibility for change. With her comment, "It was the language again, I couldn't use it, it wasn't mine" (106), the protagonist enters into the dilemma of "I": how to use a language that does not allow woman to express herself. She feels betrayed, for the words used by her lovers, present and former, have made her deny herself as woman to the point she too has made up lies to remember her past. What she initially reveals as a wedding and birth, lies she has told to many, she revises to the truth and confronts the emotional strain of her abortion, one she feels she was "talked into" by her lover. A betrayal. She refuses to use the word love as she sees it as a trap, a commitment demanded by men. She is skeptical of language's possibilities for her; she can refuse to be a victim any longer, but can she take over language for herself? Returning to civilization, and Joe, is the only way out of the realm of silence, and that demands working within the framework of the "symbolic order". Atwood's protagonist is not optimistic: "We will probably fail".

Although Atwood's text deals most directly with the problem of woman and language, Atwood doesn't seem to want to develop this female "I" outside of the formal limitation accorded her by the narrative. She seems aware of being caught up in the paradoxical stance mentioned before, i.e., that the female "I" is at once subversive, declaring itself a subject by the fact of being "I", yet dependent on the law of the text which limits her possibilities within narrative.

In *The Color Purple*, Walker's young narrator Celie, as a poor, black, female, is multiple-marginalized. Her language is not the socially standard English of the dominant culture, but instead it is a colorful, emotional, expressive dialect. Celie not only asserts herself as subject in the text, but specifies an audience. I think it is important to distinguish that Celie writes letters, not diary entries, and addresses them to a (male) God, this Other of the opposite sex, almost as a plea for him to recognize her existence. The point at which Celie changes her addressee to Nettie, her sister, coincides with the point at which she sees herself outside of male authority. She has redirected her sense of self into an all-female context, and consequently the tone of her letters changes as they become longer, more explanatory and at the same time more emotional.

The narrative path Walker has chosen does not run parallel to Atwood's. Celie never questions the system of language as such, although she does question pronouns and gender. For example, recognizing that the male God, as well as all other males, have failed her, she rejects even Shug's suggestion of neuterizing God ("God ain't a he or a she, but a It").

In questioning gender, Celie finds herself outside of the male domain, outside of the heterosexual definitions of man and woman. For Walker, the lesbian symbolizes for Celie the process by which Celie becomes a subject. Her sense of self develops only after her first sexual encounter with Shug, which is also the first time she considers herself lovable. Up to that point Celie had internalized the description of herself that her step-father once voiced: "She ugly. He say. But she ain't no stranger to hard work. And she clean. And God done fixed her. You can do everything just like you want to and she ain't gonna make you feed it or clothe it. ... She ain't smart either" (18). Later her husband rephrases this to "You black, you pore, you ugly, you a woman. Goddam, he say, you nothing at all" (187). But through Shug, Celie learns first to love herself and then others, but most importantly she learns to direct her hate at those who are victimizing her, not at herself.

As her self-confidence grows, so does the length of her letters. She is learning to express herself as a woman, verbally as well as sexually. Once outside of the physical oppression and abuse accorded her by the men in her life, Celie can assert herself and fight back. Her sense of self grows, so that she can exclaim: "I'm pore, I'm black. I may be ugly and can't cook ... But I'm here" (187).

While I will not dwell on the contrast between Celie's and Nettie's styles of letter writing, it is relevant to note that Nettie's use of educated, standardized English restricts her emotional expression, and what is left is a somewhat superficial report of her activities in

Africa, that stylistically would be basically boring or uninteresting were it not for the theme involved. Celie's language remains colorful and emotional. When one of her employees tries to teach her standard English, she comments, "Look like to me only a fool would want you to talk in a way that feel peculiar to your mind" (194).

That is the crucial issue for woman as well. Celie's language is doubly-marginalized, as that of a black woman. Can woman change language to assert herself, make herself the woman-as-subject? Is she a fool for trying? By continually writing "I", Celie's drive to express her thoughts in written form over decades can be seen as an unshakable faith in her own worth.

Robinson's narrator in *Housekeeping*, unlike Atwood's or Walker's, is already a woman-as-subject in that the narrative is a story retold. The narrator Ruth is looking back. In this sort of Bildungs narrative, as in *The Diviners* in this respect, the plot would normally take over, pushing the "I" to the edge and focusing on the younger version of the "I" as a third person Other, until at the end, the character is reunited with the personal narrator. And so this text begins: "My name is Ruth" definitively announcing a female "I", but in many ways continues on the path of a traditional narrative text. The difference here, and perhaps it is slight, is that Ruth remains emotionally tied to this version of herself throughout the narrative sequences. Seldom does Ruth regard her younger self as another character. There is no real split that must be resolved. This reinforces the reader's sense that, while Robinson has her narrator begin with facts, we actually have a story of emotional rather than educational development which allows Ruth to be the earlier version of herself. Near the end, Ruth comments on her own retelling of the narrative: "All this is fact. Fact explains nothing. On the contrary, it is fact that requires explanation" (217). This serves to question everything but her emotional development and relationships (which require no explanation). This recognition of language's failure to supply explanation is one that points to the liberating factor in language for woman. For Ruth, this failure makes her capable of interpreting and defining herself in emotional rather than factual terms.

Unlike Walker, and certainly Atwood, Robinson does not consider language as a system of suppression. She conveniently removes all male influence from Ruth. Her father and grandfather are already absent. No brothers, no boy neighbors, only Ruth, her aunt Sylvie, and her sister Lucille form a familial nucleus in a small town where the feminine element, Lake Fingerbone, continually intrudes on the mountainsides. There is little direct dialogue. What is left are poetic passages of consciousness that touch on the dream, mere impressions framed by words. An example, if a long one, should convey the flavor of the style that would "go beyond words", and is pushing at the boundaries of narrative possibilities:

> Lucille would tell this story differently. She would say I fell asleep, but I did not. I simply let the darkness in the sky become coextensive with the darkness in my skull and bowels and bones. Everything that falls upon the eye is apparition, a sheet dropped over the world's true workings. The nerves and the brain are tricked, and one is left with dreams that these specters loose their hands from ours and walk away, the curve of the back and the swing of the coat so familiar as to imply that they should be permanent fixtures of the world, when in fact nothing is more perishable. Say that my mother was as tall as a man, and that she sometimes set me on her shoulders, so that I could splash my hands in the cold leaves above our heads. Say that my grandmother sang in her throat while she sat on her bed and we laced up her big black shoes. Such details are merely accidental. Who could know but us? And since their thoughts were bent upon other ghosts than ours, other darknesses than we had seen, why must we be left, the survivors picking among flotsam, among the small, unnoticed, unvalued clutter that was all that remained when they vanished, that only catastrophe made notable? Darkness is the only solvent. ... it seemed to me that there need not be relic, remnant, margin, residue, memento, bequest, memory, thought,

> track, or trace, if only the darkness could be perfect
> and permanent. (116)

In beginning this passage with Lucille, who accepts the male social conventions of woman and her place, Robinson contrasts the possibilities of perception. What Lucille calls falling asleep is, for Ruth, a richly textured, multi-layered experience at the limits of consciousness and darkness. Ruth's perceptions and yearnings are for stillness and darkness, and that which is absent, i.e., her mother. In numerous metaphors, Robinson clearly creates Ruth and her Aunt Sylvie as the embodiment of the feminine. In the end Ruth and Sylvie become as absent as Ruth's dead mother, for after their flight from the civilizing influences of the sheriff and townspeople, they are presumed dead, drowned like the mother. They become wanderers, tramps, as fluid and ungraspable as memory, the lake water, the wind. This evokes strong associations with the characterization of the feminine by Cixous and Irigaray, which is one of silence, lack, absence, chaos, darkness, irrationality, negativity, and that which cannot be represented or expressed. Similarly, Kristeva's "chora", the semiotic, is repressed by the symbolic order, and later will only be detected as disruptions of language, as silence, meaninglessness, absences, etc. In other words, her chora seems very much like "the feminine" described above. But what is relevant here is that in Robinson's text, Ruth portrays herself in these terms in the end, when she acts in defiance of the social and symbolic order. She stays with the assertive first-person pronoun, and describes her relationship to Lucille, her symbol of the patriarchally defined woman. A sampling of the closing passages conveys this well:

> If Lucille is there, Sylvie and I have stood outside
> her window a thousand times, and we have thrown
> the side door open when she was upstairs changing
> beds, and we have brought in leaves, and flung the
> curtains and tipped the bud vase, and somehow left
> the house again before she could run downstairs,
> leaving behind us a strong smell of lake water. She
> would sigh and think, "They never change". ... Sylvie
> and I do not flounce in through the door. ... We do

> not sit at the table. ... My mother, likewise, is not
> there. ... We are nowhere in Boston. However Lucille
> may look, she will never find us there, or any trace
> or sign. ... No one ... could know how her thoughts
> are thronged by our absence, or know how she does
> not watch, does not listen, does not wait, does not
> hope, and always for me and Sylvie. (218-9)

Again, the passage begins with Lucille as the counterpoint to the fluidity of air, wind, water, and the senses, and absence. She depicts herself in those terms as a subversion, for then she has moved beyond the control of the phallologos. What Robinson represents here is an image of the feminine "I" that defies a dominant cultural code by inserting herself in the text, and at the same time, through words, depicts her rebellion against the phallologos that embodies her as absence, negativity, etc. She does this using the woman-as-subject. In this sense Robinson comes close to a deconstruction of the phal-lologos, deftly confronting the paradoxes of woman's relationship to language.

These three texts come together in a spirit of defiance against a language that wants to deny them a voice. But this does not solve all the problems of woman's relationship to language in fictional texts. Subjectivity, the dilemma of the "I", is complex. If we consider identity and subjectivity as a plot of the phallologos and accept the idea that the concept of the "self" is a complex of structures and mani-festations that inevitably diminishes sexual identities, then this "I" that announces the female sentence is caught in a dead-end. In Moi's words again, the "self" is itself a trap of "Western male humanism" (7) that makes the subject a central concept.

The Dilemma of We

Given this dilemma of the female "I", it is not surprising that two of the texts attempt to circumvent those problems, as well as those of traditional narrative by working through a collective protagonist. However, attractive such a possibility might be, it poses yet another dilemma regarding the nature of the subject-object relationship in narrative.

In *Wanderground*, Gearhart has attempted to create female characters beyond any phallologocentrism. In choosing to portray a collective protagonist, and thus rejecting an individual woman-as-subject, Gearhart moves beyond the bounds of any female "I" who might announce a "woman's sentence". DuPlessis, again, calls this the "choral protagonist", which she sees as

> a means of empowering narrative if one chooses to
> depend neither upon the romance and personal *Bildungs* plots nor upon some of the assumptions (beginning with gender polarization and the dichotomy of male and female, public and private spheres, and moving to heroine and the 'hard visible horizon' of the isolated individual) underlying those plots. (162)

In other words, Gearhart has applied such an organic process to the structure and style of her work as well.[13] In *Wanderground*, there are some twenty stories and at least twenty female main characters. None of the characters are "well-rounded", in the traditional literary sense through speech patterns, thoughts, actions or through other characters. Nevertheless some individuality is minimally suggested, by attributing characteristics, talents and interests to them. That is, some wish to have children and others don't; some wish to develop certain powers rather than others, etc. This type of individuality and their sexuality are part of their commitment and their rituals, their culture.

Although the absence of a main protagonist in the foreground makes the characters seem less individualized, this structuring of the stories suggests that an organic society is the only appropriate form capable of dealing with the misogyny and destructive tendencies of the hierarchal-patriarchal dystopia. DuPlessis sees this type of protagonist itself as a critique:

> The communal protagonist operates, then, as a
> critique both of the hierarchies and authoritarian

> practice of gender and of the narrative practice that
> selects and honors only major figures. (163)

If Gearhart had not created her Wanderground in opposition to the
City, that paragon of male domination gone wild, she could have gone
beyond the dualism she sets up in the narrative. Consequently, her
attempt to go beyond phallologocentrism ultimately fails.

Similarly, in *The Women of Brewster Place*, Naylor leads the
reader through a depiction of place, rather than character, an intersection of women's lives in their struggle for self-definition. Naylor's
women are less "collective" than Gearhart's, more individual:

> They were hard-edged, soft-centered, brutally de-
> manding, and easily pleased, these women of
> Brewster Place. They came, they went, grew up, and
> grew beyond their years. (5)

They are individuals, who "each in her own time and with her own
season had a story" (5). As individuals, they create a community, and
Naylor uses this emphasis on community to undermine gender
institution.

What this implies for the protagonists is the development of
a closely focused sense of social connectedness. Although each of the
seven stories that make up the novel focuses on one character, each is
put back into Brewster Place at the conclusion of her story. Brewster
Place is physically cut off from the mainstream of the city by the wall,
that metaphor for many things, and its destruction is a collective
action.

What strikes me with these two uses of the choral protagonist
and all the critical implications surrounding them, is that the authors
must again deal with their women in the objective case. The contradictions and paradoxes involved here must lie in the essence of narration.
As discussed in the previous section, in these texts there is either the
woman-as-subject, female "I", first-person narrator, in which the focus
is on a female protagonist expressing her subjectivity through the act
of narration, and the acceptance of the assumptions underlying the
romance and Bildungs plots, but applied in a special way to woman;

or we have the choral protagonists in "organic" narrative structures that critique the assumptions of the more traditional plots and narrative structures, but move in the realm of the objective Other.

Neither possibility, or strategy, breaks through the barriers of a dualistic language system. The one allows the emergence of woman-as-subject, but she is a gender-particularized subject; the other defies both the terms of the subject as a central concept and the terms of individualization in fictional narrative, but reverses to the "omniscient" viewpoint to do so. Even if they are not powerful enough to completely counteract the phallologos (if that is even possible), it is clear that in these fictional narratives, the process of making language work for woman has already begun. What we certainly have here are ranges of possibilities, both potent and eloquent, to build on that might eventually solve this dilemma. For the moment, this might be the answer to the questions asked previously: What is the nature of women's entry into literary discourse? To what extent must women submit to phallologocentricity as the price for this entry? Let it be noted here, however, that although Gearhart fails to eliminate dualistic constructs, she does envision a society that could function outside of traditional linguistic structures, a society of women who have succeeded in disrupting language, one which like Kristeva's "chora" emerges through a feminine non-order outside the framework of symbolic language.

The problem of subjectivity and the confrontation of language that these authors cope with in their fictional texts have some important implications for the reconceptualization of woman and nature. It seems we are concerned with entry problems; and it seems that most of the authors here are aware of this initial jump into the literary discourse on woman and nature because of their particular emphasis on the protagonist's relationship to language. In our context, the extensive use of first-person narrator, and modified first-person narrator, all female, is a sort of challenge to the phallologos that would deny subjectivity to woman. With this strategy, the authors are creating, or reconceptualizing, woman as one that might eventually move outside the boundaries of narrative laws or change the textual customs in order to deconstruct the phallologos. Also, there is the feeling that the authors leave the endings open to new possibilities in these directions — an emphasis perhaps on the subject-as-process.

In the texts concerned with language and nature, a similar phenomenon is evident. Shifting nature away from its place of Otherness/Object involves changing perceptions of nature embedded in the dualism of language that is man-centered. For Atwood, this is neutrality; for Piercy, this involves the use of holistic language in which natural elements can function as subjects; for Gearhart, nature must be allied with the feminine regardless of biological gender.[14] And, as regarding the concept of woman, there is a feeling for the process involved and a direction delineated.

Ideology and Metaphor

If we looked only at the issue of subjectivity in the texts, it would seem that the attempt to put a woman at the center of language still upholds gender as the signifying system. A few seem to be satisfied in changing the points of reference. But at least some of the authors (Atwood, Piercy, Naylor, Gearhart) assume a multilayered approach and question this dualism through the lexical and semantic levels in the texts. In this way they come closer to breaking through the paradox of language, part of which concerns the use of metaphor. Ecofeminism is also a critique of metaphors which have associated woman and nature in dualistic opposition to man and culture, images of oppression and domination.

When Alice Walker's Celie comments that during the beatings she got from Mr.____ "I turned into a tree"; when Atwood's protagonist submits to the rules of the spirits of the woods, briefly becoming like them ("I lean against a tree, I am a tree leaning. ... I am not an animal or a tree, I am the thing in which the trees and animals move and grow, I am a place" [181]); when Daphne turns into a tree to protect herself from Apollo's ravishment;[15] when Robinson's Ruthie and Sylvie become the wind, they are all attempting to escape man's domination by spiritually and psychologically entering another world. There is an expectation that nature will protect them from man and a culture that allows man to beat them, exploit them, ravish them and take them away. From the point of view of feminist ideology, if we see these particular metaphors as ingredients of fictional narrative that define the boundaries of experience,[16] then we can say the authors are approaching the limits of language within the narrative fictional form. On the level of the narrative there is this metaphorical link that would enclose these characters within objects of nature — the tree, the wind.

From the point of view of ecofeminist discourse, these metaphors are counterproductive and ineffectual. Trees and the wind cannot protect because they are subject to the same system of exploitation as woman. The metaphor reinforces the association again and emphasizes the dualistic split. Again the opponent is man. Can woman's relationship to language be circumscribed by nature metaphors? Can the metaphor in this case offer a path outside of the limits of narrative? In all of the instances suggested above, the function of the metaphor is to take the protagonist out of the realm of her physical being where she can no longer be reached by man, where he can not inflict pain. However, this state in another realm of existence would deny herself as woman, for by becoming something else — tree, wind — she gives up the physicality that makes her woman, including the capacity for language. It seems significant in the literary process that those metaphors that imply the woman/nature vs. man/culture opposition become reinforced at the same time that language itself is seen more clearly as a tool of domination.

Thus we can look at metaphor as an element of fiction that is ideologically influenced or determined. Referring back to the Althusserian definition of ideology as "a system of representation by which we imagine the world as it is",[17] we can also see the ideologies clashing in the fictional texts through this element of metaphor. This holds for the individual metaphor, like the examples above, or for the system of metaphor the author chooses for the text, for the metaphor is used to extend the imaginative structure of the concept of I/woman to the limits of fictional narrative. Beyond this, language — the "Symbolic Order", "Law of the Father" — fails.

The Limits of Silence

The clashing ideologies are basically ecofeminism and feminism on one level and the phallologos on another; each level vying with the other through metaphor. These authors have relied on some rather traditional metaphors and symbols of woman, representing the level of the phallologos ideology working in the text. At the same time the authors are trying to fuse new meanings into their metaphors which represent new levels of ecofeminist/feminist ideology. What this does to the language of these texts is to create a new perceptual frame of reference: absence becomes presence; silence becomes communication.

Only Atwood, and to a certain extent Robinson, takes this possibility to its near-end. In narrative, Atwood portrays the state of non-language. Her protagonist realizes that language oppresses ("It's that language again, I couldn't use it, it wasn't mine"). She renounces her physicality during her stay alone in the woods ("The animals have no need for speech, why talk when you are a word"). She imagines that the spirits of the woods spoke "in the other language". The protagonist rejects language altogether then. Silence. Isolation. To her imaginary baby she will teach no words. Animals and trees have no need of language and remain true to themselves. Her entry into the wilderness alone that lasts for a couple of days can also be seen as exploring the possibilities of silence. But, from the point of view of the phallologos, silence relegates woman to absolute powerlessness, and/or madness. It is a rejection of language, or in Kristevan/Lacanian terms, a rejection of the "Symbolic Order", which results in the psychosis symptomatic of the failure to enter into communication and to establish relationships.

However, this silence also represents communication on a different level, a more direct emotional level that does not require words for interpretation. Silence becomes in Atwood's text a rejection of the phallologos (read "languages", read "Symbolic Order") for however short a time. In this sense a rejection of the "Symbolic Order" is not a failure in Lacanian terms, but rather this silence becomes a commitment to a relationship that does not depend on communication through the phallologos. Atwood is approaching the boundaries of consciousness in her protagonist's aching need for silence.

Robinson also explores the limits of consciousness and dream through images of absence that mark the ends of the state of the "Symbolic Order". The primary metaphor of absence is Ruth's mother.

She becomes ever more present for Ruth in and through Silvie, who brings her to transcend the "puzzling margins" of darkness and light, presence and absence, consciousness and dream, death and life. Ruth and Sylvie as well become "absent" from the confines of patriarchy by running away, for everyone assumes they're dead. And finally it is their absence that fills Lucille's thoughts and prompts her actions. It is, then, through these uses of metaphor that Atwood and Robinson create a new perceptual frame of reference, one that more closely corresponds to ecofeminist/feminist ideology.

Metaphorical Cliches

These authors explore another possibility for using metaphor, which is similarly effective in undermining the ideology of the phallologos: this is cliche. Robinson uses images, symbols, and metaphors in her initial scenes in order to exaggerate the ideology of the phallologos. The clashing of meaning through metaphor, in which the traditional metaphors associating woman and nature belong to the realm of the phallologos, is handled in a way that allows Robinson to work through these metaphors. Through repetition, exaggeration and cliche the symbolic meaning is changed, and the feminine is allowed to triumph and survive. For example, the traditionally feminine element of water is absolutely pervasive and has numerous layers of reflections:

> It is true that one is always aware of the lake in Fingerbone, or the deeps of the lake, the lightless, airless waters below. When the ground is plowed in the spring, cut and laid open, what exhales from the furrows but the same, sharp, watery smell. The wind is watery, and all the pumps and creeks and ditches smell of water unalloyed by any other element. At the foundation is the old lake, which is smothered and nameless and altogether black. Then there is Fingerbone, the lake of charts and photographs, which is permeated by sunlight and sustains green life and innumerable fish, and in which one can look down in the shadow of a dock and see stony, earthy

bottom, more or less as one sees dry ground. And
above that, the lake that rises in the spring and turns
the grass dark and coarse as reeds. And above that
the water suspended in sunlight, sharp as the breath
of an animal, which brims inside this circle of mountains. (9)

The mountains (jagged peaks, phallic symbol) are the obvious
masculine element; the impinging lakes, the feminine element. To
further enhance the mutual exclusivity, Robinson eliminates all male
characters right in the beginning. To ensure the right identification for
Sylvie, the lake, as if to greet an ally, floods their house the first
weekend Sylvie arrives to take care of the children. At the end, Ruth
and Sylvie set fire (masculine element) to their house (their last vestige
of subordination to "culture") and run away. Robinson works through
a great deal of ideology in her choice of metaphors and images of
woman as nature.[18] Similarly, society and culture are represented by
symbols of power like the sheriff, and the socially proper groups of
ladies of the town. And these symbols of power attempt to put
restrictions on Ruthie and Sylvie, give them boundaries, and try to
enclose them.

    In a similar manner, Atwood seems to exaggerate both the
nature metaphors she employs as exclusively feminine and the
metaphors of destruction and civilization she uses as exclusively
masculine. This phenomenon can be seen in the other texts as well,[19]
and leads to the issue concerning the essence of metaphor as ideological. With metaphor, the author uses images that are generally under-
standable, or that will evoke another set of images in the reader to
enhance the author's intention. These images would have a broad consensus of meaning, and are socially determined.[20] The feminist author
then, being limited to those metaphors that have meaning through the
ideology of the phallologos, must rely on such traditional metaphors.
Her only recourse is to negate, marginalize, and deconstruct them, or
make them meaningless through cliche. This is the tactic Irigaray
suggests as miming the master discourses: a critique of metaphor
through its very use.

Ecofeminism as discourse is interested in the processes by which woman and nature have been associated over the centuries in order to liberate both concepts from their clearly defined dualisms, man and culture. This association is worked out through language. Two aspects of language, subjectivity and metaphor, become central to ecofeminist considerations of woman and language in the fictional texts. Together subjectivity and metaphor frame many of the possibilities of fictional expression; they are the major elements that define the boundaries of fictional experience and so perceptualize meaning. As such, they can do much to undermine the power of the phallologos.

Now, having moved through ecofeminism as first a possibility for developing a self-critical stance regarding woman's participation in culture, then looking at elements of nature, gender and language within the discourse of ecofeminism, there does seem to be a common direction through these texts toward a wider concept of woman, one that is not restricted to a particular social construct and one that is attempting to break through the boundaries of dualism. However, ecofeminism is only one approach that attempts to challenge these boundaries of dualism in a way that leads to a reconceptualization of woman and nature. The second part of this project deals then with the discourse of gynocriticism, which also challenges the accepted limitations on woman and nature in fictional narrative.

NOTES

1.cf. Jacques Derrida, "Le Facteur de la verité", *Poetique*, 21 (1975), 96-147; Namascar Shaktini, "Displacing the Phallic Subject: Wittig's Lesbian Writing", *Signs*, 8/1(1982), 29-44. Both spellings, "phallologocentrism" and "phallogocentrism", seem to be interchangeable.

2. All three trained in Freudian psychoanalysis via Lacan, and through Derrida began looking into structuralism as a literary discourse. All are based in Paris, and have made important contributions to the feminist movement there, and in turn have greatly influenced the direction of American feminist criticism after their introduction into the American scene by such philosophy and Romance language critics as Alice Jardine,

Domna Stanton, Hester Eisenstein, and psychoanalysts like Jane Gallop, Carolyn Burke, and Nancy Chodorow.

3. Alice Jardine points out that for these theorists in France "'Woman', 'the feminine' and so on have come to signify those *processes* that disrupt symbolic structures in the West", and that they "continue to emphasize the effects of the human subject's inscription in culture through language — the recognition, for example, that the signifier 'woman' does not necessarily *mean* the biological female in history". (*Gynesis*, 42). On the other hand Toril Moi in *Sexual/Textual Politics* suggests that for Kristeva the pre-oedipal, semiotic *chora* is linked to the mother, but is not necessarily "feminine" (7, 165).

4. She does not confine these possibilities to female writers however, and in fact, concentrates primarily on Joyce, Proust, Kafka, Soller, Burroughs, as "feminine" on the basis of their attempts at writing the unconscious, much to the dismay of particularly American feminist literary critics and her French colleagues like Cixous and Wittig all of whom are concerned exclusively with women's fiction.cf. Kristeva, "The System of the Speaking Subject"; "Word, Dialogue and the Novel"; "Semiotics"; "Revolution in Poetic Language"; "A New Type of Intellectual: The Dissident". all in Toril Moi, (ed). *The Kristeva Reader*, (N.Y.: Columbia UP, 1986).

5. Rich, "Teaching Language in Open Admissions", in *On Lies, Secrets and Silence,* (N.Y.: Norton, 1979); Daly, *Gyn/ecology*; Domna Stanton, "Language and Revolution: The Franco-American Dis-Connection", in Eisenstein and Jardine (eds.), *The Future of Difference*, pp. 73-87; Jacobus, "A Difference of View", in Jacobus (ed.), *Women's Writing and Writing About Women*, (London: Croom Helm, 1979), pp. 10-21.

6. I bring these two prominent feminists as examples of the importance given to language change outside of the academic fields.

7. Rich, pp. 51-68.

8. Mary Jacobus, Elaine Showalter, Alice Jardine, Annette Kolodny, Nina Baym, Nancy Miller etc. are among the prominent Anglo-American feminist critics who propose such and similar questions.

9. Kristeva, *The Revolution of Poetic Language*, chpts. 2 and 7. cf. also Toril Moi, *Textual/Sexual Politics*, pp. 160-163.

10. See chapter 7 for discussion on woman's relationship to fiction.

11.Morgan, "Humanbecoming: Form and Focus in the Neo-Feminist Novel", in Susan K. Cornillon (ed.), *Images of Women in Fiction: Feminist Perspectives*, (Bowling Green, OH: Bowling Green UP, 1973), p. 183.

12.Moi, *The Kristeva Reader*, p. 13.

13.Elsewhere I have developed the idea of organicism related to these utopian texts. cf. Devine, "*Woman on the Edge of Time* and *The Wanderground*: Visions in Ecofeminist Utopias", in Arno Heller, Walter Hölbling, and Waldemar Zacharasiewicz (eds.), *Utopian Thought in America: Untersuchungen zur literarischen Utopie und Dystopie in den USA*, (Tübingen: Gunter Narr, 1988), pp. 131-146.

14.See chapter 7 for further discussion.

15.cf. Pratt, *Archetypal Patterns*, "Introduction".

16.cf. DuPlessis, p. 9.

17.Althusser, p. 233; cf. Zima, *Ideologie und Theorie*, pp. 236-8; and DuPlessis, p. 9.

18. See chapter 6.

19. Some such examples can be found in chapter 6.

20.Also Derrida in *On Grammatology* is concerned with the function of metaphor, but maintains in his sub-chapter "The Originary Metaphor" that language is all-metaphor: "Metaphor must therefore be understood as the process of the idea of meaning (of the signified, if one wishes) before being understood as the play of signifiers." (275) His complex analysis seems to question the ideology of language expressed in metaphor, while suggesting in Rousseauian terms that language functions only metaphorically. cf. pp. 270-80.

PART II

Gynocriticism

Gynocriticism as discourse focuses on the relationship between woman and fiction. As with ecofeminism, it has developed out of a feminist ideology that has concentrated on defining a literary tradition in a feminist context, and the use of language and thematics in fiction by women writers. Specifically defined as gynocritics by Elaine Showalter, it is

> concerned with *woman as writer* — with woman as the producer of textual meaning, with the history, themes, genres, and structures of literature by women. Its subjects include the psychodynamics of female creativity; linguistics and the problem of a female language; the trajectory of the individual or collective female literary career; literary history; and, of course, studies of particular writers and works. (128)

Although most feminist literary critics are engaged in gynocritics, and numerous texts claim it as discourse and use it to define literary traditions, the idea of a "feminist literary criticism" is a troubling one considering the aspect of dualism we are confronting here. Just as the point where dualism is approaching its deconstruction, a particularizing of gender-based readings and critiques emerges that insists that women writers are different, and approach writing from a completely different background, thus challenging the universality of the masculine "weltanschauung" in fictional narrative. These points of view are, however, not necessarily contradictory, and in some respects such a particularizing of gender serves to undermine dualism to make way for the "multiplicity" in literary criticism that many critics demand. The authors I am concerned with are also involved in discovering a relationship between woman and fiction beyond the boundaries of dualism, and in doing so also take up the concept of nature as a crucial element of fiction. Gynocriticism, as I suggested in "Preliminaries", is concerned with a dialogue of the texts emanating from and between gynocritics texts, the "trans-Atlantic" critical circle, and the fictional texts.

Gynocriticism as discourse must also consider how woman-as-writer influences fiction, not so much in the individual texts, but as a writer approaching the boundaries of fiction within the limits of language and gender. As in Part I, the discussion here concentrates on nature, gender and language as the planes of intersection where feminist literary criticism and the fictional texts meet — each in conjunction with what I call "literarity". Literarity refers to the various strategies and elements authors use to confront issues concerning woman and to encode meanings about woman within the boundaries of fictional narrative, meanings that can provide a key to the overriding theme of this project. Thus in this second part, the focus is on gynocriticism's contribution to reconceptualizing woman and nature.

...the truth is the world is very much out of order.

(James I)

As much land as a man tills, plants, improves, culti-
vates, and can use the product of, so much is his
property. He by his labor does, as it were, enclose it
from the common.

(John Locke)

To make a prairie it takes a clover and a bee,
One clover, and a bee,
And revery.
The revery alone will do,
If bees are few.

(Emily Dickinson)

5

Literarity and Nature

Of the many elements of fiction that writers must attend to,
one is the representation of nature as setting and landscape in which
the characters move. This aspect takes on further connotations when
considering the type of relationship between woman-as-protagonist and
nature-as-landscape in texts that begin an attempt to deconstruct this
relationship within the narrative boundaries of the text. We have
already looked at single elements of metaphor in an ecofeminist
context as a possibility for moving beyond those boundaries, when
they became restrictive, and we have also already seen that a text like
The Wanderground falls back on an almost nostalgic view of nature as
the feminine Mother, protector of women against masculine transgres-
sions. There is a certain self-righteous mechanism involved here in the
women allying themselves to their natural environment in such a —
utopian — way. However, my primary interest here is the literarity of
the texts in relation to nature, that is, the strategies and elements of

fiction the authors use to refer to woman in relation to nature; specifically, how the authors portray landscape, through this portrayal the extent to which these authors are attempting to take gender out of nature, and for what narrative purposes. In the overall context of this study, the emphasis is on these issues as a contribution to a reconceptualization of nature. In this chapter, we will focus on the author's use of both landscape as metaphor and nature as thematic device.

Landscape as Metaphor

Behind the common metaphors of the environment or natural landscape as home, which stresses an interrelatedness and sense of community with it (equivalent to the Garden of Eden), and the metaphor of the environment as a household to be economically managed and kept in shape (equivalent to wild untamed nature needing to be tamed, or the "wise use" school), lies a range of attitudes that reflect the human relationship to that environment — from explaining to controlling. Even the contemporary interest in ecology — a word meaning "house", but later in history referred to as "oeconomy",[1] grows out of this need to control and to decide who shall control what, for which purposes, i.e., a power struggle whose object is the natural environment. As discussed in ecofeminism, the tendency to refer to environmental nature in feminine metaphors reflects a primarily Western, philosophical, religious and scientific bias that is now being questioned by feminists as part of a process of revising and questioning the concept of woman, the extension of which is to revise the concept of nature.

As we have seen, too, the authors of the texts here have gone far to reconceptualize woman. Also important to the texts is the environment or setting chosen by the authors and the attitudes and actions of characters toward it, and the symbolic language of the literary texts relating to nature. Vera L. Norwood in "The Nature of Knowing" makes a case for a woman's tradition in nature writing

> reaching back at least to the poet Emily Dickinson
> and forward to Nobel Prize-winning Barbara
> McClintock, a tradition celebrating not narrow

> "domesticated" nature, but the expanding conceptions
> of nature as home and family to include appreciation
> and respect for the uncontrollable, unknown — even
> the never-to-be-known — aspects of the world. (743)

Although Norwood uses the word "tradition" in mentioning only these two women and Rachel Carson, she does point to an alternative to the existing feminine metaphors and to a possible way of looking at the problem of symbolic language. Both Annette Kolodny and Ellen Moers take up this issue as well. Kolodny, in her analysis of the letters and diaries of early pioneer women, suggests that women had a different relationship to the pioneer life and environment than their menfolks, "and struggled to find some alternate set of images through which to make their own unique accommodation to the strange and sometimes forbidding New World landscape" (3). Moers postulates that there is a specifically female landscape as metaphor in literary texts from Mary Wollstonecraft onward, with such examples as George Eliot, the Brontës, Isak Dinesen and George Sand on one side of the Atlantic, Willa Cather, Kate Chopin on the other, and suggests that women have a stronger attraction to prairie, moor, or desert landscapes than to "phallic" Alpine settings. This intriguing idea of the relationship between topology and gender only holds to a certain extent, not absolutely, in the texts here. However, the psycho-sexual connotations of many metaphors of nature suggests some sort of gender-differentiated perception of landscape.

"A Complicated Topography"

In psycho-sexual terms, Moers brings the landscapes described by many female authors into context with Freud's comment that female genitalia, to him a "complicated topography", "are often represented as landscapes" (254), and thus makes her point that prairie, moor, and desert are more to women's liking than the more phallic mountainous landscapes. Indeed, of all the novels considered here, only *Housekeeping* is set in the mountains, and that primarily for the effect of the strong contrasts to the "feminine" lakes. For Laurence, on the other hand, the Manawaka landscape in *The Diviners* — the town is on a river that flows among gently rolling hills in Manitoba — plays a significant role in the development of Morag, so that despite her wanderings to other parts of the world, she settles in an Ontario counterpart of the prairie town, Manawaka. McConnell's Landing typifies the grassy wide-open landscape, sloping gently to the riverbanks, that she constantly returns to in memories of her childhood. Through this movement from past to present, also reflected in the motion of the river that "seemed to be flowing both ways" (453), Morag comes to recognize her divinations, her possibilities and gifts as a woman which she can pass on to Pique. In understanding the reality of her present, Morag can look out the large wide window by her writing desk and look across the meadows to the river and beyond — a boundless openness of possibilities reflecting her own openness and independence. Cathy Davidson, in writing on this aspect in Laurence, comments that

> inner and outer landscapes merge into each other, and
> even Manawaka itself becomes as much a state of
> mind as a place on a map. But by *recognizing the
> complex interrelationship of geography and psychol-
> ogy*, Laurence's characters survive and a few even
> manage to achieve art. (129-130, emphasis mine)

The very openness of the prairie, its undulating surface, its windswept grasses are the attributes of landscapes that Moers suggests "have been good for women" (262). In this, Laurence is similar to Willa Cather in her use of landscape, one in which the openness of the prairie is representative of richness, freedom and independence for her heroines. Similar too is their use of gardens as negative elements, so that in *The Diviners* Morag ends up selling off much of her property at McConnell's Landing for others to use, because she herself wouldn't take the time (420), the precious time she needs for her writing. On the other hand there is Morag's fascination with the early pioneer women of the area, Mrs. Cooper and Catharine Parr Traill, and not least with her own ancestors who moved farther west, and how they fared and survived the harsh conditions — the prairie as a place of hope and fulfillment, but not of the easy life.

Significant, too, is that Pique goes off to Galloping Mountain in search of her father's family, to find the image of her father. If we consider the mountainous areas symbolic of her relationship to the masculine, then this use of landscape is quite obvious for its contrast to the prairie as a reflection of Morag's state of being, marked as it is by careful hope, rich creativity, freedom and independence. This is all quite contrary to a comment by (male) critic Laurence Ricou that the true prairie landscape is "a perfect metaphor for existential, universal meaninglessness for man [sic]."[2] Rather than a perfect metaphor, this is a perfect illustration of the perceptual problems of a gender-differentiated depiction of landscape. If, as Jardine suggests, nature and the feminine are cast in similar terms as "representation of the *space* at the end point of Man's symbolization" (87), then presumably such a space might indeed represent meaninglessness, as Ricou suggests the prairie does for man. For woman the prairie is many things but certainly not a metaphor for universal meaninglessness. Its topography is complicated exactly because the authors accord the prairie land-scapes multiple meanings.

In *The Diviners*, Laurence molds a unity of character, rural setting and natural time. The very tone of the text in the city scenes (Toronto and London) becomes disjointed, clipped, reflecting Morag's fear and claustrophobia there. The contrast to the rural scenes is pointed. There the descriptive elements take over in terms of the landscape, even though in the case of Manawaka, the descriptions are not of beautiful pastoral scenes. In referring to the sense of unity of character and rural setting, Clara Thomas in "The Wild Garden and the Manawaka World" writes of Morag that

> She is substantially free of the confines of man-measured time, and she is living largely in natural time, the flowing of day into night into day again, the changing of the seasons, spring into summer into autumn; and in her riverwatching she has the constant companionship and awareness of the water's cease-less mixing flow. Specific signals like the ringing of the telephone recall her to man-measured time and

> return her to the anxieties that impel her to set out on
> her remembering journey. (403)

Similarly, Morag's garden becomes in the end, not an island of isolation keeping out the surrounding elements, but a garden of wild flowers. It signifies a joining rather than a separation, a unity of subject and object. So too does she come to realize that her divining powers are not her possession, but rather inherited temporarily and then passed on to future generations. Again, a sense of joining rather than of separation is significant here. Through the essence of her natural surroundings, signified among other images by her garden of wildflowers, Morag learns to live as a diviner in harmony with her womanness and mystic gifts — a diviner — that also give her universality.

The landscape of *Surfacing* is a wilderness area of woodlands and lakes; mountains and jagged peaks are absent. The woods extend right down to the water's edge, or are separated by the transitional swamps. The shores are muddy. Only the cliffs, ancient Indian dwellings, rise out of water occasionally, dotting the lakes with more islands, and significantly, mark the scene of her father's death. The intrusion of the male element (the father) into the mysteries of the primitive (the now-submerged cave dwellings with their ancient drawings) is eliminated by drowning. While the protagonist's personal identification with the wilderness is a catalyst for her psychological development, the point I want to make here regarding the author's use of landscape is that Atwood, too, chooses a setting of gentle fusions rather than strong contrasts — lakes and low-lying islands, swamps and marshes. A garden had been fenced off and carefully tended by her mother, but it is clearly an inroad of cultivation against the wild environment. The protagonist uses it while her friends are there, but alone, she avoids it, and gets her nourishment from the woods. Both Laurence and Atwood in the end avoid making the identification with nature as sympathetically feminine. Both protagonists take a neutral stance. For Morag the river as always seems to run in both directions, the rolling grassy hills divulge nothing of their secrets. For Atwood's protagonist, "It does not approve of me or disapprove of me, it tells me it has nothing to tell me, only the fact of itself" (187). She can thus gain the distance from her nonhuman environment in order to deconstruct the male ideology imposed on it and accept it as a non-genderized element. Both Laurence's and Atwood's protagonists understand and respect the power of their landscapes. This is one particular reflection of the Canadian ties to the European tradition of nature which is more neutral, or, at least, balances an awe to the wilderness with a sense of danger to humans.

Similar to Laurence's and Atwood's depictions of landscape are those Walker makes of the African landscape in *The Color Purple*, which she uses as a setting for Nettie's experiences: bushlands and forests, gently rolling or flat, and easily cleared for the road that approaches, the symbol of colonial destruction. More significant, however, is the rift, the scene of the mbeles encampment where the young Olinkas escape the encroachment of the whites. To preserve their ancient customs, they seek enclosure and protection hidden deep in the earth they identify with. Walker's descriptions of the rift is metaphorically similar to Freud's "topography of the female genitalia": "It is a place set so deep into the earth that it can only really be seen, ... from the air, and then it would seem just an overgrown canyon" (242). So diametrically opposed to the earlier African landscape of the village taken over by colonial civilization, the rift is used to rally the ancient, archaic elements and to serve as a meeting place, a secret place of power. But, Walker reduces the nostalgic sentimentality attached to the area, for it is also the place where the women undergo genital mutilation. Unlike the landscape of the Wanderground that provides absolute protection for the women, Walker's depiction of this rift is ambivalent in its relationship to the feminine. It is as if, with so much feminine symbolism surrounding this area, that woman is "deprived" of her sexuality. The topographies become complicated indeed.

Balance and Contrast

Adding to the complexity of the representation of landscape, contemporary writers have inherited the pastoral images of literary symbolic language, traced by Leo Marx back to Virgil, which he calls "the root conflict of our culture" (365). It is all the more challenging to women writers to depict alternative relationships to nature using such symbolic language, and indeed the variety of feminist views on women also indicate a heterogeneous attitude toward the natural environment. Typical of these widely contrastive views of nature are the two utopian texts, which offer a wide variety of views of women.

In creating the Mattapoisett of *Woman on the Edge of Time*, Piercy adopts a utilitarian viewpoint that approves a well-organized, highly-productive and highly-technical land use (the "wise use" philosophy) based, of course, on organic principles, such as the elimination of wasteful practices, and self-sufficiency. The "grand council" decides the use and production of the land, but all community members must be in agreement. Humans are also responsible for keeping the balance in the natural environment in Mattapoisett, although they inherited an environment badly out of equilibrium. In *The Wanderground*, on the other hand, Gearhart has the women manifest an attitude of wonderment and awe at their mystical mother nature, in keeping with her idea that the earth has had enough of *Homo sapiens*.[3] Running through the work is also the idea of the power and unpredictability of nature, which can easily overpower man's technology, such as the mystical shield that prevents factories from running and electricity from working outside the City, etc. There is no overall plan in dealing with the environment in the Wanderground, as there is in Mattapoisett; the women interact with their natural environment but do not control or plan it. While these two visions are connected by a non-exploitative, non-destructive, organic relationship to the environment, the approaches are very different. They exemplify on a wider level two feminist views of nature that are roughly congruous with those suggested by Norwood and Kolodny.

The authors of the other novels incorporate these approaches in various ways into the symbolic level of the texts. In *Surfacing,* there is certainly the tentative acknowledgement that the landscape is out of balance. The intruding machine in the garden takes the form of the motorboat on the lake, the fishing poles, and the bullets in the body of the heron, all cast in feminine images as victims of violence. The protagonist's escape to the woods is her escape from the masculine but she finds little protection there. Her destruction of the cabin is symbolic ritual as well as a practical move. She encounters both female and male principles in the woods in the visions of her mother and father, but also ambivalence.

Similarly in *Housekeeping*, with its initial image of the machine in the garden being the sleek black train sliding into the lake (6), thus eliminating masculine influence on the next generations of the family, there is awe expressed throughout at the power and wonder of nature's happenings. The train has disappeared so thoroughly that nothing of it or from it was ever found. Early on, there is the destructive flood that even reaches their house set high on the hillside. Then, after the ritual on the island, Ruthie and Sylvie have considerable difficulty on the lake returning home, and the wind and the current bring them far from their goal. But the description of the setting implies considerable respect for the uncontrollable and unknown of nature's ways, and appreciation of its power:

> ... there are mountains, uncountable mountains, and where there are not mountains there are hills. The terrain on which the town itself is built is relatively level, having once belonged to the lake. It seems there was a time when the dimensions of things modified themselves, leaving a number of puzzling margins, as between the mountains as they must have been and the mountains as they are now, or between the lake as it once was and the lake as it is now. Sometime in the spring the old lake will return ... The earth will brim, the soil will become mud and then silty water, and the grass will stand in chill water to its tips. (4-5)
>
> *****
>
> ... the bridge pilings were set in the crest of a chain of flooded hills, which on one side formed the wall of a broad valley (there was another chain of hills twenty miles north, some of them islands) and on the other side fell away in cliffs. Apparently these hills were the bank of still another lake, and were made of some brittle stone which had been mined by the water and fallen sheerly away. (7)

Lastly, this setting claims the lives of her grandfather and mother. Because of the startling contrasts, nature here is puzzling and unpredictable.

The "landscape" of *Brewster Place* is a "cityscape" of similar importance, for Naylor devotes the first chapter to the development of this street and neighborhood, and significantly its enclosure and dead-end atmosphere symbolized by the wall, this wall that the women in Mattie's dream revolt against and tear down. The contrast between the urban and rural landscapes is provided by the stories of the women, especially that of Mattie Michael, for to her the Southern landscape of rolling hills and sugarcane fields signify lost youth and innocence. The particular scene of her lovemaking is chosen for its lush image of fertility: "the edge of the thick, tangled dogwood, and the deep green basil and wild thyme formed a fragrant blanket on the mossy earth" (15) and the images of her feelings for Butch are those of the sensual feminine element of water:

> ... she felt that she had somehow drifted too far into
> strange waters and if she didn't turn around soon, she
> would completely forget in which direction the shore
> lay ... (15)
>
> *****
>
> Mattie found herself floating far away in the brown
> sea of his irises, where the words, shoreline and
> anchor became like gibberish in some foreign tongue.
> (18)

These are the last scenes of carefree happiness for her, and are in a particularly romantic setting, but these scenes also provide the contrast to Brewster Place, which is grim, gray, enclosing, decaying.

The literary tradition, relative to the representation of nature that Norwood, Kolodny and Moers point to, suggests that women writers on the whole, and this group of writers in particular, relate to an idea of nature that is beyond dominance and control, is powerful but not overpowering; in other words, an idea of nature that goes beyond the cliches of garden, virgin and mother to include, as Norwood suggests, an appreciation of and respect for nature's unknowable capacities and secrets. Just as our fiction writers are intent on freeing the concept of woman from cliched images, they focus on representing nature in their texts in ways that also free it from cliches. However, for these writers, the psycho-social aspect of landscape as metaphor for these writers is more conventional than one would have thought.

Nature as Thematic Device

In addition to the landscape as metaphor aspects, some of the authors use nature, the environment, or the relationship to the environment as an important thematic device. It is not only the particular landscape the authors choose to represent setting, but the impact this setting has on the characters and protagonists and the importance of the interaction between character and setting that frames nature as a theme. That these texts concern the interactions with nature as environmental issues is clear from the discussion so far. In terms of literarity, however, the focus will now turn to the various narrative strategies the authors use to confront issues concerning nature.

Complicity and Ideology

Important to literarity in connection with nature as thematic device, for example in Atwood's text, are such issues as the uniqueness of Atwood's final neutrality towards nature. Why does her protagonist arrive at this stance at the particular point in which she decides she must return to civilization? Are the changes in attitude evidenced in the text compatible with the obvious ecological ideology emanating from it? From close reading of the text, Atwood's strategies seem to initially oversimplify any relationship to nature. Of course, the other characters, Anna, Joe, and David, are repulsed at the sight of the dead heron strung up to a tree. Of course, they are irritated at the sound of the outboard motors on the tourists' boats screaming across the lake in the pristine forests while they are portaging their canoes. These are the obvious intrusions.

The protagonist's movement away from her friends' points of view begins with her understanding that they themselves are just like those hunters, killers, tourists who exploit the environment for their pleasures. David's camera and his "Random Samples" film is an example of this, demonstrating his lack of empathy and identification first with his environment, and then with his wife, Anna, when he forces her to pose naked for the film. David, Anna, and Joe can only relate intellectually to their natural environment, and their emotional relationships, to each other as well as to nature, are severely lacking or encased in terms of degradation and exploitation. But the protagonist turns away from them emotionally and towards nature. It would be at this point, I think, that the reader would expect the absolute feminine identification between the protagonist and her nature/environment. In fact, it is here that Atwood diverges from the obvious ending.

In keeping with a feminine portrayal of nature as she has done up until the end, Atwood would be expected to extend the protagonist's identification with nature. However, to show the protagonist's complicity in the destruction of the environment, Atwood has her remain part of civilization. She does not reject it, but returns to it. Nor can nature remain feminine, for that, too, would be a confirmation of an oversimplified idea of dualism working in the text. Instead, Atwood attempts to expose the obvious ecological ideology she began with as naive. The nature spirits envisioned by her protagonist require certain rules of behavior in the woods that she eventually understands:

> There must be rules: places I'm permitted to be,
> other places I'm not. I'll have to listen carefully, if I
> trust them they will tell me what is allowed. I ought
> to have let them in, it may have been the only chance
> they will give me. (175-6)
> *****
> Now I understand the rule. They can't be anywhere
> that's marked out, enclosed; even if I opened the
> doors and fences they could not pass in, to houses
> and cages, they can move only in the spaces between
> them, they are against borders. (180)

As representatives of nature, these spirits, or gods, determine what is permissible in her initiation rite (or, at least the protagonist interprets them so). On the textual level, it is here that Atwood begins to push against the boundaries of narrative, when the protagonist explores the possibilities of silence as a last act of rebellion against language. Once the gods of nature recede, put at rest by the protagonist, she can come out of the intense identification experience to see nature, the gods, the environment, trees, as neither allied to her as feminine elements, nor against her as masculine elements; they are only neutral elements. In this text, the protagonist can leave only when they have become neutral for her, but at that point she must leave, for they no longer hold anything for her development. The sophistication with which Atwood deals with the issue of ecological ideology belies the compromised ending. Atwood backs down in the end rather than break through the boundaries; it is as if she had touched them, found a wall, and decided to stay comfortably within.

In *Housekeeping*, Robinson's strategies for employing nature as theme begin similarly to Atwood's, for she too begins from an obvious ecological ideology that she proceeds to examine, but her Ruth and Sylvie, faced with a decision similar to Atwood's protagonist, do not return to civilization in the end. In employing nature as thematic device, Robinson goes beyond the descriptive and metaphorical levels so that character interacts with the environment/nature. We are dealing with principles of holism in this text, as the title implies, for "house-keeping" means "economy", later developed into "ecology". Robinson ironically turns the plot on this issue, for actually it is Sylvie's form of housekeeping that is the catalyst of their conflict with the society of the townspeople.[4] Aside from this, Robinson's use of the lake as a place of interaction is a primary device that unites the characters of Ruth's mother and grandfather with the narrator and Sylvie. It is equally significant that Ruth's education by Sylvie involves a passage on the lake during which the water continually laps up around them as if wanting to claim them too. The impervious smell of water in the air, on the wind, becomes part of them, and, in the end, Ruth and Sylvie "leave behind us a strong smell of lake water" (218).

While Atwood's strategy in the end becomes one of turning back, Robinson moves Ruth and Sylvie through to a "logical" end in which Ruth describes themselves in terms of wind, smell, or as nature's spaces. By moving elements of nature/environment out of the landscape-setting aspects into the predominance of theme, Robinson can ally Ruth and Sylvie to these elements as if to another character. This reasserts gender into the text, making the major nature-character, the lake/water, absolutely feminine. In this sense, Robinson retains or reinforces the ideological stance she begins with, that of a feminine nature. Atwood affirms a neutral stance toward nature's elements, but turns back; Robinson, by asserting the feminine, accrues the power to move beyond the narrative boundaries, and Sylvie and Ruth become spiritual elements.

Nature as thematic device is nowhere more evident than in the utopian texts, and of these two, *Wanderground* is most unwaveringly committed to employing nature as a primary literary device. This situation is due to the essence of utopian fiction that allows it to stretch representation into the fantastic, not limited to time or space as "imitations of reality".[5] Gearhart is obviously committed to such ecofeminist ideology that demands complete identification of the feminine and nature, as strong, active (rather than weak and passive) elements. Thus, one of her narrative strategies is to create this character out of nature. In the episode titled, "The Revolt of the Mother", we see the active mystical happenings that hinder machines and telecommunications, and encircle the city to infringe on any misogynistic tendencies that might escape from there. Gearhart also uses interactions with nature — talking to the animals, asking the help of the trees and streams, etc. — to personify these natural elements. Through this device she defines the feminine, and reinforces the proximity of woman and nature, both for the purpose of depicting a conceptual world structured differently from the City, or the masculine.

Gearhart's literarity includes other narrative strategies that take on important symbolic functions of gynocriticism. Just as Kolodny suggests that some women writers encode in their texts "a fictive rendering of the dilemma of the woman writer"[6], I would like to suggest that Gearhart, in a parallel move, approaches her rendering of this dilemma through her use of nature. The women of the Wanderground move in both worlds, in the City albeit dangerously, for they must disguise themselves for protection. Just so have women readers learned to read feminist texts as well as the literary greats of a tradition structured differently from their own conceptual world (but having thought for a long time it was not different). When the woman writer discovers that her world has a different conceptual structure, she can only escape to her own nature, this "differently structured conceptual world" of woman, which Gearhart depicts as the Wanderground, a place of mystical powers protected by an even more mystical "Mother". To go back to the masculine world of fiction, the woman reader must assume a disguise, but can and does so successfully. Indeed she must. But this position is unbalanced, with women always making the move to become sensitive readers of the "mainstream" traditions, always trying to understand a world different from their own. The men immersed in their mainstream "City" of literary traditions prefer to discount, ignore, or even destroy the existence of other literary worlds. But some men, those Gentles, do acknowledge the existence of the Wanderground and then want to find out more about such an alternative, and so begin also to break through their own culturally defined (literary) boundaries and "can learn to apprehend the meanings encoded in texts by and about women".[7] But, letting the men read or not read whatever they wanted to comprehend about women's writing within their own conceptions is a new situation for the women who have always carefully guarded their own secrets. Suddenly, some, men, having discovered there is a feminine conception, want to comprehend its encoded meanings. But, the consequences of this situation are complex. Obviously, there is a danger in opening up this world, this Wanderground of feminist literary richness. There may come a point at which male readers and critics might begin criticizing women's writings, not biased by their own perspective, but based on feminist criteria within feminist theory. A few "Gentles" have already made it to the Wanderground; they are the ones who help by interpreting women's writing in the "City". It seems natural that they want to read women's writing from the woman's point of view. Ignoring them, hindering them, getting angry at them, forbidding them to develop these "powers" of nature — which can incidentally only be realized outside the male paradigm — might be tactics, but ones that time itself will make obsolete. The "Gentle" readers and critics have already begun to "read" gender outside the male paradigm. Gearhart herself seems undecided; there is a great safety for women in the isolation of the Wanderground.

In addition to using the nature theme to encode the dilemmas of woman writers, Gearhart reflects on the disparity of gender and the possibilities of mediation and complicity. Unlike Robinson, she does not exclude masculine possibilities, nor like Atwood, does she want to neutralize the gender significance of nature. Cohabitation seems a bit utopian even for her utopian women, but she does not reject it out of hand. What she tends to reject for the Wanderground is cohabitation under false premises, which in terms of gynocriticism is ignoring the existence of "differently structured conceptual worlds", not "reading" or comprehending the meanings of woman writers.

These authors by depicting nature/environment as a major thematic element in the texts demonstrate alternatives to traditional concepts of nature. Because the texts themselves are examples of gender-differentiated perceptions of nature, it seems possible that the reconceptualization of nature can only proceed from woman's consciousness capable of representation beyond "man's symbolization".[8] But, this reconceptualization must break through the dualism paradigm. Norwood's and Moers' suggestion of a woman's tradition of depicting nature in fiction that is decidedly different from the male mainstream is only of limited value here, because it reinforces the dualistic element. Most of the authors are explicitly dealing with the gender aspect of nature, in such a way as to question its validity: nearly to the point of cliche, like Walker; of valorizing the feminine aspects, like Robinson and Gearhart; or de-genderizing nature like Atwood and Laurence. All are narrative strategies used to deal with nature and the feminine from a perspective that at least questions that paradigm.

NOTES

1.The etymology is suggested in a publication of the respected Sierra Club: Donald Worster, *Nature's Economy: The Roots of Ecology* (San Francisco: Sierra Club Books, 1977), p. 37.

2.cf. Laurence R. Ricou, "Empty as Nightmare: Man and Landscape in Recent Canadian Fiction", *Mosaic*, 6/2 (1973), 148.

3.cf. Gearhart, "An End to Technology", pp. 180-181.

4.cf. Bachinger, "The Tao of *Housekeeping*".

5.Piercy on the other hand keeps a rather traditional strategy of nature as the objective landscape-setting in Mattapoisett.

6.Kolodny, "A Map for Rereading: Gender and the Interpretation of Literary Texts", in Showalter (ed.), *New Feminist Criticisms,* p. 58; she analyzes Charlotte Perkins Gilman and Susan Glaspell short stories from such encodings.

7.Kolodny, "A Map for Rereading", p. 58.

8.Jardine, p. 87.

tell all the truth
but tell it slant.

(Emily Dickinson)

for those of us whose language is not heard, whose
words have been stolen or erased, those robbed of
language, who are called voiceless or mute, ... for those
of us who speak our own language ...

(Susan Griffin)

There are no opposites: only from those of logic do we
derive the concept of opposites — and falsely transfer
it to things.

(Nietzsche)

6

Literarity and Gender

Gynocriticism as a dialogue among critical and fictional texts,
interested as it is in the why's and how's of women's writing, must
somehow come to terms with the variety of representations of gender
in fictional narrative. One of the many challenges to the feminist writer
is the portrayal of gender, for as a social construct, gender is a
representation of roles conferred on the social groups depicted in the
fictional context. Consequently, feminist writers have a spectrum of
possibilities for creating female characters. Three possibilities are
prominent in the texts: the androgyne, the lesbian, the mother. These
"types" and the issues that emerge from them are not mutually
exclusive. Why the authors make use of particular gender representations, and, in terms of literarity, the narrative strategies they employ to
do so, are central to the problematization of the concepts of woman
and nature. But the authors' more traditional use of gender in
metaphorical terms — attributing traditional feminine and masculine

characteristics to other elements — often seems to contradict their narrative strategies in the depiction of character. This conflict is most obvious in the ways the authors make use of androgyny.

The Androgyne

Androgyny has been, and to a certain extent still is, a much-discussed concept in feminism. It is relevant to our discussion of gender because the problem of working through paradoxical stances seems more transparent in androgyny than in the other aspects of ecofeminism and gynocriticism discussed thus far. The controversy centers on the definitions of the term, and the interpretations themselves have provided two opposing points of view on the relevance of androgyny for present society: some critics accuse androgyny advocates of being trapped, as one put it, "in an atomistic science that pretends to understand a whole by an examination of the heap of its disembodied parts",[1] while others claim androgyny is a means of transcending gender roles. The paradox becomes more transparent concerning the idea of androgyny as transcendence because its advocates have relied on quantifiable and empirical definitions of gender which indicate that androgyny is trapped in a static and essentialist relationship to gender, rather than a dynamic one.

Moving briefly to a psychoanalytical paradigm, androgyny is the union of feminine and masculine characteristics, but it is also seen as a principle by which men become grounded or centered, in tune with themselves by acknowledging feminine characteristics in their psyche. Theories concerning the relationship between androgyne and the psyche are primarily associated with C. G. Jung.[2] Ultimately he saw androgyny as a possibility for the transcendence of gender; he identifies the unconscious, the anima "as an inner-aspect of the masculine personality", but the animus, as an aspect of the feminine personality, is less clearly defined. The anima offers the male a possibility of "a completion of his individuality" whereas the corresponding animus of the female personality prevents her eroticism from developing. In other words, although Jung sees androgyny as essential to human development, it is precisely because the animus is an element of restraint and the anima of development that the male is favored and the female disadvantaged in this paradigm.[3] Pratt comments ironically that "logical, spiritual, and in association with the powerful creativity of the sun when present in the male psyche, the animus only makes a woman opinionated, masculine, and shrill" (7).

To date, despite a few attempts to define it as a holistic system,[4] androgyny lies deeply imbedded in dualistic thought and undermines the possibility of gender being non-discriminating. For example, Beauvoir contended that gender is learned and so each newborn is androgynous until the oedipal stage when the child learns the importance and implications of gender identity. Thus, in this descriptive interpretation, infants have male and female traits, and the learning of gender-identity causes the suppression/rejection of the set of traits identified with the "Other". However, as a prescriptive interpretation, feminist psychoanalytic theory proposes that the development of the self depends on an identification with, rather than a rejection of, the "Other", so that the rigid dichotomy self/other would become invalid. But, androgyny, as a concept that depends on rigid dichotomous opposition to a set of characteristics that are masculine and those that are feminine in order to offer the possibility to each of embracing and uniting with the "other", obscures the possibility of gender being non-discriminating and undermines feminist goals of gender-equality.

For feminism, androgyny is a double-edged sword — to stay with gender symbols. The characteristic traits of "masculine" and "feminine" lose their complexity in such reductionist formulas, while the symbolism of masculinity and femininity prevents, in Rosemary Reuther's terms, "the liberation of women, as well as men, from sexist hierarchicalism" (57). But, on some very complex levels, even some of the more consistent feminist authors seem to be unclear as to their stance.

As a literary concept, androgyny is often associated with Carolyn Heilbrun, who began working on her analyses of androgyny in literature in the early 1960's, and developed — and revised — her ideas over the period in which the feminist movement became very vocal in its questioning of the social constructs of gender. In keeping with Heilbrun's later stance, that androgyny should be a "stopping place on the road to feminism" (265), the texts discussed here do seem to stop only briefly at a place of androgyny before moving on towards feminism. Androgyny, represented in the use of gender symbols, is predominant in these texts, and the protagonists measure their growth as women against the background of such gender symbols. As we will see later, this growth involves women either acknowledging masculine aspects in themselves, which however are expendable and not crucial to their development as women, or rejecting the idea of androgyny out of hand. Half of the novels discussed here have androgynous elements or androgyny as a theme, which testifies to its importance as a literary element. However, only the two utopian texts treat androgyny and gender specifically and thematically as a viable possibility for gender transcendence.

As Heilbrun admits, it is fairly easy to dismantle the concept of androgyny as a gender paradigm by simply denying the validity of gender stereotypes. Indeed, most of the writers would probably deny this validity suggesting, like Heilbrun, that androgyny might only be a convenient stopover on the way to feminism. As my overall focus in this project is the way authors are reconceptualizing woman and nature, ideally outside of dualisms and oppositions, I am suggesting that succumbing to the dualisms involved in androgyny is a crucial process for a critique of androgyny on a literary level. There seems to be an initial point at which the authors see androgyny as the resolution of the problem of gender, and proceed to work their way through the paradox of androgyny to dismantle dualism. They are more successful with characterization than with metaphor. The use of gender symbols in metaphor, especially in depicting the environment or natural elements, remains astonishingly traditional despite the trend in the other direction in characterization. In other words, these authors often utilize narrative strategies that rely on androgyny on a metaphorical level while attempting to deconstruct gender on a thematic level.

Keeping in mind Jehlen's suggestion for handling contradictions — either resolving them or tapping them for their energy — that seem especially pertinent here, this internal textual contradiction need not be detrimental to the dynamics of feminism in the texts. The authors' relationships to the concept of androgyny in terms of characterization, metaphor, and the themes derived from them points to a literarity through which the authors critique androgyny, and question the role of gender attributes in coming to terms with "Woman" and "Nature".

Mimesis and Entanglements

Particularly Atwood, Robinson, Piercy and Gearhart at times mimic gender attributes as a form of critique that through exaggeration usurps their power in the text. But this approach does not solve all the problems.

Atwood's text *Surfacing* offers a particularly rich field for investigating androgyny in literature. In this quest narrative, which easily lends itself to psychological interpretations, the protagonist is searching for her father, in Jungian terms, seeking her *animus*. While she does in fact find him, what becomes more important for her development is that she discovers the legacy of her mother. (So, again in Jungian terms, she is actually reunited with her *anima*.) But she must resolve her gender conflicts first before she can emerge whole. Initially these conflicts involve her relationships to her male-dominated world which have proven only destructive, and her own self-deceptions about this world.

Atwood seems almost to go out of her way to insert strongly dualistic gender symbols and metaphors in the text. For example, in returning to the primeval forest of her past, the protagonist must reconcile her images of masculine and feminine, father and mother, sister and brother. But the setting is stereotypically feminine — wild, chaotic nature, the primeval forest. In attempting to find a connection between her remembered past and her present, she searches through photo albums, jacket pockets, scrap books, and books on the shelves. The contrast of herself to her brother is particularly poignant in drawings she finds, in which her brother's drawings are of symbols of destruction (war, bombs, swastikas) and her own are of fertility symbols (Easter bunnies, eggs, grass), balanced by the masculine sun in the left corner and the feminine moon in the right hand corner.[5] The sun/moon images, carefully placed to create balances of power, are first connected to her childhood drawings of "an almost impossible innocence" (98): the sun in the right corner, the moon in the left. This symbolism evolves to the "moon on my left hand and the *absent* sun on my right" (161, emphasis added) in the impregnation scene, in which her feminization begins. We will return to this scene in a moment.

The protagonist, as a woman already engendered as the feminine principle, should be searching for her masculine pole, here represented by her father. But by the time she finds him, her feminine principle has been doubly reinforced, through the spirit of her mother and her recognition of her own femininity which she has been denying through the years. After destroying her links to civilization (masculine), she re-enters the forest to meet with her ancestors. Here Atwood creates partly Shamanistic visions of her mother as nature goddess, caring, nourishing, preserving, protecting, and her father as nature spirit, indifferent, quiet eternal.[6] Having encountered them, and put them to rest, she can then emerge "the natural woman" (190).

Atwood also addresses the contrast between civilization (masculine) and nature (feminine). The protagonist returns to her feminine nature from which she has been alienated by her embrace of the masculine culture, in which she had played out the role of passivity and acquiescence expected of her. Her ultimate rejection of her own lies about her past concerning marriage and childbirth is expressive of her rejection of the masculine in favor of the feminine. Her memories are not of the courthouse ceremony and the maternity ward, but of the abortion clinic. These experiences she associates too with the masculine culture that demands passive acquiescence of her. Another example of her relationship to masculine culture concerns her profession as an artist, an illustrator of children's books. Her publisher does not allow her to use the color red, symbol of sexuality, because it is too costly to reproduce (54); in the wilderness, however, she finds the primitive Indian rock paintings all done in red, which affirms her recognition of her earlier repression. In trying to cast off these unsatisfying roles she must come to terms with herself in a feminine element — again in the primeval forest.

To a certain extent, although the novel is pervaded with strongly dualistic gender symbolism and metaphor, the masculine-feminine elements are not complementary as suggested by the term androgyny — they are not transcended, cannot be united. They remain separate, retaining their oppositional character.

On a superficial level, Atwood is certainly not attempting to overcome gender dualisms here. It almost seems as if she is indulging in a bit of playful (metaphorical) mimesis. Barbara Rigney takes the stand that

> Androgyny is not a meaningful concept in Atwood. The male principle here is ultimately expendable, the female principle alone and in itself incorporates and resolves opposites. Life and death, good and evil, exist within the protagonist, within all women as they exist in nature. (111)

This would all work out very nicely, triumph of the feminine, masculine principles irrelevant, except for the conclusion, where the protagonist decides to return to civilization, and Joe.

I would like to suggest that Atwood is pointing up all the possible cliched gender oppositions, not to resolve them, but to mimic them and use them as contradictions, taking the energy from them (as Jehlen would say) to turn them back on themselves. The conclusion, and the character Joe, need some elucidating on this point. Far from being, as DuPlessis suggests, "the woodsy impregnator, set aside when his task is done" (98), he becomes the mediator between the protagonist and civilization, because he really belongs to neither. She can trust him in the end because, "he isn't anything, he is only half-formed" (192). Atwood does not depict him through any gender stereotypes — he is masculine through biology not through social construct. "He isn't an American" (192), the metaphor she uses for all (negative) aspects of the masculine, and in the impregnation scene, described previously, she remarks specifically while looking over Joe's shoulder, that the sun, that symbol of the masculine principle, is *absent*. His use of language, an important indicator of masculine culture is minimal and primarily used to express emotion. In the very last paragraph, Joe is "balancing on the dock which is neither land nor water" (192). To this character, a neither-nor neutral, the protagonist returns. The primeval forest, previously the symbol of wild, chaotic, feminine, is also neutral at the end. The closing line of the text suggests a neutral stance: "The lake is quiet, the trees surround me, asking and giving nothing."

Finally amidst all this neutrality at the end, the protagonist willingly returns with words that suggest caution and the process of negotiation: "not running away, but cautious ... we will have to talk ... we will have to begin.   ... probably fail ... that's normal", etc. For Atwood, androgyny is not a meaningful concept, but neither is feminine nor masculine. Given this interpretation, Atwood has not resolved the contradictions of gender, she has successfully turned the energy generated from the tension of the contradictions back on itself, to negate them. In going beyond the concepts of the feminine and masculine as social constructs, Atwood "deconstructs" the basis of androgyny.

Another text that offers an equally rich field for the study of the author's literarity regarding androgyny is *The Wanderground*. Like Atwood, Gearhart seems to purposely set up a variety of dualistic oppositions regarding gender roles, which, at first glance, suggest that only the feminine is a viable choice for survival. But, unlike Atwood, she resolves these oppositions using androgyny.

The major dichotomy Gearhart deals with is the City and the Wanderground, the one a bastion of masculine domination and violence, individualistic, industrialized, mechanistic and scientific, and the other of feminine equality and peace, communal, primeval, holistic and intuitive. These two poles, in every way diametrically opposed to each other and within the value system in the narrative also morally opposed to each other, are also limited by each other. The feminine cannot exist in the City, the masculine cannot exist outside of the City, as the women risk confinement and death in the City, and the men and their machines do not function on the outside. Left as mutually exclusive principles, there would be no particular basis for fictional narrative, no tension around which to build a narrative. Consequently, Gearhart structures the tension in the narrative around the bridge between the two, one that becomes essential for the survival of the women. This bridge is the group of the Gentles, secret male allies whose function is to protect the women of the Wanderground in the City, but not to interfere in the Wanderground. These Gentles reveal to representatives of the women at a secret meeting that they too have begun to develop powers similar to those the women have developed.

Here we have the masculine principle striving for and beginning to achieve feminine characteristics.

Up to this point, Gearhart has constructed quite a traditional narrative of androgyny. She demonstrates just that relationship to androgyny that would completely support Jehlen's thesis that "androgyny, in the novel, is a male trait enabling men to act from their male side and feel from their female side" and that "the novel as a genre precludes androgynously heroic women while, and indeed *because* it demands androgynous heroes" (90, 92) and, further, that narrative fiction takes on the conflict between the interior life and the outer world, and "that this interior life, whether lived by man or woman, is female" (90). The Gentles develop this "interior life", the feminine powers of the women; the women are more or less confined to this realm, while "their ability to act in the public domain", the City, is suppressed. What Gearhart changes in her scenario is a shift in value judgments, which suggests that the outer world and the order it signifies is unworthy of the conflict of interest; whereas in Jehlen's theory, the novel makes a basic acceptance of a traditional social order it considers natural. In her unmistakably dualistic moral stance, Gearhart depicts the masculine as absolutely negative, androgyny a necessary evil, and the feminine as absolutely positive, in fact, the only possible mode of survival. By embracing such definitive moral stereotypes, Gearhart cannot have the women incorporate any masculine principles, whereas the Gentles must incorporate feminine ones as a matter of moral imperative. Androgyny is thus portrayed as a threat to the identity of the women, because one is restricted to thinking in dualistic categories. Unfortunately Gearhart's shift in value judgments is not strong enough to question the basic assumptions fiction, according to Jehlen, makes about androgyny, and to a certain extent underscores these assumptions. Unlike Atwood, who goes beyond gender definitions and can thus disregard androgyny, Gearhart becomes so ensnared in categories of gender stereotypes that she needs androgyny as a male trait to find her own way out of the dilemma. Androgyny becomes more than a mere stopping off point on the way to feminism, as Heilbrun suggests. It becomes the vehicle.

Woman on the Edge of Time is more successful in its attempt to come to terms with androgyny, gender roles, and dualism in the utopian mode. Here Piercy takes an approach just the opposite of Gearhart's. In her depictions of Mattapoisett, she develops the idea not of an androgynous society, but a genderless one. My point here is that androgyny pre-supposes gender identification on the basis of social roles rather than on biology; genderlessness, however, while acknowledging male and female biologically, rejects any cultural construct or attributes on the basis of biological differences. Sexuality is pleasurable and unrestricted in Mattapoisett. Keeping these differences in mind, then, the contrast between the protagonist Connie's environment and that of Mattapoisett becomes more clear-cut: the one organized completely around gender distinctions, the other around genderlessness. In this construction, androgyny does not have a place, equality is the catchword in utopia. Through her protagonist, Piercy accomplishes the depiction of the destructive tendencies of gender dichotomy. Unlike in *Surfacing* and *Wanderground*, there are no male characters of any importance, except as symbols of repression (the doctors, the pimp, the brother), and we only see the result of their actions on Connie. In Mattapoisett, there are males, but gender is irrelevant.

Piercy develops the dramatic tension in her text through Connie's projections of utopia which parallel the intensity of her repression in her "present". If we consider the progression of the narrative, somewhat in Jehlen's terms, then it is Connie, rather than a male character, who develops this interior life — her projections of Mattapoisett — and the crucial point of the narrative is Connie's accumulation of power in order to act. This might imply that Connie moves toward androgyny, taking on this male characteristic of action, casting off her feminine characteristic of passivity. But she is not rewarded. In fact, she is basically destroyed by the system's revenge. (This aspect coincides with Jehlen's comment that female characters have power only in their interior lives, and that the novel suppresses only woman's ability to act in the public domain, defined as masculine). Connie, however, has derived her ideas of activity and passivity from the genderless Mattapoisett. Within the terms of the text, these characteristics are not gender-identified and Connie does not become androgynous. Also, Piercy does not set up any male contrasts by which to measure Connie's development; there are certainly no androgynous tendencies in the masculine depicted here.

In Mattapoisett, Piercy shows a firm stance against androgyny as well, in that psycho-social characteristics are divorced from biological ones. For instance, Connie cannot differentiate between male and female Mattapoisettians through speech, dress, attitudes or sexual preference, nor often through appearance. Critic Patricino Schweickart, in commenting on the Mattapoisettians success in doing away with gender-based roles including those connected with conception and child-rearing, writes that "...they have eliminated fatherhood and made motherhood available to everyone" (205), indicating that the feminine principle has triumphed. However, her comment reintroduces the dualism Piercy tries so hard to eliminate in her depiction of utopian life, making it neither masculine nor feminine, but stridently egalitarian, in the purest sense of the term, both socially and politically, including the very basis of communication, language itself.

The issue of androgyny is played out on two levels in Robinson's *Housekeeping*. Like Atwood, there is much to suggest a playful mimesis in the use of gender symbols on the metaphorical level. Her depiction of setting is especially full of complementary gender symbols, like Lake Fingerbone and the mountains, which Robinson describes in minute detail on numerous occasions. Gender-role expectations are emphasized in the narrative, as well. But while Atwood ultimately seems to suggest neutrality as the key to development, Robinson emphasizes the feminine more strongly.

Her description of the setting brings in a format of androgyny in which masculine and feminine elements combine and overlap: There is the contrast between Lake Fingerbone, clear and deep, metaphorically feminine, and the surrounding mountains, with their jagged peaks, metaphorically masculine. The marks of delineation are unclear, as the lake floods and encroaches on the surrounding mountains, and as Lake Fingerbone contains a ridge of ancient hills and peaks that formed the banks of yet another ancient lake. The railroad bridge spanning the lake is used as a primary symbol which becomes both a means of death and escape.

Against this backdrop, the characters are all female, the male characters having been eliminated in the first few pages. This could lead to an interpretation about androgyny, such as Bachinger's comment that the female characters in *Housekeeping*, are "mentally incorporating the masculine in themselves, thus making compensatory and finally revolutionary retribution for the ejection of the male characters" (15). However, in the end, it is the feminine, embodied in Sylvie and then in Ruth that triumphs, not an androgynous character. Through Sylvie's "education" of Ruth, Ruth comes to understand the meaning of nature, civilization, and her own nature as woman, which, with the wisdom of youth, she accepts as part of the impermanence of everything. If they have mentally incorporated the masculine element in themselves, as Bachinger suggests, it becomes an intermediate step in their development.

That the feminine element is the more powerful one here is supported by the fact that a week after Sylvie's arrival in the household, Fingerbone floods the surrounding hillsides to a height never before experienced, flooding the ground floor of the house. Previous flooding had left their house with, at most, a puddle in the basement, because the house was built up so high on the hillside. But with Sylvie there, the feminine symbol, the lake, intrudes and remains in the form of puddles long after the floodwaters have receded. That Sylvie is greatly attached to the lake is evident in her day-long trips on the lake, and even her near suicide dive into the lake from the train bridge, an image of leaping away from the link to the masculine principle into the feminine. Also in the passage in which she shows Ruth the secrets of survival, they go out on the lake to an island where she leads Ruth to a deserted homestead in ruins — the civilizing cultural (masculine) element gone. Having left the masculine elements, Sylvie can show Ruth the secret of her feminine nature as permanence. In a sense, in contrast to the timelessness of the lake, Ruth comes to see material values as symbols of impermanence. If nature is feminine, and culture and civilization, masculine, then Sylvie teaches Ruth to let go of the masculine, and she learns to break "the tethers of need, one by one" (204). The symbol of the train bridge becomes the ultimate boundary of heterosexuality which Ruthie and Sylvie must cross, and the townspeople presume they are dead, rather than admit the possibility of feminine life beyond cultural (masculine) control.

In their texts, Atwood, Gearhart, Piercy and Robinson deliver a fairly definitive critique of androgyny that would indicate that the concept is not really relevant for feminist texts that are attempting to reconceptualize woman. Nevertheless they employ androgynous principles in abundance, at times to achieve the opposite effect through mimesis, taking the energy out of the metaphor. More problematic is Jehlen's contention that the novel as literary form demands androgyny, but these authors in their literary treatment of androgyny seem to take issue with this in subtle ways as well, either by rejecting the idea of an underlying identification with the dominant society, or by eliminating the influence of male characters. Only Gearhart remains somewhat problematic with her strongly moralistic stance that keeps her entangled in dualism. Thus, once androgyny is seen to be more static than dynamic in relationship to the problem of gender, the idea of transcending the oppositional character of gender through androgyny seems revisionist. Indeed, together these texts suggest that conceptualizing gender is a continual process.

Woman-in-process

These authors, in questioning the terms of gender depiction in narrative, are, to a certain extent, still struggling with the literary legacy of woman. At the same time, they would no longer agree with Miles, that "there is an implicit and inescapable antifeminism in any insistence upon the difference between the sexes" (110), for these texts have taken decidedly new directions. Gearhart could even be called "misoandrist", (although it seems that the very idea is so unthinkable that there is no word like its common equivalent "misogynist"!). Instead, these authors acknowledge that the sexes are quite decidedly different, that striving for the animus in the female is a waste of energy (although the androgynous male has not yet been entirely eliminated in fictional texts).

The accumulated literary legacy, "the 'masculine', objective, fictional stance of George Eliot" and "the 'feminine' subjective novel of Jane Austen and the Brontës", as Miles comments on the choices available to women writers (195), or Virginia Woolf's search for the feminine sentence, have been held up for scrutiny and found to be wanting and invalid for the contemporary debate. Similarly, the stock stereotypes have been invalidated. Kolodny, for example, in "Some Notes on Defining a Feminist Literary Criticism", identifies the use of

stereotypes of women as parody in women's novels as one of the
possible characteristics feminist critics can focus on:

> On the one hand, the stereotyped, traditional literary
> images of women — as, for example, the loving
> "Mom", the "bitch", the Sex Goddess — are being
> turned around in women's fiction, either for comic
> purposes, to explore their inherent absurdity, or, in
> other instances, to reveal their hidden reality, though
> in new ways, not previously apprehended. (43)

Nor do our authors accept androgyny, as Heilbrun suggests, as a
stopping place on the way to feminism. An examination of the various
types of characters these authors portray indicates how the authors treat
androgyny, perhaps unconsciously, as a dead end. They have gone
beyond this type of gender dichotomy and moved towards defining
women in "new" non-normative ways. The texts that do not treat
androgyny as directly as those already mentioned also subtly critique
it (on this point by using stereotypes as parody) and define their
female protagonists outside of these stereotypes. In *Housekeeping*,
Lucille becomes the socially acceptable female, the stereotype Ruth
finally decides against. Lucille manifests her gender in keeping with
the expectations of society, whereas Ruth and Sylvie define themselves
as different. It is society, in the form of the sheriff and the ladies of
the town, that eventually forces them to escape.
      Ann of *Surfacing* is the stereotype of the liberated sex-kitten,
applying her layers of makeup everyday in the woods to please David,
fearful of ever stepping outside her role. The protagonist sees Ann is
beyond recovering herself, for she has dedicated herself to David, and
together they seem united in their mutual opposition. The protagonist
prefers the man who is "not yet formed", if any man at all, because he
might be able to bridge the worlds of opposition she sees around her.
Probably few authors manage to define their characters outside of
gender stereotypes as thoroughly as Margaret Laurence does in *The
Diviners*. Morag Gunn, as a child, was always the outcast, the other;
but in developing her identity with others rather than in opposition to

others, she becomes her own person, one who rejects gender markers as discriminatory.

Collectively these authors are suggesting that such concepts as androgyny are more deterrents than aids in developing characters with a sense of self. Thus working through the paradoxical stances that androgyny implies, there is a definite tendency to work within the implied contradictions to expose the metaphor as essentially suppressive to the meaning of woman.

The Lesbian

The second gender stereotype that the authors confront is the lesbian. It seems clear that in texts strongly challenging the very essence of a patriarchy that demands heterosexuality as a form of dominance, the lesbian becomes a figure of liberty, and the depiction of the lesbian becomes a political statement. Of this group of texts, only *Surfacing* and *The Diviners* do not deal directly with the concept of the lesbian. Which space the lesbian occupies in gynocriticism and why are the main considerations to be dealt with now.

To begin with, there are a number of "definitions" of the lesbian and her significance in feminism. I am relying here on lesbian critic Bonnie Zimmerman in "What Has Never Been: An Overview of Lesbian Feminist Literary Criticism",[7] for the complex definitions that frame her own work. She delineates three viewpoints of the lesbian. The first is an inclusive connotation preferred by Adrienne Rich, who maintains that lesbian implies a continuum:

> I mean the term *lesbian continuum* to include a range
> — through each woman's life and throughout history
> — of woman-identified experience; not simply the
> fact that a woman has had or consciously desired
> genital experience with another woman. If we expand
> it to embrace many more forms of primary intensity
> between and among women, including the sharing of
> a rich inner life, the bonding against male tyranny,
> the giving and receiving of practical and political
> support ... we begin to grasp breadths of female

history and psychology which have lain out of reach
as a consequence of limited, mostly clinical, definitions of "lesbianism".[8]

A second definition suggested by critics like Catharine
Stimpson is a more exclusive one; that is, sexual experience with or
affectionality for a woman that distinguishes the lesbian viewpoint
from other "gestures of political sympathy for homosexuals" and
"affectionate friendships in which women enjoy each other, support
each other, and commingle their sense of identity and well-being"
(205). Zimmerman herself prefers a third one, Lillian Federman's more
precise definition in her study *Surpassing the Love of Man: Romantic
Friendship and Love Between Women from the Renaissance to the Present*:

> "Lesbian" describes a relationship in which two
> women's strongest emotions and affections are
> directed toward each other. Sexual contact may be a
> part of the relationship to a greater or lesser degree,
> or it may be entirely absent. By preference the two
> women spend most of their time together and share
> most aspects of their lives with each other. (206)

What is important for my purposes, however, lies not so much in
definitions, but in the literary portrayals at hand. Piercy, Gearhart,
Walker and Naylor depict lesbian relationships as also sexual, whereas
Robinson depicts one as affectionate. It is not so much that they
choose the lesbian as why, and what perspective they adopt.

Politics as Escapism

It is probably clear from the discussion thus far that these four
authors (Robinson excluded momentarily) deal with the lesbian as a
political sexual alternative to heterosexuality, which the protagonists
have found to be a stifling and painful, if not degrading or humiliating,
experience. Certainly in the time span I am dealing with here, heterosexuality is a central feminist issue, even if most feminist critics prefer

to confront it only implicitly. One means of attempting to avoid domination and control by man on a personal level is avoiding sexual contact, although as we will see in the texts, avoidance is not enough, for heterosexuality is only one means (although a powerful one) of domination in patriarchal society.

Walker in *The Color Purple* depicts the lesbian sexual relationship between Celie and Shug as sexual liberation for Celie, who had never experienced her sexuality positively. The lesbian Shug embodies political and psychological enlightenment. Celie falls in love with Shug well before their first sexual experience. Celie is fascinated with Shug's independence from most social restrictions that she herself feels enclosed by. Shug's relationship to Celie's husband provides for the emotional ups and downs of jealousy, but also contributes to the unusual conclusion in which Celie and her husband feel an emotional camaraderie, united as they are by their love for Shug over the years. Shug is the free spirit, loves men and women, and is dominated by no one. As Celie's first positive sexual mate, Shug is the catalyst for Celie's further development which is very crucial for Celie's sense of self. Walker, however, portrays Celie as turning to Shug because every man she has known has horribly abused her; whereas for Shug, a lesbian relationship is part of a playful sexual multiplicity. Shug enjoys sexuality with men and women, but for Celie, lesbianism is an escape. These two characterizations are typical of what we find in the other texts. However, each case in which the portrayal of the lesbian is an escape from patriarchal domination is problematic.

The utopian *Wanderground* provides another case in point. The lesbian environment of the Wanderground is affectionate and sexual, and the women have all escaped from the City. Within their own society, sexual relationships are not problematic. Gearhart portrays a harmonious lesbian (woman-oriented) community where woman's sexuality is connected with its own rituals and celebrations. But these women will eventually have to confront homosexuality when the Gentles join them; they will have to confront homosexuality and eventually heterosexuality because it is what they fear most. However, these speculations take us "beyond the ending".

Naylor touches on a more sinister fear in *Brewster Place*. While fear is Lorraine's main reaction to men and this fear that brings on her horrible end, more relevant to this discussion is the fear of the other women directed at Lorraine and Theresa, the lesbian couple; it mounts and seems inexplicable. Naylor increases the tension around this fear by having the other women react to it, and this in turn brings Lorraine and Theresa to the center of their story. The reason some of the other women fear them is suggested in a few lines: "The quiet that rested around their door on the weekends hinted of all sorts of secret rituals, and their friendly indifference to the men on the street was an insult to the women as a brazen flaunting of unnatural ways" (131).

In these passages, Naylor addresses one of the serious problems in feminism, that is, the marginal space the lesbian has in the feminist movement. Although many see lesbianism as a legitimate intellectual and political stance against patriarchal heterosexuality, the personal, emotional, and sexual bonds tend to be overlooked or ignored. Naylor brings all these tensions and fears into the open, not in the remarks of her male characters, but through the women who turn against Lorraine and Theresa. After the first direct public verbal confrontation between Lorraine and her neighbors (the scene of the block meeting to organize a rent strike), it is clear that the women unconsciously feel challenged, and must question the security they feel with heterosexuality, even though these women have not been dealt with kindly by their own men. In a dialogue between the characters Mattie and Etta, Mattie sums up her confusions and discomfort:

> "But I've loved some women deeper than I ever
> loved any man," Mattie was pondering. "And there
> been some women who loved me more and did more
> for me than any man ever did."
> "Yeah", Etta thought for a moment. "...but it's still
> different, Mattie."...
> "Maybe it's not so different," Mattie said, almost to
> herself, "Maybe that's why some women get so riled
> up about it, 'cause they know deep down it's not so
> different after all." She looked at Etta. "It kind gives
> you a funny feeling when you think about it that
> way, though". (141)

Naylor's strategies elicit sympathy for Theresa and Lorraine as the outcasts. However, Naylor's portrayal of Lorraine as the "weaker" of the two lesbian women is problematic, because she depicts Lorraine's weakness as her continual search for social approval and her desire for inclusion in a heterosexual and patriarchal community. Because Lorraine cannot have both (a lesbian relationship and social accept-ance), she is destroyed. Theresa, on the other hand, shows no interest in her surroundings or the community, and is neither dependent on Lorraine (she has had male lovers before) nor on acceptance. In this way she is more like Walker's Shug: neither use their lesbian selves for political motives.

The (male) gang resents that fact that Lorraine and Theresa do not adhere to their heterosexual rules. That Theresa does not fear them, and therefore does not acknowledge their sexual superiority, is what fires their resentment and precipitates their vicious attack on Lorraine, the "weaker" of the two. And finally it is Mattie who feels that the women, in their intolerance, have become accomplices in this attack, and thus her powerful dream of female solidarity transformed into political action ends the text. The women are accomplices not only in the attack, but all along have been accomplices in support of a system that makes them its victims. So the wall, encoded with many mean-ings, can also signify the gender barrier to sexuality, which only the women can tear down.

What Naylor represents as harsh "reality", Piercy in *Woman on the Edge of Time* handles on both of her narrative levels. Of course, Piercy's primary emphasis is on the utopian aspect, for in Mattapoisett there are no gender barriers to sexuality, and so, Luciente has lovers of both sexes, unencumbered by custom or social mores. In comparing this solution to *Wanderground*, Piercy's seems to be the more challenging: no gender restrictions at all on love relationships implies an open tolerant society, which of course is Piercy's main goal in depicting Mattapoisett. By removing the masculine element in *Wanderground*, Gearhart has, in effect, inserted gender barriers and has created a sexuality without choice. The lesbian in Piercy's New York City is represented by the character Sybil, of whom we learn only that she considers herself a witch and that she is lesbian, which is considered an abnormality and thus the reason she is in the mental hospital. Also, the doctors are particularly eager to experiment with her. This representation of the lesbian and the lesbian experience is no less harsh than in *Brewster Place*, and Sybil is just as surely destroyed by a patriarchal heterosexual system that feels threatened by sexuality it cannot control.[9] She becomes a radio-controlled being.

Piercy, Gearhart, Walker and Naylor stress the lesbian relationships they portray as a means to escape the politics of the heterosexual patriarchy, which can furthermore only retain its dominance through a violent insistence on heterosexuality. That Federman suggests a wider interpretation of a lesbian relationship, including ones that need not be sexual but based on affection, provides a basis for understanding Robinson's work as a lesbian text.

Affection as Politics

To a certain extent Robinson avoids some of the problems of heterosexuality by announcing right in the beginning that masculine influence on her family of women had already been removed by death and desertion. Thus, she announces a lesbian text, woman-centered, woman-oriented. But, as Robinson does not portray a sexual relationship between Ruth and Sylvie, their relationship is one of affectionality. The interruption of the close-knit lives of Lucille, Ruth and Sylvie comes in the form of a male-centered society, and it is only Lucille who moves away from the lesbian toward patriarchal social acceptance. Finally, threatened by the sheriff, that paragon of patriarchal law and order, Sylvie and Ruth flee. However, the lesbian contact with the social practices of Fingerbone are not so simply represented. Like the women of Brewster Place, the ladies of the town see in Sylvie and Ruth a threat to their own values. It is for these ladies that Sylvie begins her furious "housekeeping" in order to gain some sort of social acceptance that will enable Ruth to stay with her. But once Lucille's leaving has caused the town's attention to be focused on them, they are doomed to escaping, fleeing always and everywhere; the plight, symbolic or "real", of the lesbian in a heterosexual society.

Part of Robinson's narrative strategies in focusing on Ruth as the narrator is the depiction of Ruth's interpretations of her orientation to Sylvie, which is almost a symbiosis, and her amused tolerance toward Lucille. She imagines Lucille fulfilling a role demanded by society, the perfect housekeeper: "in a fury of righteousness, cleansing and polishing, all these years" (217); and "I imagine it is Lucille, fiercely neat, stalemating the forces of ruin. I imagine doilies, high and stiff, and a bright pantry curtain, there to rebuke us with newness and a smell of starch" (216). Ruth herself has left this order, "Someday when I am feeling presentable ... for such days are rare now" (217). Ruth is the ultimate lesbian then, for she has not assimilated any patriarchal values.

In terms of gynocriticism, these various representations of the lesbian serve to enlarge the possibilities for reconceptualizing woman. Trans-Atlantic critique of the lesbian elements in fictional narrative is primarily associated with Monique Wittig and Hélène Cixous, both of whom are concerned with deconstructing the language of heterosexuality, the phallologos, and developing the politics of the lesbian. However, most discussions of this type tend to be vague as to sexuality: the sex of the author has nothing to do with the sexuality of the writing, as Cixous contends.[10] "... still perceived as a minor and somewhat discomforting variation within the female life-cycle, when it is mentioned at all,"[11] lesbianism becomes a metaphor for freedom from heterosexual domination at a time when theoretical feminism is looking beyond gender differentiation based on biological sexual difference.

The Mother

The third and last aspect of gender representation we will consider is the mother as a composite of physical and psycho-sexual images. The connotation of "mother" is a place where the trans-Atlantic critical stances meet. The French viewpoint is concerned primarily with "mother" as a physical, sexual being; the American also with the psycho-sexual connotation of "mother". The numerous feminist writings concerned with exorcising matrophobia from feminist vocabulary and reuniting mother and daughter across the void of the "master discourses", which attempt to negate the mother, and the view of some feminist anthropologists and psychoanalysts on the relationships between mother and daughter, are reflected in the concern of the authors here. Regarding the prominent French critics, Jardine summarizes, "To all of these writers, the mother must be rediscovered, differently, if we are to move beyond the repetitive dilemmas of our Oedipal, Western culture" (116).

In "Towards a Feminist Poetics" Showalter writes that

> Hating one's mother was the feminist enlightenment
> of the fifties and sixties, but it is only a metaphor for
> hating oneself. Female literature of the 1970's goes
> beyond matrophobia to a courageously sustained
> quest for the mother, in such books as Margaret
> Atwoods's *Surfacing* ... As the death of the father has
> always been an archetypal rite of passage for the
> Western hero, now the death of the mother as wit-
> nessed and transcended by the daughter has become
> one of the most profound occasions of female litera-
> ture. In analyzing these purposeful awakenings, these
> reinvigorated mythologies of female culture, feminist
> criticism finds its most challenging, inspiring and
> appropriate task. (135)

Indeed, a great many of the texts discussed here have at their core a search for the mother in oneself, or the death of the mother or mother figure (whether real or symbolic), or the very direct awakening of the *Surfacing* type.

This development in literature surely results from the feminist critique of Freud and his theory of the oedipal complex. The Freudian idea that this break is a prerequisite for a healthy development, that a girl child must, in effect, also identify with the father and reject her mother, was perhaps the reason for so much matrophobia in the past. For example, Showalter gives the example of Sylvia Plath's *The Bell Jar*, in which the protagonist screams, "I hate my mother", to her analyst as proof of her cure (135). But this is a situation that feminists are attempting to rectify, and the texts all treat some elements of the mother-daughter relationhips.[12]

The Mother Ritual

The purpose or end of what I will call "the mother ritual" is not to prevent the protagonist from taking her place in patriarchal society, a place of alienation prepared for her by that society, but rather, to allow the protagonist to reach a fuller understanding of her mother's role in a patriarchal society, and to appreciate her gifts to her daughter, her woman nature. This implies neither becoming just like the mother, nor rejecting and hating the mother, but accepting the inheritance from the mother and carrying it on, modifying or even transcending it. Furthermore, it is important that the continuity of the bequest/inheritance be passed on to the next generation of daughters. Coming to terms with the mother is seen as a possibility for coming to terms with oneself as woman.

In *Surfacing*, the protagonist enters a process of coming to terms with her mother which is essential to her coming to terms with herself. The discovery that the previous rejection of the mother was necessary for her to take on a role in the city lies somehow at the core of the protagonist's dissatisfaction with her life there. This alienation is basically the alienation from the woman in herself, and the rite of passage conducted at the end of the work is a celebration of her own womanness. There are images suggesting a sort of identification between the protagonist and her mother, such as her taking the chair and the cushion her mother always used when she visited Madame (20-21), or her wearing her mother's jacket in the woods. Her alienation from her mother is well characterized in the brief hospital scene: a sterile, windowless room, the mother dying, the daughter telling her she is not going to the funeral; they talk past each other, unable to make contact (21-22).

The major connection between the rejection of her mother and her role in the city is, of course, the abortion - she herself rejecting her own motherhood. The protagonist has lied to herself about this act, referring to it as the wedding and then the birth of a son (notably not a daughter here). Thus, in order to overthrow her feelings of powerlessness and to accept the gifts of her mother, she wants to conceive a child. Her previous pregnancy and abortion she associates with her victimization (80, 143); a new pregnancy is a possibility to re-create her own womanness: she can then accept the gift of her mother.

The ambivalence toward the mother's body, which Jardine suggests is necessary for literary texts operating in contemporary thought (and, by corollary, attempting to disrupt dualisms), is taken up by Hélène Cixous. She emphasizes the reluctance to portray the mother's body as a notable lack in literary texts. She comments in "The Laugh of the Medusa" on the "taboo of the pregnant woman" in literature, as follows:

> This says a lot about the power she seems invested
> with at the time, because it has always been sus-
> pected that, when pregnant, the woman not only
> doubles her market value, but — what's more im-
> portant — takes on intrinsic value as a woman in her
> own eyes and, undeniably, acquires body and sex.
> (891)

The protagonist in *Surfacing* sees this intrinsic value of woman in defiance of male constructs; her pregnancy empowers her. Not only is she strong enough to reject the role of victim, but she also has the possibility of bequesting her newfound truths to her newly conceived child.

This type of mother ritual is evident in other texts as well. In, for example, *The Diviners*, Margaret Laurence exemplifies the ambivalent relationship between mother and daughter over three generations. For Morag Gunn, this mother ritual is less direct, more complex. Having lost her mother as a child, the death of her parents has only a minor significance in her photo-album memory of them. But interestingly enough, in the opening pages of the novel, the first photograph Morag finds is of her parents, her mother pregnant. This is also the only time her mother is mentioned by name, and Morag's relationship to this photo is extremely ambivalent:

> Morag Gunn is in this picture, concealed behind
> the ugliness of Louisa's cheap housedress, concealed
> in her mother's flesh, invisible. Morag is still buried

> alive, the first burial, still a little fish, connected
> unthinkingly with life, held to existence by a single
> thread. (7)

But this ambivalence causes her anguish at the same time:

> When I look now at that one snapshot of them, they
> aren't faces I can relate to anyone I ever knew. It
> didn't bother me for years and years. Why should it
> grieve me now? Why do I want them back? What
> could my mother and I say to one another? (11)

This anguish, reflected in her relationship to her own daughter, Pique, forms the basis for Morag's story.

Another aspect of the mother ritual in this text is Morag's own pregnancy as an act of defiance against her husband and her relationship to Jules, the father of Pique. Her pregnancy also has empowering characteristics, in that through her relationship with Jules, she recreates ties to Manawaka and her step-parents, ties that she had negated with her marriage. Equally important is the concept of pregnancy as a process of identification with the mother through motherhood, in that, as Cixous says above, woman takes on value as a woman in her own eyes. For Morag this pregnancy is a complex of emotional ties to mother and place on the one hand, and a rejection of her unhappiness with her husband on the other. Later, through Pique, these ties live on for her.

In the primary plot of the novel, Morag is concerned about bequeathing her gift of womankind to her daughter, who is intent on discovering herself, and so, in a sense, is not yet ready to receive this gift. She has a feeling for place similar to Morag's, and she retreats to the grounds of her Indian ancestors. On the other hand, there are numerous parallels set up between Morag and her daughter that center around searching for one's place, really searching for oneself.

For Morag, the identity as woman is tied to a particular place, Manawaka, but it is noteworthy that Morag's interest in her own past is centered around her father and his ancestors, rather than her mother. Her stepfather, Christie, tells her all about her father and his ancestors, but makes no mention of her mother. Morag wonders about the lives of the women who settled in that strange and frightening, isolated northern prairie. In her reveries she relocates her sense of maternal place to McConnell's Landing from her hometown of Manawaka, and finally understands the meaning of her "gift" in the terms of bequeaths of women to women. In doing so she has transcended the death of the mother, which, as Showalter suggested in the passage quoted earlier, is one of the most profound occasions in female literature.

Both *Surfacing* and *The Diviners* are also "Künstlerromane" that depict a female artist, a figure who

> encodes the conflict between any empowered woman
> and the barriers to her achievement. Using the female
> artist as a literary motif dramatizes and heightens the
> already-present contradiction in bourgeois ideology
> between the ideals of striving, improvement, and
> visible public works, and the feminine version of that
> formula: passivity, "accomplishments", and invisible
> private acts.[13]

Both artist protagonists enact the mother-ritual in creative as well as procreative terms: In *The Diviners,* giving birth to a daughter and producing a work of art (novel) at the same time; in *Surfacing*, the promise of doing both. To return again to Cixous's metaphor[14], pregnancy is the particular maternal power that *em*powers. In a twist of the usual feminist scenario, in both works, the protagonist wants her role as mother against the wishes of the male concerned. Thus the role of mother is itself seen as contradictory, but it is tantamount to giving birth to creativity, to self-expression and to a refusal of silence.

Resolving the ambivalence toward mother is an underlying current in *Housekeeping* that Robinson maintains on several levels. Through the personal narrative of Ruth, the ambivalent attitude of the protagonist toward her mother changes and she sees through the social construct of "mother". Robinson treats this "mother" with a marked lack of emotion. Ruth relates how her mother deposited her two daughters on the grandmother's porch before she drove away over a cliff into the deepest part of the lake. Unlike Atwood's text, for example, there is no sentimentality. The ensuing succession of substitute mothers (grandmother, great-aunts) leaves no impact on Ruthie and Lucille. Only Sylvie, with her strange, gentle ways, is any kind of mother figure. Defying the rules of mothering, such as keeping house and children neat and cared for, and participating in community and social functions, Sylvie is rejected by the one sister, Lucille, for her failure and neglect, but is able to reach through to Ruth, exemplifying that "mother" means love.

Sylvie wants to "teach" Ruth a sense of self as woman. But more importantly, having had to cope with the suicide of her mother, the death of her grandmother, and the escape of her great-aunts, it is what Ruth wants to learn. Robinson, too, has her protagonist Ruth participate in this mother ritual in order to transcend the death of the mother. To do this, the characters actually enact a ritual, watching for the imaginary children Sylvie has told her about. In the following passage, Ruth's reference to Lot's wife, punished for her compassion by a merciless, patriarchal God, as a mother for these imaginary children is crucial for her recognition of the importance of her own mother. The passage is also an indication of what Ruthie feels is important in a mother:

> If there had been snow I would have made a statue, a woman to stand along the path, along the tree. The children would have come close, to look at her. Lot's wife was salt and barren, because she was full of loss and mourning, and looked back. But here rare flowers would gleam in her hair, and on her breast, and in her hands, and there would be children all around her, to love and marvel at her for her beauty, and to laugh at her extravagant adornments, as if they had set the flowers in her hair and thrown down all the flowers at her feet, and they would forgive her, eagerly and lavishly, for turning away, though she never asked to be forgiven. Though her hands were ice and did not touch them, she would be more than mother to them, she so calm, so still, and they such wild and orphan things. (153)

At the close of the ritual, in which Sylvie leaves her alone for many hours in an abandoned homestead, Ruthie reconciles herself to her mother's suicide, accepting the unspoken legacy:

> If I could see my mother, it would not have to be her eyes, her hair. I would not need to touch her sleeve. There was no more the stoop of her high shoulders. The lake had taken that, I knew. It was so very long since the dark had swum her hair, and there was nothing more to dream of, but often she almost slipped through any door I saw from the side of my eye, and it was she, and not changed, and not perished. She was a music I no longer heard, that rang in my mind, itself and nothing else, lost to all sense, but not perished, not perished. (160)

Symbolically, through Sylvie, Ruthie "becomes" her mother:

> that by abandoning me she had assumed the power to bestow such a richness of grace. For in fact I wore her coat like beatitude, and her arms around me were as heartening as mercy, and I would say nothing that might make her loosen her grasp or take one step away. (161)

Ruth now knows that "mother" does not need to be equated with clothes, house, with all the social constructs of mother, but with an all-encompassing love, music, beatitude, and richness of grace that does not perish. This is the pre-condition for their flight away from the town and its restrictions, and the purpose of the ritual.

By moving her protagonist through these steps of recognition, which entail first removing the biological mother from the narrative, and then suggesting the irrelevance of the social construct of mother, Robinson has attempted to remove the concept of mother, and by analogy the feminine, to a metaphorical/semiotic level in the text (and she has been more successful than most of the authors here). This is an important step in the direction preferred by the French critics, reflecting their own images of "mother" and "feminine" as spaces outside consciousness. Indeed, the protagonist conceives of her mother as "a music I no longer heard, that rang in my mind, itself and nothing else, lost to all sense, but not perished, not perished" (160). This passage is strikingly reminiscent of Kristeva's concept of the semiotic "chora" as articulation associated with the pre-oedipal mother, that occasionally breaks through language in the form of silences, absences, disruptions, rhythmic pulsions, etc.[15] Ruthie feels her absent mother in herself.

Robinson, Atwood, Laurence, white middle-class authors, treat biological mother-daughter pairs, but Walker and Naylor seem inspired by a wider concept of motherhood, one that includes many relationships and a sense of community. The two utopian texts suggest some innovative variations on the motherhood theme as well. In her sensitive essay, "In Search of Our Mothers' Gardens", Alice Walker, ironically using comments from Virginia Woolf's *A Room of One's Own*, expresses how, for the writer, the double marginality of the black woman imposes hindrances on the mother ritual. It is clear that this same disruption is exposed in the black author's texts. The experience of "mother" for the black child is very different from that for the white middle class child, as are the conditions for the black woman artist very different from those of the white middle class woman artist. Walker makes clear the meaning of such double marginality for the black woman artist:

> Black women are called, in the folklore that so aptly identifies one's status in society, "the *mule* of the world", because we have been handed the burdens that everyone else — *everyone* else — refused to carry. We have also been called "Matriarchs", "Superwomen," and "Mean and Evil Bitches". Not to mention "Castraters" and "Sapphire's Mama." When we have pleaded for understanding, our character has been distorted; when we have asked for simple caring, we have been handed empty inspirational appellations, then stuck in the farthest corner. When we have asked for love, we have been given children.

In short, even our plainer gifts, our labors of fidelity
and love, have been knocked down our throats. To be
an artist and a Black woman, even today, lowers our
status in many respects, rather than raises it: and yet,
artists we will be. (197)

In Alice Walker's, as well as in Gloria Naylor's text, the
mother ritual is significantly different from that in the novels discussed
already. In *The Color Purple*, the role of mother is filled by various
women, for of the many children mentioned in the text, none are raised
by their biological mothers — a situation not based on ideology, but
born of necessity. The relationship between Celie and her sister Nettie
is central to the mother ritual. Having succeeded in protecting Nettie
from sexual abuse by their stepfather and later by Celie's husband,
Celie agrees to Nettie being sent away. In this situation Celie has
assumed a mother role for Nettie. In Nettie's subsequent work
situation, she is first the caregiver for children who turn out to be
Celie's, and later becomes their stepmother. For Nettie, the voyage to
Africa and her lifetime there provides the search element of the mother
ritual, as she discovers in herself the meaning of mother, and passing
it on to Celie's children.

The reunion at the end of the novel, that in many respects is
so overly sentimental, is the physical fulfillment of the spiritual mother
ritual. The children are reunited with their biological mother, and
Celie, after having taken care of so many children not her own and
having been deprived of her own, is thus united through the mother
ritual with her own biological children.

In *The Women of Brewster Place*, there is a similar situation
in that Mattie, beaten and thrown out by her father because of her
pregnancy, exploited and rejected by her son, in effect becomes a
mother figure for the tenants of Brewster Place. Confronted with the
unbelievable brutality of Lorraine's death, Mattie transcends the
symbol of mother in her dream, which unites mothers and daughters
in the single action of tearing down the wall, a deed of strength rather
than weakness.

What is also noteworthy in these two texts is the role of
pregnancy, which in both Atwood's and Laurence's texts empowers the

protagonists. The double marginality of the black texts is most explicit here. Neither Walker nor Naylor project this attitude toward pregnancy. On the contrary, pregnancy becomes for their protagonists the initiation into a terrifying world of harassment and objectification, a symbol of the loss of control over their lives as women. Ironically, the first step Celie takes to control her life is not getting pregnant, which seems to be a sheer act of will on her part: "A girl at church say you git big if you bleed every month. I don't bleed no more" (15). Naylor's Mattie never even considers the sexual act after her child is born, so drastic and negative is the experience to her. Both of these texts then turn to the possibilities of the lesbian as an alternative way of approaching the concept of woman outside of the consequences of heterosexual relationships — pregnancy, motherhood, marriage.

Similarly, the utopian texts contain a sort of mother ritual, which in *The Wanderground* returns to a mystical valorization of some very traditional values associated with the concept of mother, like the conception rituals in the story, "The Deep Cella", but, on the other hand the women have developed a child-rearing unit which has eliminated the patriarchal social construct of "mother". In this respect, both novels are united. In *Woman on the Edge of Time*, the mother rituals are associated only with the physical act of motherhood while the emotional bonding between mother and child is seen as detrimental to the development of the child. This may very well have its base in a subtle acceptance of Freud's theory of child development in which basically mother is seen primarily as a hindrance to healthy child development. To eliminate the hindrance, Gearhart and Piercy eliminate mother, rather than questioning the theory behind it. However, the feminist objection to Freud's theory[16] suggests that the continuity in identification with the mother is crucial for girls. In the utopian mode, parental identification is difficult to analyze because of the lack of individual character development. It should be noted, though, that Elaine Showalter, in connection with her gynocritics, suggests a type of mother ritual that is one of individuality and development.

Only in the case of Connie Ramos is the idea of the legacy of the mother raised, and in this case concerns not Connie's relationship with her mother but with her daughter, and the legacy Connie can give to her. This is brought out by the doubling technique, in which Angelina is cast as Dawn in the future Mattapoisett. In deciding to take on an active role in the fight for the existence of the future Mattapoisett, Connie prepares the way for a life in the future with Angelina. Without reading too much into the text, one could say that the values of Mattapoisett that do not restrict the possibilities of woman is what Connie would like to bequeath to her daughter.

The representation of the mother, then, apparent in all of the texts here, reunites women across a void created by patriarchal discourse which demands a negation of the mother and adherence to the father. On the textual level, these mother rituals represent the authors' attempts to restore the concept of mother primarily *in opposition to* this patriarchy. In this oppositional mode, however, the texts verge away from the concepts put forth by the French critics; by staying in such an oppositional stance, they cannot begin to overcome the dualisms we are discussing here. Only Atwood's and Robinson's texts might be seen as taking the initial steps out of this oppositional stance because the protagonists develop and confront a self-conscious awareness of the concept "mother". Walker and Naylor differentiate and represent "mother" in much larger contexts that might also provide a way out of "the repetitive dilemmas of our Oedipal, Western culture", as Jehlen hopes: the mother has been rediscovered, differently.

Focusing on the author's strategies to portray female sexuality and particular female experiences in the texts as core positive experiences illuminates the concept of woman emerging from this group of texts.

The literarity of gender becomes on the textual level one which leads the protagonists to a certain self-awareness of their sexuality. The use of the lesbian relationship is an attempt to move out of the oppositional stance of gender, as are the utopian attempts to remove the difference from gender and equalize sexuality, but these efforts are further problematized by the French perspective which tends to valorize difference itself as a possibility for transcending gender opposition. The androgyne seems to have run its course — through mimesis — as a literary legacy in these novels, but the representation of the mother as a figure incorporating many aspects of female sexuality and relationships is a very dynamic feature in these texts. Perhaps they are the first steps in loosening the bedrock of dualistic opposition and moving toward a reconceptualization of woman.

NOTES

1. Jane Singer, *Androgyny: Towards a New Theory of Sexuality*, (London: Routledge & Kegan Paul, 1976), p. 230.

2. cf. Jung, *Archetypes and the Collective Unconscious*, (Princeton,NJ: Bollingen Press, 1969); *The Development of Personality*. trs. R.F.C. Hull. (NY: Pantheon Books, 1954); cf. also, Alfred B. Heilbrun, Jr., *Human Sex-Role Behavior*, (N.Y.: Pergamon Press, 1981) who indicates some contradictory material from the psychological perspective, in which he states that on the one hand it is more serious for males to deviate "from stereotypic masculine role-expectations ... in our culture than is female deviation from femininity" (67), but on the other hand in his studies of college students, "Males emerge as more androgynous than females" (70). cf. also Pratt, *Archetypal Patterns*, pp. 3-10; Daniel A. Harris, "Androgyny: the Sexist Myth in Disguise", *Women's Studies*, 2(1974), 171-84; Heilbrun, *Toward a Recognition of Androgyny*; and "Androgyny and the Psychology of Sex Difference", in Eisenstein and Jardine (eds.), pp. 258-266.

3. The concept of androgyny has developed in psychology beyond Jung's initial investigative and theoretical writings to the point that it is possible to rely on a number of other analyses of sex-role behaviors that are based on androgynous concepts of society. (Ellen Piel Cook for instance lists literally dozens of studies in *Psychological Androgyny*, pp. 18-36; see also Alfred Heilbrun.) But the greater emphasis is given to the masculine personality who has accepted the expression of his anima, rather than to the female acceptance of her animus — although this may, of course, be due to the built-in bias of the investigators.

4. Singer suggests that if thought of as a holistic system, androgyny might offer possibilities out of the maze of gender categories, but what she discusses is basically the aspects that feminist theory has adopted/adapted from systems theory - "androgyny" then is replaced by "feminism"!

5. cf. Barbara Hill Rigney, *Madness and Sexual Politics in the Feminist Novel*, (Madison: Univ. of Wisconsin Press, 1978), p. 98.

6. cf. Heller, p. 47.

7.Bonnie Zimmerman, "What Has Never Been: An Overview of Lesbian Feminist Literary Criticism", *Feminist Studies*, 7/3 (1981); rpt. in Showalter (ed.), pp. 200-224. Page numbers are from the Showalter version.

8.Rich, "Compulsory Heterosexuality and Lesbian Existence", *Signs*, 5 (summer, 1980), 648-49; qtd. in Bonnie Zimmerman, "What Has Never Been: An Overview of Lesbian Feminist Literary Criticism", in Showalter (ed.), p. 205.

9.It must be noted, however, that Piercy's homosexual character in the mental hospital fares no better than Sybil, and, in fact, commits a gruesome suicide. The homosexual, though, does not have the same status as the lesbian in heterosexual patriarchal society, because homosexuality is in effect an affirmation of the phallus and thus is more tolerated, and has been at least from the time of the Greeks. The lesbian, however, rejects this power of the phallus.

10.cf. Cixous, "The Laugh of the Medusa", pp. 878-879.

11.Zimmerman, p. 217.

12.In addition to Chodorow, Mitchell and Irigaray, cf. Carol Gilligan, *In a Different Voice: Psychological Theory and Women's Development*, (Cambridge: Harvard UP, 1982); and Jane Gallop, *The Daughter's Seduction: Feminism and Psychoanalysis*, (Ithaca: Cornell UP, 1982).

13.DuPlessis, p. 84.

14.cf. Cixous,"Laugh of the Medusa", p. 891.

15.cf. Kristeva, *Revolution in Poetic Language*, pp. 43-48; rpt. in Moi (ed), pp. 93-98.

16.See chapter 3.

The girl or woman who tries to write ... is peculiarly
susceptible to language. She goes to poetry or fiction
looking for her way of being in the world ... she is
looking eagerly for guides, maps, possibilities, and over
and over ... she comes up against something that
negates everything she is about ... but precisely what
she does not find is that absorbed, drudging, puzzled,
sometimes inspiring creature, herself.

(Adrienne Rich)

It's rare, but you can sometimes find femininity in
writings signed by men: it does happen.

(Hélène Cixous)

The problem may not be woman's speech, but men's
hearing.

(Helen Grace)

7

Literarity and Words

Gynocriticism, concerned as it is with the relationship between
woman and fiction, must confront the issues of the language of fiction
from woman's perception. In this context, literarity becomes central to
a discussion of narrative fiction that explores its own limitations, for,
as we have seen so far, many of the texts concern woman approaching
the boundaries of fictional narrative. Whether the feminist authors can
influence fiction by extending its boundaries and language barriers to
include woman and her meanings is the focal question of literarity.
Surely, woman's relationship to fiction brings up a variety of issues,
problems, and questions that also go beyond the scope of this project[1]
and we have already considered the concept of the subject and meta-

phor in relation to the fictional texts.[2] But indeed, by exploring the relationship between woman, language, and fictional narrative we can more precisely define gynocriticism's contribution to the reconceptualization of woman and nature. Woman's writing, or "l'écriture féminine", incorporates a number of important aspects, for the problematization of language in these texts is one possibility of extending fictional boundaries and language barriers to include woman.

L'écriture féminine

Primarily associated with Hélène Cixous, who explores the relationship between woman and feminism and fictional texts, "l'écriture féminine" is a recognition that language frames our perceptual possibilities, and, for writers, language is the artist's tool. After recognizing that a language is man-centered and sexist (phallologos), women writers become especially sensitized to using this language. In the framework of this project, this sensitivity manifests itself by using and changing the dominant phallologos to express conceptions of woman and nature. Also of special relevance here is the number of writers who have criticized language in their own narratives, by creating a thematics of language that also includes problematizing woman's relationship to fiction.

Cixous's theory of woman's writing would seem, at first, not to be a rejection of "patriarchal binary thought" as she terms it, but rather a reinforcement of it. She herself would strongly deny this, and indeed states in "Laugh of the Medusa" that woman's writing need not have a woman as author, but only that a woman, because of her space in patriarchal thought processes, would be most likely to produce such texts.[3] Admitting that such writing is rare, and that from the body of female writers, one must "first deduct the immense majority whose workmanship is in no way different from male writing, and which either obscures women or reproduces the classic representations of women as sensitive-intuitive-dreamy, etc." (878), Cixous also maintains that this woman's (feminine) writing is impossible to define:

> It is impossible to *define* a feminine practice of
> writing, and this is an impossibility that will remain,

> for this practice can never be theorized, enclosed,
> coded — which doesn't mean that it doesn't exist.
> But it will always surpass the discourse that regulates
> the phallocentric system: it does and will take place
> in areas other than those subordinated to philosophic-
> theoretical domination. It will be conceived of only
> by subjects who are breakers of automatisms, by
> peripheral figures that no authority can ever sub-
> jugate. (883)

There is definitely a problem in naming processes that are difficult to define within the logic of the phallologos as "feminine" simply due to the fact that the phallologos demands a differentiation coded by the cultural construct of gender. Cixous's tenuous comment that at present only women are "bisexual" in a sense that manifests rather than negates differences only clouds the terminology, and encloses her theories in contradictory "biologism" and "anti-biologism", which returns to the essence of dualism again. As a great deal has been written on this topic already,[4] it is perhaps sufficient to suggest that the purpose is to expose the male bias of writing based as it is in the phallologos, and to suggest that women writers have the possibility of developing out of these confines. Indeed, the whole concept of using narrative strategies to express woman's experiences with and through the text is a result of this recognition of the power of male bias in writing. What Cixous and, certainly, Kristeva are concerned with is the gender of the text rather than the gender of the writer.

Another concern of Cixous' is that entry to the feminine is typically through lyrical writing:

> But only the poets — not the novelists, allies of
> representationalism. Because poetry involves gaining
> strength through the unconscious and because the
> unconscious that other limitless country, is the place
> where the repressed manage to survive: women, or as
> Hoffmann would say, fairies. (880)

Thus, for her, representation is a delusion, for it implies a reality, which within her framework, is already an ideological perceptual construction. But this project concerns exactly such texts that deal with their own marginality and exclusion from language, worked out through, and thus undermining, language itself. These texts deny universality through fictional representation — not always consistently but sufficiently, I think, to establish their distrust of language.

Indeed, the narrative strategies these writers have developed to cope with the representations of woman and nature that in effect deny their universality and their dualistic cultural constructs seem to be "evidence" of the type of woman's writing Cixous says is undefinable. It might well be that women writers have been coping all along and undermining the cultural codes of language, unrecognized by theorists who are more caught up in phallologocentric thinking. A number of recent rediscoveries of women writers, newly critiqued in the light of such theories of woman's writing, seem to indicate this.[5] In the body of texts here, nearly all the authors can be seen to have problematized their own relationship to their texts, encoded in and through the process of writing. This is especially forceful in the three texts that have the woman-as-artist as their protagonists.

The conflicts a woman-as-artist faces which hinder her relationship to her art, whether "high art" (like writing or painting) or "crafts" (like quilting, gardening, cooking, etc.), can be seen as the conflicts the woman faces in becoming herself, wading through the sea of cultural restrictions that deny her creativity. Not taken seriously by a culture that does not take empowered woman seriously, the woman-as-artist develops a relationship to her art outside of the social expectations accorded her. DuPlessis writes on this problem in her chapter on the "Künstlerromane":

> Using the female artist as a literary motif dramatizes
> and heightens the already-present contradiction in
> bourgeois ideology between the ideals of striving,
> improvement, and visible public works, and the
> feminine version of that formula: passivity, "ac-
> complishments" and invisible private acts. (84)

and suggests that in such novels, the writers "present a radical oppositional aesthetics criticizing dominance" (104). While DuPlessis moves her analysis in other directions, for this discussion the encoding of this critique of dominance is the starting point for a woman's writing, or "l'écriture féminine". The woman-as-artist/woman-as-writer become one in this study, for through the creation of the protagonist-as-artist the authors encode their own relationship to their texts.

Laurence, in choosing as her protagonist a writer who throughout the text is in the process of writing, is a prime case in point. In *The Diviners*, in some ways the more conventional of the texts we're looking at, Laurence portrays a woman on the margins of society, probing the strands of her memory and her dreams of the past. Her past becomes a non-linear reconstruction of events evoked from scraps of artifacts, photographs and memory associations from which she tries to gather strength to approach her writing, those "private and fictional words" (453) born of her "magic tricks" (452). Laurence does not genderize her writing, but mysticizes it as a psychic gift like that of Morag's friend and neighbor, the old diviner Royland. Morag keeps a talisman, refers to Royland as shaman, accepts the unexplainable like the water that "kept its life from sight" (453) and the river that flowed both ways. She sees divining as "the gift, or portion of grace, or whatever it was" but writing for her is even more mystical:

> At least Royland knew he had been a true diviner.
> There were the wells, proof positive. ... Morag's
> magic tricks were of a different order. She would
> never know whether they actually worked or not, or
> to what extent. That wasn't given to her to know. In
> a sense, it did not matter. The necessary doing of the
> thing — that mattered. (452)

This mystification of writing is an entry into the unconscious realms of association, which Laurence uses as the structure of her text. Thus, although some of the plot concerns the difficulties the woman-as-writer faces in society, Laurence does not directly confront woman's writing as a problematizing of language. Instead, she encodes the relationship of Morag to her writing in images of "the feminine" as spiritual, mystical, unexplainable.

Atwood accomplishes something similar in creating a protagonist as artist; and while I will discuss *Surfacing* in the following section because it is the text that most explicitly problematizes language, a few comments about it concerning woman's writing are necessary here. Atwood carefully constructs the ties which link her woman-as-artist to the primitive, spiritual, mystical ("feminine") elements of the past: the protagonist cannot use the color red for her drawings because it is too expensive to reproduce well, whereas the cave drawings of the ancient local tribes are red; the clue to her father's disappearance lies in his own copies of the cave-drawings, which she comes to understand only after she has broken a few of her ties to her companions and her present; the desired birth of her child, signifying her own creativity, is planned to take place outside the boundaries of civilization. All these indicate the problematization of the woman-as-artist not only in society, but also to her art: that until she releases the cultural barriers to her development, she will remain trapped because she has to produce her art on male/cultural terms. In rejecting the cultural construct of "woman", as in rejecting the cultural construct of "art", the protagonist becomes rooted in her own creativity — creating herself and her works of art. This is the emphasis Cixous places on her "l'écriture feminine": writing as a process of "the feminine" encoded as spiritual, mystical, unconscious forces.

Finally, Walker's *The Color Purple* must be seen as writing-in-process in the context of woman's writing. She creates for Celie an invincible sense of herself as woman that is manifested in Celie's writing. Its ungrammatical, raw emotional style is very marginal to the standard dominant language. With her language, with her sexuality and with her art Celie creates herself outside of male domination. In her essay "In Search of Our Mothers' Gardens", Walker argues that the dominant cultural definitions of art, and its split into "high art" of writing, painting, sculpting and creative "crafts" like gardening, cooking, quilting, needlework have codified women, but especially black women, out of art. In the contextual dilemma of "what is art?", while at the same time undermining such an essentialist question, Walker has her Celie make pants: fanciful, imaginative, colorful pants. Initially, of course, Celie designs them after completing the field work, housework, and servicing of her husband and step-children. This seems to be Walker's decided critical response to Virginia Woolf's demands for "A Room of One's Own" that separates and isolates the woman-as-artist from her own pulsating creativity within the life- and love-giving community.[6]

But more crucial to the topic here is the much overlooked aspect of Celie as writer, her writing being as fanciful, imaginative and colorful as her pants. Initially, Celie's main reason for writing is to record the unspeakable. Nettie writes to her,

> I remember one time you said your life made you
> feel so ashamed you couldn't even talk about it to
> God, you had to write it, bad as you thought your
> writing was. (122)

Writing becomes her path through the feminine silence, a way of circumscribing her inability to articulate the feelings she "couldn't even talk about". Exactly because Walker's protagonist is very much a marginal character in terms of the dominant culture, Celie's writing is full of the linguistic disruptions, contradictions, rhythm and pulsation, and "absences" (in that what she does not explain is more meaningful than some of the comments) that mark her as marginal. Up to the point in the text where she enters into her lesbian love affair with Shug, her letters primarily concern events, and the most expressive passages are those of her repression of her emotions, like "I know what I'm thinking bout, I think. Nothing. And as much of it as I can" (116); or "Mr.___ feelings hurt, I say. I don't mention mine" (106). However with the beginning of her relationship to Shug, she becomes capable of expressing her emotions, both positive and negative ones and begins to see herself in positive terms.

Celie's style is not representational, as for example is her sister Nettie's whose letters are meant to "represent" the "reality" of colonial repression in Africa. However, Celie's style conveys the same repression, while it undermines the dominant rules of "symbolic order". In contrasting the two styles in her text, Walker encodes the possibilities for woman's writing, giving it meaning outside the restrictions of representational narrative.

Laurence, Atwood, and Walker testify to Cixous's problematization of "l'écriture feminine", ambiguously genderized. Although here
both protagonist and author are of the same "gender", each of these
texts expose the dominant male bias towards art and writing, by
reconnecting, on the textual level, the protagonist with her own self
from whom she had been culturally disconnected. And on another
level, the authors undermine the cultural codes of language, as
suggested by Cixous, by portraying such characters; for the woman-as-
artist defies some of the very cultural codes that deny woman a place
in art, and simultaneously, the authors-as-artists problematize their own
relationship to their art.

Whereas in these texts the focus is on the woman-as-artist
attuned to her gender and its relationship to art, a woman writer is also
concerned with her tools, not just creating a "feminine" text, but
creating it with language, a phallologos bent on depriving her of her
voice. Authors are still caught in the paradox of using the very
language-as-discourse they rebel against. Women's access to discourse
obviously involves a certain submission to phallologocentricity, the
masculine, the symbolic;[7] refusal of that discourse relegates woman
to silence, madness, or nonsense.[8] If feminists proceed to consider
their theories of the feminine through language, then some care must
be taken to avoid a dead end, a silence. So again, woman is in a
situation that demands a use of what is simultaneously the object of
criticism, and the very discourse that makes it possible. As one critic
comments, because they want to

> destroy the male hegemony of language, the writers
> experience a rage that is all the more intense because
> the writers see themselves as prisoners of the dis-
> course they despise. But is it possible to break out?[9]

If one sees this as a continual process played out within language and
across its boundaries, then women could, as Kristeva, Cixous, and
Irigaray suggest, work in this process to deconstruct it,[10] "to write
what cannot be written". What these fictional texts reveal is a central
concern, and doubt, that this man-centered language the authors use is
capable of expressing the new realities of woman, and, what is of

central importance to this paper, how the authors nevertheless struggle with this language to reconceptualize woman and nature.

Language as Theme

When the protagonist in *Surfacing* says, "It was the language again, I couldn't use it because it wasn't mine" (106), she vocalizes a fundamental distrust in a phallologos that she feels has betrayed her. It is not only the lexical and semantic factors, but language as a complex system that "ignores, defines and deprecates women."[11] It is as if man's language had pre-formed certain slots for the protagonist that she feels she had to fit into, and now discovers that these don't fit her. This attitude is characteristic of a number of the texts. One of the narrative strategies used by the authors is the direct thematic problematizing of languages, constrictions and restrictions on woman. However, there is also a focus on language's possibilities for woman and its possibilities for change. These themes figure prominently in such works as *Woman on the Edge of Time*, *The Wanderground*, and *Surfacing*. While Atwood questions the adequacy of language to express woman's experience or emotions, or needs, Piercy and Gearhart suggest that language use is essential for social changes and experiment with the use of different meanings and communication in their utopian "countries".

The Adequacy of Language

In *Surfacing*, the ambivalent relationship between woman and language is indeed the protagonist's central problem. Initially her language problem is characterized by her inability to use French to communicate with her French-Canadian neighbors. This contact with a foreign language sensitizes her to situations in which "people would say words that would go into my ears meaning nothing" (11), a problem she eventually realizes she has as a woman within her own (English) language. As a Canadian, she also associates American English with an alien society, one bent on the destruction of the Canadian environment and consciousness. Finally Atwood draws the circle more closely around her protagonist, as she realizes that not even her own Canadian English is hers. Thus sensitized to language problems, she realizes that language is powerful, it controls experience, "a language is everything you do" (129), but that it is also dangerous for a woman. The protagonist feels "paralysis of the throat" (19) when she tries to speak, she is silenced and alienated, unable to express feelings.

What Atwood is suggesting is that language, as a cultural construct, however "universal", is, in fact, produced only by men. Irigaray writes of this indirectly asking,

> A language which presents itself as universal, and
> which is in fact produced by men only, is this not
> what maintains the alienation and exploitation of
> women in and by society? (62)

Thus, Atwood's protagonist, in an intermediate move, chooses silence, which she qualifies as "the other language" (158), rather than betray herself with words. This withdrawal from communication, the feminine silence, or being silenced, represents the dualist mode of thinking. The text is full of such references to language as inadequate for expressing her feelings, but also her awe of the power of language, which she feels excluded from. Her silence is one of her own choosing, but one she finally realizes is counter-productive. Before coming to this conclusion, however, Atwood creates a parallel movement in the text, similar, I think, to the level of Kristeva's semiotics, or the pre-oedipal (pre-verbal) identification with the mother. This metaphor is used to portray opposition on the basis of gender, and the ambiguity she feels when she realizes that her acquisition of her father's system of expression — his language and civilization — is at the expense of her female relationships.[12] She sees her father as "the voice of reason" (88). She becomes more drawn to her dead mother whose silences impressed her:

> My father explained everything, but my mother
> never did, which only convinced me that she had the
> answers but wouldn't tell. (74)

She finds her mother's non-verbal legacy to her in the form of "pictographs" (158), and these non-verbal significations become her guides; she must "immerse myself in the other language" (158). To do this she escapes from her companions and stays on the island in the woods. Her vow not to teach her child any words and her own silence, which is a refusal of language (the phallologos), during her time in the woods, interrupted only by her own laughter, are both finally rejected as counterproductive.

Atwood is ambiguous here about the limitation and liberation of language for woman. She has created a highly complex text as a dialogue on language and presents the paradoxes clearly, but at the critical point she withdraws. When in the final chapter the protagonist emerges as the non-victim, a natural woman, she resolves to use language again. Instead of having her protagonist, in Kristeva's terms, "rethink the unrepresentable", Atwood sends her back to "civilization", "reality", "normality", etc. The possibility of creating a "woman's language" beyond silence is lost. It seems that Atwood, in having her protagonist return to her Joe, and her resolution that "for us it's necessary, the intercession of words; and we will probably fail" (192), reaffirms the law of the fathers, but also the inadequacy of that law for woman's needs and desires.[13] In this aspect, Atwood stays within the paradoxes she creates, rather than trying to break through them. Keeping in mind that this is chronologically the earliest of the works here, published in 1972, and to a great extent precedes most of the critical works on feminism and language, I think it is important to note that in this text she initiated a discourse on language in fictional texts that has been taken up and carried on by many writers. In the utopian texts, for example, Piercy and Gearhart consider the effect of language on social relations within the whole society, rather than just the individual's relationship to language.

Pronouns and Social Change

Marge Piercy, in *Woman on the Edge of Time*, certainly questions the capacity of language to simultaneously experience and include the female. In her novel, the contrast between utopia and the present revolves around just this point. Piercy concentrates on the social and political consequences of language. What sort of society would use a language in which categories of sex do not exist? How are social relationships constructed in a society where relationships are not indicated by names? What political systems develop out of such a society? What values are important to such a society? etc.[14] Her Mattapoisettian attempts to answer these questions are, of course, problematical, but are important for the views offered here on the concepts of woman and nature.

These types of questions have also been taken up by French writer and critic Monique Wittig. Beginning with the use of the personal pronoun, Wittig explored the oppression of the male signifiers on the perceptual associations of woman in her novel *Les Guérrillères*, published in 1969, in which she uses the third person plural pronoun "elles" as a universal signifier. In attacking the use of gender as a means of oppression for women — the normal use of grouping woman under the universal "he" — Wittig suggests the problems lie in the genderized pronouns. This is rather a deceptively simple solution at best. However, in her novel she tried to universalize the female gender in a reversal strategy that was only partially successful. Furthermore, the attempt was completely negated by the [male] English translator, who proceeded to translate "elles" as "the women"! In her later essay, "The Mark of Gender", she again takes up the issue of gender:

> The result of the imposition of gender, acting as a denial at the very moment when one speaks, is to deprive women of the authority of speech, and to force them to make their entrance in a crablike way, particularizing themselves and apologizing profusely. The result is to deny them any claim to the abstract, philosophical, political discourses that give shape to the social body. Gender then must be destroyed. (66-67)

While her polemical rhetoric is self-serving here, Wittig overlooks a more fundamental simplification in her argument, that is, "destroying" gender in language automatically implies "destroying" social gender signification. It is not clear here to what extent she accounts for gender in language and if this corresponds to biological sex in the social context. Her description of the result of gender in language as depriving woman of authority and subjectivity is more accurate.[15] These are also the points that Piercy and Gearhart touch on.

In her utopian setting of Mattapoisett, in *Woman on the Edge of Time*, Marge Piercy experiments with gender usage, in the form of personal pronouns, as an indicator of a society free of gender signification. Connie — and, by implication, the reader — initially finds such usages as "per" for the third person pronominal adjective somewhat uncomfortable and strange. The implications however are far-reaching. For Piercy, it seems, the issue is "not simply to change language, but to examine language for its ontological assumptions, and to criticize those assumptions for their political consequences."[16] This goes a step further than, for example, Monique Wittig's insistence on changing/destroying linguistic gender. Gender usage can certainly be challenged, as Piercy does, but it is only one of numerous factors involved in a complex system of signification.

If we look at Mattapoisett from the view of language, we cannot determine which occurred first, the change in language or the change in society, but certainly each reflects the other. Piercy does not seem to want to enter into the discussion on which precedes the other, although the idea that changes in language use can effect changes in society is the underlying assumption behind efforts to change at least English and German and French to more gender-neutral languages.[17] The question remains open; do the introduction and use of non-sexist expressions precipitate social change? In other words, is our relation to language one of function only or also one of transformation?[18] What is more evident in Piercy's text is that language clearly reflects present social situations, and Piercy has invented new words to reflect Mattapoisett's "gender free" society.

The protagonist Connie is at a loss to understand the insignificance of gender in Mattapoisett, confused at not being able to tell men from women. In her New York, it is the major social division, and there she is neither heard nor understood, in effect has no language; the situation is thus a precondition for the projection into the future of a genderless language. Also significant in Piercy's portrayal of Connie is that the protagonist's mother tongue is Spanish, which further removes her from the dominant culture of her immediate surroundings. In other words, her marginality is defined through language as well as gender. But because of this, Connie is sensitized to the power of language.

Piercy has created a genderless pronoun to indicate how thoroughly one relies on gender signification. Initially, "Per" and "pers" are not pronouns that clarify for Connie, but cover up the issue until she realizes there is no issue. It is at this point in the novel that Connie realizes that in her New York, gender signification in language is indicative of gender oppression.

Although the pronoun is only one of the linguistic indicators Piercy employs to suggest an egalitarian society, it is the most important one. For Wittig, as one French critic who is deeply troubled by the pronoun, it is not only the third-person pronouns that indicate gender opposition. She points out that in the other persons, especially first person, gender is evident, and that as a woman, the "locutor" must "make her sex public" (65) and in doing so particularizes herself "under her proper physical form and not under the abstract form, which every male locutor has the unquestioned right to use" (66). While Wittig advocates the destruction of gender through the exercise of language (and indeed in her own texts, personal pronouns are her primary subject matter), we see certain implications of her theory at work in Piercy's text: Luciente, for example, does not make her sex public, and so is assumed by Connie to be a man.

Connie's relationship to Luciente, her counterpart in Mattapoisett, is linguistically troubling. Initially, she accords Luciente the abstract universal significance of being "he", because Luciente does not "make her sex public" in Wittig's terms. Indeed, under her own linguistic obligations, Luciente is unable to, the concepts do not exist for her. To a great extent, Connie's misunderstandings in Mattapoisett revolve around these pronoun uses. Having no gender designations in the language, no sense of sexual domination, and no specific societal gender roles confuse her. Piercy avoids the chicken-and-the-egg discussion of which came first in Mattapoisett — language or social change.

A parallel development to the change in pronoun usage is the change in name designations, a situation reflecting Mattapoisett's social groupings: No patronyms because there are no fathers, and first names can be changed at will. There is no sense of "belonging" to one or another person through name designations.

Reading *Wanderground* offers a much more radical view of woman's language than the other texts. To a great extent the women of the Wanderground have attempted to ignore the phallocentrism of language by developing other means of communication. Schweickart comments that this represents a move to "recover powers and faculties which have atrophied as a result of the hegemony of scientific reason" (201). By replacing "scientific reason" with "dominant discourse" the basis of the argument is transferred more specifically to language. Kristeva sees "the feminine" in the pre-oedipal semiotic, Cixous in the unconscious, but both are interested in "the feminine" as the time and space of pre-verbal communication. Gearhart, in her utopia, creates a time and space for non-verbal possibilities for communication. For example, history is preserved in the remember rooms, where the women can go to re-experience historical events in trance-like "unconscious" states. Only a very few books were rescued from one of the libraries that were destroyed, but as we can conclude, the written word is for them another form of the dominant discourse that had oppressed them for so long. Gearhart is attacking the issue with the women's conscious refusal to use language as a means of domination. This is obviously not the possibility Kristeva and Cixous conceive of, for their "feminine" spaces have not yet entered the realm of the phallologos. However, their ideas converge in this "feminine" as a time and space where the "Law of the Father" and the "Symbolic Order" do not function, and therefore do not dominate or oppress women.

In *Wanderground*, Gearhart envisions the savior of the earth as the feminine, completely cut off from the still-existent phallocentric society, which she has embodied as "the City". For Gearhart, the feminine is equivalent to "woman", while for some critics, the feminine is a principle metaphor for "that which exceeds the grasp of the Cartesian subject — be it called nonknowledge or nontruth, undecidability or supplementarity, even writing or the unconscious."[19] Gearhart has succumbed to a paradoxical situation in depicting the women of the Wanderground in absolute opposition to the men of the City and as having developed a unique system of communication and powers to ensure their autonomy. The women of the Wanderground exist only because of their opposition to the men of the City. This is in keeping with the traditional categories of thought described by Alice Jardine as, "women can (have) exist(ed) only as opposed to men. Indeed, women, especially feminists, who continue to think within those categories are, henceforth, seen as being men" (63). And so we come through language back to a discussion of dualism, in which Gearhart seems particularly ensnared. However, Gearhart leaves herself an opening through her treatment of the "Gentles", who, in developing similar non-verbal, psychic and communicative powers, incur the wrath of the women. For the feminist theorists like Kristeva, Irigaray, Cixous, and particularly Wittig, these Gentles would pose fewer problems than the women themselves, for if they consider these women who only live in opposition to phallologocentrism as "men", then they would consider the Gentles as "women", because they completely negate the issue of phallologocentrism. The Gentles refer to themselves as "a special breed of men [who] may be on the brink of discovering [their] own nonviolent psychic powers" (179). The women fear the Gentles will usurp their subjectivity, the ultimate form of violence against them, but certainly for the French feminist critics, the Gentles would be the real "heroes" for showing the way to femininity.

Until now, we have been primarily concerned with the problem of language from woman's perception, and in particular, the narrative strategies the authors use to problematize language in their texts. Before concluding, however, it should be noted that both of the utopian texts bring in the additional aspect of perceptualizing elements of nature through a language that is liberating rather than restrictive and oppressive. The idea seems to be that once oppositional dualism, so intricately ensconced in language codes, is eliminated — as in their utopian spaces — then individuals can perceive their environment in non-dominating, non-hierarchal, value-free ways. Gearhart and Piercy portray this utopian possibility by having their characters establish communicative relationships with animals. Both authors are suggesting that it would be not only gender relationships that change with a changed language system, but that one's perception of everything would be realigned under the new forms. Thus, a nature can be explored that is beyond dualistic, oppositional connotations.

Gearhart has infused nature with the feminine by allying the women with "Mother nature" and creating a special relationship with animals that includes communication. Curiously, Daly suggests something similar in her *Gyn/ecology*. First she argues for a metaphysical language as ontological discourse, one that asserts the primacy of an *a priori* female Being. She sees herself creating that language, because our present language is so male dominated that it breaks every female who uses "I". Her language would not differentiate or classify objects of reference. Finally she insists — surely in a utopian sense — that lesbians must initiate and learn the language of animals "whose non-verbal communication seems to be superior to androcentric speech" (19).[20] All of which the women of the Wanderground have done. But in so doing they have not managed to appropriate nature for themselves: The birds respond to the attempts of the Gentles to understand them (177-79). In other words, for "nature" (taking the birds as representative of "nature") gender itself is not as important as the concept of the feminine, which the Gentles embody as well.

In *Woman on the Edge of Time*, however, Piercy has created a gender-free society that still has a production-oriented relationship to agriculture (though on a more ecologically conscious scale). In Mattapoisett, there is a difference between the relationship to animals and the relationship to the land and forests. Again, much like Daly suggests, the Mattapoisettians communicate with the animals:

> 'I mean in sign languages. For instance, Tilia and I talk sign language based on cat signs but modified because many things must be said between cat and human different from what is said cat to cat. ... Now we have rudimentary sign languages with many mammals. Some, like apes, use sign language with each other. Most, like cats and dogs, have other ways of communing and only sign to us.'
> 'Tell me, what do you say to a cow you're about to eat?'

> 'Exactly. It's changed our diet. So has the decision
> to feed everyone well. For each region we try to be
> ownfed and until the former colonies are equal in
> production, mammal meat is inefficient use of
> grains.' (98-99)

This interchange between Connie and Luciente is indicative of the two
levels Mattapoisett functions on, objective production efficiency
coupled with a respect for the subjectivity of animals. It also character-
izes the textual problems of nature in Piercy's utopia that are, on the
one hand, based on a dominant discourse of Marxism interfaced with
a metaphorical, metaphysical approach to communication. Although its
didactic tone does much to dull the dynamic possibilities of a utopian
text, Piercy understands nature as a cultural construct to a much greater
extent than, for example, does Gearhart. In the Mattapoisettian culture,
nature plays a different role than in *Wanderground*. However, both
authors envision far-reaching changes in societies in which language
does not emanate from a phallologocentric system, and these differences include the demise of hierarchies in which mankind dominates and
exploits nature.

    These five authors (Laurence, Atwood, Walker, Piercy,
Gearhart) and their texts are representative of the intense confrontation
feminist writers have initiated by using their own language and in their
efforts to make this language sensitive to woman. This is an act that
only woman can complete, since it demands woman's voice and
woman's writing. The narrative strategies these authors develop in this
confrontation pose a challenge to the limitations of fiction structures.
The utopian mode is one possibility for stretching the imaginative
order, especially when "the medium is the message" and different
language systems come into play. Atwood develops another mode by
depicting silences. Problematizing one's relationship to art, through the
artist-protagonist, is another possibility. However, one might challenge
that these fictional modes are peculiar not only to woman: utopian
fiction began centuries ago with such authors as Thomas More,
Tommaso Campanella, Johann Andreä, Francis Bacon, etc.; stream-of-
consciousness "silences" have been around for decades, as has the
fiction of art. The use of particular fictional modes is not what

determines the qualitative "gender" of the text, but rather the voice coming through that challenges language as the dominant, oppressive phallologos.

NOTES

1.I'm referring to such semiotic and post-structural themes and questions as the relationship between the "Symbolic Order" and fiction; can or does fiction negate language as a signifying system text for text by substituting another set of signifiers in the fictional text?; is fiction a symbolic system representing the "Symbolic Order"? can woman influence the qualities that make a text fictional?

2.See chapter 4.

3.Cixous, "Laugh of the Medusa", and "Castration or Decapitation?", *Signs*, 7 (1981), 41-55; also cf. Verena Andermatt Conley. *Hélène Cixous: Writing the Feminine.* (Lincoln: Univ. of Nebraska Press, 1984), pp. 129-161; and Moi, *Sexual/Textual Politics*, chpt. 6.

4.Moi, *Sexual/Textual Politics*, chpt. 6; Conley; Jardine, *Gynesis*; Stanton, "Language and Revolution", and "Difference on Trial"; Margaret Homans, "'Her Very Own Howl': The Ambiguities of Representation in Recent Woman's Fiction", *Signs*, 9/2 (1983), 186-205; Jacobus; Kolodny, "A Map for Rereading", to name just a few.

5.cf. DuPlessis, Gilbert and Gubar, and Kolodny, "A Map for Rereading", etc.

6.Walker criticizes Woolf's elitist attitudes about woman and art in "Search for Our Mother's Gardens."

7.cf. Kristeva, "System and the Speaking Subject", in Moi, *The Kristeva Reader*, pp. 29-33.

8.cf. Jacobus, "A Difference of View".

9.Elaine Marks, "Women and Literature in France", *Signs*, 3/4 (1978), 836.

10.Jacobus elaborates these ideas in "A Difference of View", pp. 11-13.

11.cf. Nancy M. Henley, "This New Species That Seeks a New Language: On Sexism in Language and Language Change", in Joyce Penfield, ed. *Women & Language in Transition* (Albany: SUNY Press, 1987), p. 3.

12.cf. Homans, "'Her Very Own Howl': The Ambiguities of Representation in Recent Women's Fiction", p. 199.

13.Sally Robinson points out further that Atwood's "language at the end signifies negation rather than affirmation: she 'refuses', she 'recants', things are 'finished'." cf."The 'Anti-logos Weapon': Multiplicity in Women's Texts," *Contemporary Literature*, 29/1 (1988), 114.

14.These are formulated by Jane Flax as: "Could/would gender relations wither away in egalitarian societies? <and> "What are the relationships between forms of male dominance and gender relations?" cf. "Postmodernism and Gender Relations in Feminist Theory", *Signs*, 12/4 (1987), 627.

15.See discussion in chapter 4.

16.Benhabib, p. 141.

17.Notable here are the Modern Language Association Guidelines for Non-Sexist Use of the Language. cf. Penfield, ed. *Women & Language in Transition.* Also, Wittig comments on the difference in French and English, especially regarding the English translation of her novel *Les Guérillères* in "The Mark of Gender".

18.Robin Lakoff, in her *Language and Woman's Place*, (N.Y.: Harper & Row, 1974) takes the view that social change precedes language change, and uses among others the introduction of the term "Black" for "Negro" in the mid-1960's; on the other hand Nan Van Den Bergh, in "Renaming: Vehicle for Empowerment", takes the stand that forcefully changing language will bring about changes in social attitudes and awareness. In linguistic circles this is known as the Sapir-Whorf hypothesis.

19.Stanton, "Difference on Trial", p. 158; cf. also, Jardine, *Gynesis*, chpt. 2.

20.Elshtain ironically remarks on this passage: "Daly cites several conversations she has had with animals and translates a few of these; needless to say, all the animals shared her perspective and none contested her position." (611)

... there are ways of thinking that we don't know about.
Nothing could be more important or precious than that
knowledge, however unborn. The sense of urgency, the
spiritual restlessness it engenders, cannot be appeased.

(Susan Sontag)

8

Intertextuality and Reconceptualization

Ecofeminism and gynocriticism intersect at critical points on
the literary reconceptualization of woman and nature, and through
these points of gender, language and nature, their intertextuality
emerges from the fictional texts. Kristeva's concept of intertextuality,
which she began developing from Bakhtian literary theory, provides a
place to begin backtracking somewhat to questions I suggested in
"Preliminaries", i.e., how do the fictional texts affect the discourse,
how does the discourse get transformed in the text? Regarding intertextuality, Kristeva writes,

> ... each word (text) is an intersection of words (texts)
> where at least one other word (text) can be read. ...
> [This is] an insight first introduced into literary theory
> by Bakhtin: any text is constructed as a mosaic of
> quotations; any text is the absorption and transfor-
> mation of another. The notion of *intertextuality*
> replaces that of intersubjectivity, and poetic language
> is read as at least *double*.[1]

The encounter of the two discourses of ecofeminism and gynocriticism
can produce a broader understanding of feminist fiction on the issues
of woman and nature, and their relationship to dualism.

Ecofeminism is about connectedness; as discourse, it exists and
functions outside of the theoretical and fictional texts which connect
to it. Particularly regarding the historical-political emphasis of

ecofeminism there is a rich overlay working through the texts, but also
the literary level provides a new dimension for the working of
discourse.

When Ynestra King writes,

> eco-feminism supports utopian visions of harmonious,
> diverse, decentralized communities, using only those
> technologies based on ecological principles, as the
> only practical solution for the continuation of life on
> earth. (125)

she is opening up possibilities for ecofeminism on a level that suggests
new contexts. When Marge Piercy has her Mattapoisettians suggest
that they themselves might not exist in the year 2137, unless the
Connie Ramoses begin the struggle for change and that is the reason
for their reaching out to the past centuries, she is creating the
possibilities for alternative futures and does indeed offer a dystopian
vision as well. Both Piercy's and Gearhart's utopian societies fall into
the set pattern of visions that ecofeminism "supports", but, because
they develop these visions beyond reality, they are not bound by
King's political limitations. Nor are they the "practice" for ecofeminist
"theory". In political terms, King's utopian visions, found again in
these utopian texts, address the issues of dualism and the problems of
gender and language. They also touch on such political issues as the
use of technology, community life, and enlarging human possibilities.
If one voice of ecofeminism is a protesting, negative one (what we are
not, what we don't want, what we shouldn't do), another voice emphasizes positive political goals that attempt to separate the liberation
of woman and nature "from the anthropomorphic and stereotypic labels
that degrade the serious underlying issues".[2]

It strikes me that the fictional texts succeed in refocusing the
debate on woman and nature begun by ecofeminism. While Merchant,
King, Ortner and others concentrate to a great extent on woman-as-
object (how she was associated with nature, how she was oppressed,
how she was defined, how she was given a cultural code, and
concomitantly, how nature is defined and culturally constructed, etc.),
these feminist authors are exploring the woman-as-subject and how she

copes with présent cultural norms, or deconstructs them. This is surely one of Merchant's serious underlying issues. As a whole, these texts create a new context for the ecological debate of ecofeminism.

King is also interested in the forms "our culture" must take in order to restructure it in the name of nature. Again I turn to the utopian texts which seem to explore King's prescriptive visions, at least in a superficial manner, in order to portray the sort of patriarchal societies that make women victims. It is clear here that there is a tendency to valorize the relationship between woman and nature, instead of deconstructing it. In doing so, such utopias can then more easily cast technology, the symbol of patriarchal power structures, as the cause of all social demise. However, both utopian writers acknowledge that complex social challenges must be met. Piercy depicts a strictly egalitarian Mattapoisett, in which women have also had to sacrifice even their biological functions (birthing) in order to attain such equality. Gearhart creates women who are challenged by the Gentles who perhaps no longer recognize the women's moral superiority, and with whom the women will ultimately have to share. Thus, in a further development of the discourse, the process of structuring the plot continues beyond the use of clear oppositional dualism.

Utopias however are a special case in imaginative writing, exploding our conceptions and expectations of probability and reality, and because of this they can give the discourse added dimensions. It is in the texts less removed from our conceptions, however, that the real challenges of ecofeminism are to be found. When Sylvie and Ruth become the wind, when Atwood's protagonist communes with the spirits of the woods, when Mattie's women friends tear down the wall, when Celie's family and extended family are all united, in all of these fictional situations our sense of probability and reality are challenged. These final or near-final scenes in the novels suggest new possibilities for viewing womanhood as powerful, spiritual, and active. The process of acquiring these characteristics, in other words, going from the weak, mundane, passive female to the powerful, spiritual, active one involves a deconstruction of the cultural constructs of woman and nature. This deconstruction takes place through a language capable of questioning its own value system. In all of the situations sketched above, the authors are very much aware of the images and metaphors that cast woman as weak, mundane, passive. Celie's dialect becomes her most colorful, emotional weapon in divulging herself to god or Nettie, exactly because it lies outside the standard "Law of the Father". Atwood's protagonist wants to reject language altogether and her "silences" provide entry to the spiritual. Naylor's scene is put in a dream, operating in the unconscious, metaphorically beyond the "Symbolic Order". Ruth, having "never distinguished readily between thinking and dreaming" (215), moves with Sylvie completely outside the social order, even of language. Laurence's Morag, however, as a writer has command of expression and language and has crossed the line of intimidation, for her writing becomes an act of rebellion against those who would keep her silent. All of these authors have thus directly or indirectly entered into a dialogue with language as the cultural medium, with the discourse of ecofeminism.

Thus, aware of woman's relationship to language and its use as an instrument of power, ecofeminism as discourse would have the texts deconstruct the system of metaphor that keeps woman bound to nature, or at least consider how the symbolic language of nature metaphors is problematized. But the fictional elements do not push through the barriers of tradition, and in fact, to a certain extent, the texts reassert metaphors that at first appear to be an attempt at valorization that seems to undermine their own theoretical stance.

There have been few attempts to find an alternative to the tradition of using feminine metaphors for nature. In this area contemporary French criticism has not been as thorough in its questioning of the "Big Dichotomies" as in its insistence on taking the opposition out of gender. While my concern here lies in the direction of deconstructing, if you will, the traditional images of nature in feminine metaphors, there are other directions to investigate. In summary, Jardine suggests that the phallologos couches nature and the feminine in similar terms, both nature and the feminine as "representations of the *space* at the end point of Man's symbolization or utopia" (87). It is perhaps from this (metaphysical) space that woman can review the essence of fictional narrative.

The element of nature in the texts is, with the exception of Atwood's conclusion, bound fairly completely with woman, even though this association (because it is no longer the oppressed object of patriarchal culture) accrues the power to change. So while ecofeminism also demands the dismantling of dualism through a critique of metaphor, the fictional texts, in general, withdraw into their boundaries on this point, relying on traditional use of woman and nature images but trying instead to create a new positive context of power relationships. This hesitance in a sense does not detract from the discourse, but is rather an indication of the power of the phallologos and its established literary conventions. The writers seem to be working around this convention, deconstructing it from within rather than openly challenging it. It is within this process that the texts begin to reconceptualize woman and nature.

The mutual influence of gynocriticism and the fictional texts is most discernable in the issues concerning the nature of narrative and the essence or qualities of woman's writing that cover the three areas discussed here: nature, gender, language. Both gynocriticism and the fictional texts address the relationship between woman and fiction, such as author and art, representation, narrative structures, etc., that help to circumscribe the qualities of woman's writing that Cixous maintains is not definable within our culture codes.

We began with Showalter's idea of gynocritics as connected with the "woman as the producer of textual meaning, with the history, themes, genres and structures of literature by women" (128). To be sure, this concerns gender and fiction, with the underlying assumption that woman approaches the imaginative realm from a perspective very different from man's. The writing in this imaginative realm involves the interference and overlay of the masculine logos. As we have seen, the authors are struggling to work through a layer of paradox in their texts, using their writing as a process of disentangling itself from the phallologos, while depicting characters and situations that are attempting to break through this dilemma in fiction. While critics like Kristeva and Cixous would like to have "the feminine" connected with everything disruptive to the vast "Symbolic Order", and therefore tend to see so-called narrative fiction also tied to representationalism and a codified reality as part of "the feminine", it seems to me their views negate the subtleties of woman's writing too quickly. Critics like Gilbert and Gubar, Spacks, Kolodny, Moers, and Showalter have discovered that disruptive forces have been carefully coded by woman writers to problematize their relationship to their art in decades and centuries past.

Against this background, the role of the fictional texts discussed here, written at a time when the explicit quality of gender and its cultural significances have come under decidedly deconstructionist criticism, would be to find a way out of these paradoxes to further question the validity of gender and nature constructs as part of the ideology of fictional narrative discourse. Fictional narrative, because it is depictive, descriptive and imaginative, can create a space for woman to act in, but it is limited by narrative structures and conventions. The authors can also criticize these confining structures, and, as Robinson does, move her characters beyond these confinements so that only a voice detached from the material remains, and then absence. But, the paradox of using the means to criticize the goal remains. And, as Atwood suggests, silence deprives woman of participation in change, however painful the process of change might be.

All in all, there is a great variety of narrative strategies that intersect with dualism critique. But in spite of these, the problem of breaking through the central paradox remains. The tendencies toward the lesbian, the choral protagonist, and communities of women, all of which might develop into a fictional form out of genderized conflicts, are seminally present, and all serve to shift the conflict out of dualistic genderized elements. The process is an on-going dialogue between the discourse of gynocriticism and the texts.

The discourse takes on additional aspects through the fictional texts, for the authors are exploring possibilities for woman outside of the axis of man, although in all of the texts the antagonists are male. This runs parallel to the criticism of Cixous that her "l'écriture feminine" is defined only in relation to the masculine, and takes an initial step toward breaking the strong dualistic basis of the narratives. A number of the authors through the course of the plot realign the axis so that the male element is not the point around which the female protagonists move. Jehlen suggests in her analysis of eighteenth and nineteenth century novels, "Archimedes and the Paradox of Feminist Criticism", that narrative fiction takes on the conflict between the interior life and the outer world, and "that this interior life, whether lived by man or woman, is female" (90). This would imply that the very stuff of novels is a genderized conflict. And while the general tenor of Jehlen's thesis is that feminist criticism has reached the Archimedean dilemma — "Give me a point outside and I will move the world" — it seems clear from these texts that, while the Archimedean point remains as elusive as it was 4000 years ago, there is a definite shift to a new center around which the narrative revolves. This would imply that the only possibility is not moving the world of fictional narrative from outside, but changing it from within.

This has many implications for gynocriticism as discourse which the texts both incorporate and challenge. By displacing man from the center of the text, the authors do not simply insert woman in his place; they are reshaping the center altogether. This, of course, is a challenge to gynocriticism to consider feminist voices that go beyond woman as the center of narrative. The process of reshaping a center of narrative, however, depends on reconceptualizing the elements of narrative, in our case, specifically the reconceptualization of woman and nature.

I began this study with some specific questions of the texts within the framework of reconceptualization, such as, what concepts of woman and nature do these authors create, one freed from the constraints of dualism, i.e., without oppositional functions to man, to culture? What other contributions have the texts made to this possibility of reconceptualizing woman and nature? How do the contemporary theories of language and gender interplay with the fictional texts? It seems to me that there are clear tendencies in the texts, clear movements away from the confines of the dualism of gender, clear movements towards open-end possibilities.

The representation of woman is breaking away from, or need no longer revolve around, a masculine center, implicit or explicit. Protagonists have been "set free", so to speak, of "troubling" masculine influences. Robinson, Laurence, Naylor and Walker· indicate their intentions clearly as do the utopian authors, Piercy perhaps more successfully than Gearhart. Surprisingly, it is Atwood's text that proves least resourceful in this respect, whereas in most other aspects her text makes strong statements. The suggestion that the dualistic aspect of gender no longer "works" in fictional representation in these texts

refers primarily to the most obvious character level, and only to the
"woman" part of the dualism issue.

Deconstructing one level of the dualism female/male has not
resulted in a dramatically similar displacement of the nature/culture
dichotomy — perhaps because nature generally operates on a different
level of representation in fiction. It remains a dominant theme
incorporated into the ideology of the feminist texts. Again, the utopian
works in using the nature/culture dichotomy as a real "issue" focus
attention on it, but Gearhart's sympathies run clearly to the
valorization of every aspect of the feminine. Valorization becomes a
very problematic approach in feminist texts, because it simply reverses
the tactics of opposition and otherness that operate in dualism. However, the temptation to valorize woman and nature is one that all the
authors come to terms with in one way or another. But because nature,
as landscape and setting, operates differently in the texts than
character, the authors have to resort to more subtle techniques of
fiction.

It is ecofeminism with its insistence on liberation from
dualistic labels that leads to a critique of the language of dualism in
fiction: the metaphors and images which underscore the association
between woman and nature, and their opposition to man and culture.
It is this insistence that is challenging because it is so closely allied
with the "ingredients" of fiction: challenging to the authors to redefine
the boundaries of fiction, using such ingredients in new ways. The
authors' attempts to deal with metaphor and images tend to support
rather than displace dualism; most effectively used is mimesis that
takes the power out of the metaphor by exaggeration, and criticism of
the images in the text, or a purposeful misuse or no use of an expected
use of metaphor. These are certainly the significant contributions of the
texts to reconceptualizing woman and nature. Also, as ecofeminism
problematizes the subject-object dyad of language that challenges
woman out of her object position in the phallologos in order to
deconstruct that dualism, one primary indication of dismantling that
dyad is how the authors create woman as subjects in their texts. All the
authors deal with first-person narrative form, either mixed with "omniscient", or first-person singular, or choral protagonists, that in turn
problematize the very concept of subject, which focuses on the

interplay between language and gender in the texts. These new uses of such fictional ingredients contribute to the reconceptualizations that are the focus of this study — nature and woman no longer mutually associated, and no longer in oppositional dualistic stances to man and culture.

Gynocriticism, problematizing the relationship between woman and writing, brings in the further dimensions of the author and the narrative strategies she uses to encode meaning in her texts that explore the boundaries of fiction within the limits of language and gender.

The author's relationship to language is in these texts often encoded in the protagonists' use of and problematization of language. Beginning with Atwood's protagonist's comment that "It was the language again. I couldn't use it, it wasn't mine" at the beginning of the decade in question, and continuing to Walker's Celie's comment that "Look like to me only a fool would want you to talk in a way that feel peculiar to your mind" at the end of the decade, these authors have attempted to work through the issues of what Cixous calls "l'écriture feminine", trying to make language work for them in their fictional texts. Again, this brings us back to the issue of gender and language, and the difficulties inherent in gender perceptions of language in terms of displacing the dualism of gender.

For each of the discourses, the dialogue between the Anglo-Saxon and French feminist critics has been a dynamic and fruitful one. Perhaps major contributions of the French critics are the disregard of biological sex, the importance of gender as a cultural phenomenon that plays through fiction, and the role of the unconscious in imaginative writing. The Anglo-Saxon critics, more closely tied to political agendas, are concerned about the French tendency to use dualistic terminology that reinforces man and the masculine as the determining point in the discussion, around which all other points revolve.

The reconceptualizations of woman and nature exhibited in these texts suggest that we are only at the beginning of a dynamic process. The novels discussed here collectively point to a multiplicity that does not attempt to essentialize either woman or nature, but "deconstructs" dualistic constructs and focuses on displacing the masculine as the center of the text. But, this "text" is not finished: the

issues involved in ecofeminism and gynocriticism are the continua-
tions, as too are the reconceptualizations of woman and nature. This
displacing of the masculine elements does not demand a replacing with
feminine elements; but it does demand a recognition of acknowledg-
ment of all the relationships, characteristics, and roles that are being
developed outside of gender-specificity. The qualities of fictional narrative that explore the boundaries and limitations of fictional narrative
structures have also only begun to be considered in relation to "the
feminine". These and similar aspects deserve close consideration and
analysis in the future, for the reconceptualizations addressed here can
only suffice as a beginning.

NOTES

1."Word, Dialogue and Novel", in Moi, (ed.), p. 37. cf. Bachtin, *Die Ästhetik des
Wortes*, ed. Rainer Grubel, (Frankfurt/M.: Suhrkamp, 1979): "Jedes Verstehen ist das
In-Beziehung-Setzen des jeweiligen Textes mit anderen Texten und die Umdeutung
im neuen Kontext (in meinem, in gegenwärtigen, im künftigen)" (352). To avoid
confusion: the name is spelled "Bakhtin" in English, but "Bachtin" in German.

2.Merchant, p. xvii.

Index

Bibliography

Abel, Elisabeth. "(E)merging Identities: The Dynamics of Female Friendship in Contemporary Fiction by Women," *Signs*, 6/3 (1981), 413-35.

-----, and Emily Abel, Eds. *The Signs Reader: Women, Gender and Scholarship*. Chicago: Univ. of Chicago Press, 1983.

-----, Marianna Hirsch, and Elisabeth Langland, Eds. *The Voyage in: Fictions of Female Development*. Hanover and London: Univ. Press of New England (Dartmouth College), 1983.

Allen, Mary. *The Necessary Blankness: Women in Major American Fiction of the Sixties*. Urbana: Univ. of Illinois Press, 1976.

Althusser, Louis. *For Marx*. trs. Ben Brewster. London: New Left Books, 1977.

Atwood, Margaret. *Surfacing*. London: Virago Press, 1979.

-----. *Survival: A Thematic Guide to Canadian Literature*. Toronto: Anansi, 1972.

Bachinger, Katrina E. "The Tao of *Housekeeping*: Reconnoitering the Utopian Ecological Frontier in Marilynne Robinson's 'Feminist' Novel". in Truchlar, Ed. *Für eine offene Literaturwissenschaft: Erkundungen und Erprobungen am Beispiel US-amerikanischer Texte*. Salzburg: Verlag Wolfgang Neugebauer, 1986.

Bachtin, Michail. *Aesthetic des Wortes*. ed. Rainer Grubel. Frankfurt/M.: Suhrkamp, 1979.

Bakan, David. *The Duality of Human Existence*. Boston: G. K. Hall, 1966.

Bakhtin, Mikhail M. *The Dialogic Imagination*. ed. Michael Holquist, trs. Caryl Emerson and Michael Holquist. Austin: Univ. of Texas Press, 1981.

Barr, Marlene S. and Nicholas D. Smith, Eds. *Women and Utopia: Critical Interpretations*. Lanham, MD: Univ. Press of America, 1983.

-----. Ed. *Future Females: A Critical Anthology*. Bowling Green, OH: Bowling Green Univ. Press, 1981.

Baym, Nina. *Woman's Fiction: A Guide to Novels by and about Women in America, 1820-1870*. Ithaca: Cornell UP, 1978.

Bazin, Nancy Topping. *Virginia Woolf and the Androgynous Vision*. New Brunswick, NJ: Rutgers Univ. Press, 1973.

Beach, Joseph Warren. *The Concept of Nature in Nineteenth Century English Poetry*. NY: Macmillan, 1936.

Benhabib, Seyla and Drucilla Cornell, Eds. *Feminism as Critique: Essays on the Politics of Gender in Late-Capitalist Societies*. Cambridge, UK: Polity Press, 1987.

Bernstein, Basil. *Class, Codes and Control*. St. Albans: Paladin, 1973.

Booth, Wayne C. "Freedom of Interpretation: Bakhtin and the Challenge of Feminist Criticism", *Critical Inquiry*, 9 (1982), 43-62.

Brod, Harry. Ed. *The Making of Masculinities: The New Men's Studies*. Boston: Allen & Unwin, 1987.

Brooks, Paul. *Speaking for Nature: How Literary Naturalists from Henry Thoreau to Rachel Carson Have Shaped America*. Boston: Houghton Mifflin, 1980.

Brown, Cheryl L. and Karen Olsen, Eds. *Feminist Criticism*. Metuchen, NJ, and London: Scarecrow Press, 1978.

Brownmiller, Susan. *On Femininity*. N.Y.: Ballantine Books, 1984.

-----. *Against Our Will: Men, Women and Rape*. N.Y.: Simon and Schuster,1978.

Brumm, Ursula. *Geschichte und Wildnis in der amerikanischen Literatur*. (Grundlagen der Anglistik und Amerikanistik, 11) Berlin: Erich Schmidt Verlag, 1980.

-----. "Nature as Scene or Agent? Some Reflections on its Role in the American Novel". in Tuet Andreas Riese, Ed. *Vistas of a Continent: Concepts of Nature in America*. Heidelberg: Carl Winter Universitätsverlag, 1979.

Butler, Judith. "Variations on Sex and Gender in Beauvoir, Wittig, Foucault." in Benhabib and Cornell, Eds. *Feminism as Critique*, 128-142.

Caldecott, Leonie and Stephanie Leland, Eds. *Reclaim the Earth: Women Speak Out for Life on Earth*. London: The Women's Press, 1983.

Campbell, Joseph. *The Hero with a Thousand Faces*. Princeton: Princeton Univ. Press, 1972.

-----. *The Masks of God: Occidental Mythology*. NY: Viking Press, 1970.

Campbell, Josie P. "The Woman as Hero in Margaret Atwood's *Surfacing*". *Mosaic*, 11 (1978), 17-28.

Chodorow, Nancy. "Family Structure and Feminine Personality" in Rosaldo and Lamphere, Eds. *Woman, Culture and Society*, 43-66.

-----. "Gender, Relation and Difference in Psychoanalytic Perspective", in Eisenstein and Jardine, Eds. *The Future of Difference*, 4-19.

-----. *The Reproduction of Mothering: Psychoanalysis and the Sociology of Gender*. Berkeley: Univ. of California Press, 1978.

Christ, Carol P. *Diving Deep and Surfacing: Women Writers on Spiritual Quest*. Boston: Beacon Press, 1980.

Christian, Barbara. *Black Women Novelists: The Development of a Tradition, 1892-1976*. Westport, CT: Greenwood Press, 1980.

Cixous, Hélène. "Castration or Decapitation?". trs. Annette Kuhn, *Signs*, 7/1 (1981), 41-55.

-----. "The Laugh of the Medusa: Viewpoint". trs. Keith Cohen and Paula Cohen. *Signs*, 1/4 (1976), 875-893.

-----."Sorties" in Cixous and Catherine Clément. *La jeune née*, (Paris: UGE, 1975), 115-246.

-----. *Weiblichkeit in der Schrift*. trs. Eva Duffner. Berlin: Merve Verlag, 1980.

Clark, Mara T. "Margaret Atwood's *Surfacing*: Language, Logic, and the Art of Fiction", *Modern Fiction Studies*, 13/3 (Summer 1983), 3-15.

Cook, Ellen Piel. *Psychological Androgyny*. Pergamon General Psychology Series, 133. N.Y.: Pergamon Press, 1985.

Cornillon, Susan Koppelmann, Ed. *Images of Women in Fiction: Feminist Perspectives*. Bowling Green, OH: Bowling Green Univ. Press, 1973.

Coward, Rosalind. "This Novel Changes Women's Lives: Are Women's Novels Feminist Novels?" *Feminist Review*, 5(1980); rpt. in Showalter, Ed. *The New Feminist Criticism*. N.Y.: Pantheon Books, 1985, pp. 225-240.

----- and John Ellis. *Language and Materialism: Developments in Semiology and the Theory of the Subject*. London: Routledge and Kegan Paul, 1977.

Crowder, Diane Griffin. "Amazons and Mothers? Monique Wittig, Hélène Cixous and Theories of Women's Writing", *Contemporary Literature*, 24/2 (Summer 1983), 117-144.

Curti, Merle. *Human Nature in American Thought: A History.* Madison: Univ. of Wisconsin Press, 1980.

Curtis, James M. *Culture as Polyphony: An Essay on the Nature of Paradigms.* Columbia: Univ. of Missouri Press, 1978.

Daly, Mary. *Beyond God the Father.* London: The Women's Press, 1978.

-----. *Gyn/ecology: The Metaphysics of Radical Feminism.* London: The Women's Press, 1978.

Davidson, Cathy N. "Geography as Psychology in the Writings of Margaret Laurence". in Toth, Ed. *Regionalism and the Female Imagination*, 129-138.

----- and E. M. Broner, Eds. *The Lost Tradition: Mothers and Daughters in Literature.* N.Y.: Frederick Ungar, 1980.

Davis, Angela Y. *Women, Race, and Class.* N.Y.: Random House, 1981.

Davis, Thadious. "Alice Walker's Celebration of Self in Southern Generation", *Southern Quarterly*, 21/4 (Summer 1983), 39-53.

d'Eaubonne, Françoise. *Le Féminisme ou la mort.* Paris: Pierre Horay, 1974.

de Beauvoir, Simone. *The Second Sex.* trs. H. M. Parshley. NY: Random House/Vintage Books, 1974.

Demetrakopoulos, Stephanie A. "Laurence's Fiction: A Revisioning of Feminine Archetypes", *Canadian Literature*, 93 (Summer 1982), 42-57.

Derrida, Jacques. *Of Grammatology.* trs. Gayatri Chakravorty Spivak. Baltimore, MD: The Johns Hopkins Univ. Press, 1976.

-----. "Le Facteur de la verité", *Poetique,* 21 (1975), 96-147.

Devine, Maureen. "*Woman on the Edge of Time* and *The Wanderground*: Visions in Eco-feminist Utopias". in Heller, Hölbling, and Zacharasie-wicz, Eds. *Utopian Thought in America: Untersuchungen zur literarischen Utopie und Dystopie in den USA,* 131-145.

----- and Gudrun Grabher, Eds. *Women in Search of Literary Space.* Tübingen: Gunter Narr Verlag, 1991.

Díaz-Diocaretz, Myriam. "Bakhtin, Discourse, and Feminist Theories". *Critical Studies: A Journal of Critical Theory, Literature & Culture,* 1/2 (1989), 121-139.

Donovan, Josephine. "Feminism and Aesthetics", *Critical Inquiry,* 3 (1977), 605-8.

-----. *Feminist Literary Criticism: Explorations in Theory.* Lexington: Univ. of Kentucky Press, 1975.

Dufresne, Eva Fauconneau. *Das Problem des Ich-Romans im 20. Jahr-hundert.* Europäische Hochschulschriften, Reihe 18. Frankfurt am Main: Peter Lang, 1985.

DuPlessis, Rachel Blau. *Writing Beyond the Ending: Narrative Strategies of Twentieth-Century Women Writers.* Bloomington: Indiana Univ. Press, 1985.

Eagleton, Terry. *Marxism and Literary Criticism.* Berkeley: U. of California Press, 1976.

Earnest, Ernest. *The American Eve in Fact and Fiction, 1775-1914.* Urbana: Univ. of Illinois Press, 1974.

Ecker, Gisela. "The Politics of Fantasy in Recent American Women's Novels", *English and American Studies*, 3 (1984), 503-510.

Eisenstein, Hester and Alice Jardine, Eds. *The Future of Difference*. Boston: G.K. Hall, 1980, rpt. 1986.

Elder, John. *Imagining the Earth: Poetry and the Vision of Nature*. Urbana: Univ. of Illinois Press, 1985.

Ellman, Mary. *Thinking About Women*. London: Virago, 1979.

Elshtain, Jean Bethke. "Feminist Discourse and Its Discontents: Language, Power, and Meaning", *Signs*, 7/3 (1982), 603-21.

Erkkila, Betsy. "Dickinson and Rich: Toward a Theory of Female Poetic Influence", *American Literature*, 56/4 (December, 1984), 541-559.

Evans, Mari, Ed. *Black Women Writers, 1950-1980: A Critical Evaluation*. Garden City, NY: Anchor-Doubleday, 1984.

Evans, Mary. "Simone de Beauvoir: Dilemmas of a Radical Feminist", in Dale Spender, Ed. *Feminist Theorists*, 287-309.

Fabre, Michel. "Words and the World: *The Diviners* as an Exploration of the Book of Life", *Canadian Literature*, 93 (Summer, 1982), 60-78.

Fassler, Barbara. "Theories of Homosexuality as Sources of Bloomsbury's Androgyny", *Signs*, 5/2 (1979), 237-251.

Féral, Josette. "The Powers of Difference". in Eisenstein and Jardine, Eds. *The Future of Difference*, 88-94.

Ferguson, Marilyn. *The Aquarian Conspiracy*. London: Routledge & Kegan Paul, 1981.

Firestone, Shulamith. *The Dialectic of Sex: The Case for Feminist Revolution*. London: The Women's Press, 1979.

Flax, Jane. "Postmodernism and Gender Relations in Feminist Theory", *Signs*, 12/4 (Summer 1987), 621-643.

Florby, Gunilla. "Escaping This World: Marilynne R. Robinson's Variation on an Old American Theme", *Moderna Språk*, 78/3 (1984), 211-216.

Freibert, Lucy M. "World Views in Utopian Novels by Women", *Journal of Popular Culture*, 17/1 (Summer 1983), 49-60.

Freud, Sigmund. *Civilization and its Discontents*, Standard Edition of the Complete Psychological Works of Sigmund Freud. 24 vols. James Strachey, Gen. Ed. London: Hogarth Press, 1953-1974; (hereafter SE) SE, 21: 59-145.

-----. "Female Sexuality", SE, 21: 223-243.

-----. "Femininity", SE, 22: 12-35.

Friedan, Betty. *The Feminine Mystique*. N.Y.: Bell, 1963.

Gallop, Jane. *The Daughter's Seduction: Feminism and Psychoanalysis*. Ithaca: Cornell Univ. Press, 1982.

----- and Carolyn Burke. "Psychoanalysis and Feminism in France", in Eisenstein and Jardine. Eds. *The Future of Difference*, 106-121.

Gardiner, Judith Kegan. "Self-Psychology as Feminist Theory", *Signs*, 12/4 (Summer 1987), 760-779.

Gearhart, Sally Miller. *The Wanderground: Stories of the Hill Women*. Watertown, MA: Persephone Press, 1979; and London: The Women's Press, 1986.

-----. "An End to Technology: A Modest Proposal". in Rothschild, Ed. *Machina ex Dea*, 171-182.

Gilbert, Sandra M. "What Do Feminist Critics Want?: A Postcard from the Volcano", in Showalter, Ed. *The New Feminist Criticisms*, 29-45.

----- and Susan Gubar. *The Mad Woman in the Attic: The Woman Writer and the Nineteenth Century Literary Imagination.* New Haven: Yale Univ. Press, 1979.

Gilligan, Carol. *In a Different Voice: Psychological Theory and Women's Development.* Cambridge: Harvard Univ. Press, 1982.

Gilman, Charlotte Perkins. *Herland.* N.Y.: Pantheon Books, 1979.

Gom, Leona M. "Laurence and the Use of Memory", *Canadian Literature*, 71 (1976), 48-58.

Gornick, Vivian and B.K. Moran, Eds. *Women in Sexist Society: Studies in Power and Powerlessness.* N.Y.: Mentor, 1971.

Grabher, Gudrun and Maureen Devine, Eds. *Women in Search of Literary Space.* Tübingen: Gunter Narr Verlag, 1991.

Greene, Gayle and C. Kahn, Eds. *Making a Difference: Feminist Literary Criticism.* London: Methuen, 1985.

Greimas, A.J. and J. Courtés. *Semiotics and Language: an Analytical Dictionary.* trs. Larry Crist, *et al.*, Bloomington: Indiana UP, 1982.

Griffin, Susan. *Woman and Nature: The Roaring Inside Her.* San Francisco: Harper & Row, 1978.

Gubar, Susan. "'The Blank Page' and the Issues of Female Creativity", *Critical Inquiry*, 8/2 (Winter 1981), 243-263.

-----. "Sapphristries", *Signs*, 10/1 (1984), 43-62.

Hales, Leslie Ann. "Spiritual Longing in Laurence's Manawaka Women", *English Studies in Canada*, 11/1 (March, 1985), 82-90.

Hall, Nor. *The Moon and the Virgin: Reflections on the Archetypal Feminine*. London: The Women's Press, 1980.

Halliday. M.A.K. *Language as a Social Semiotic: The Social Interpretation of Language and Meaning*. London: Edward Arnold, 1978.

Harris, Daniel A. "Androgyny: The Sexist Myth in Disguise", *Women's Studies*, 2 (1974), 171-184.

Harris, Trudier. "On *Color Purple*, Stereotypes and Silence", *Black American Literature Forum*, 18/4 (Winter 1984), 151-161.

Heilbrun, Alfred B., Jr. *Human Sex-Role Behavior*. N.Y.: Pergamon Press, 1981.

Heilbrun, Carolyn. "Androgyny and the Psychology of Sex Difference". in Eisenstein and Jardine, Eds. *The Future of Difference*, 258-266.

-----. *Reinventing Womanhood*. N.Y : W. W. Norton, 1979.

-----. *Toward a Recognition of Androgyny*. N.Y.: Alfred A. Knopf, 1973.

----- and Margaret R. Higgonet, Eds. *The Representation of Women in Literature*. Baltimore, MD: The Johns Hopkins Univ. Press, 1983.

Heller, Arno. "Literarischer Öko-feminismus: Margaret Atwood's *Surfacing*", *Arbeiten aus Anglistik und Amerikanistik*, (AAA) 9/1 (1984), 39-50.

-----, Walter Hölbling, and Waldemar Zacharasiewicz. *Utopian Thought in America: Untersuchungen zur literarischen Utopie und Dystopie in den USA*. Tübingen: Gunter Narr, 1988.

Henley, Nancy M. "This New Species That Seeks a New Language: On Sexism in Language and Language Change", in Penfield, Ed. *Women and Language in Transition*, 3-27.

Hernandi, Paul, Ed. *What is Criticism?* Bloomington: Indiana Univ. Press, 1981.

Homans, Margaret. "'Her Very Own Howl': The Ambiguities of Representation in Recent Women's Fiction", *Signs*, 9/2 (1983), 186-205.

Huth, Hans. *Nature and the American*. Berkeley: Univ. of California Press, 1957.

Irigaray, Luce. "And the One Doesn't Stir Without the Other", trs. Hélène Vivienne Wenzel, *Signs*, 7/1 (1981), 60-67.

-----. *Ce sexe qui n'en est past un*. Paris: Minuit, 1977.

-----. *The Sex Which Is Not One*. trs. Catherine Porter and Carolyn Burke. Ithaca: Cornell Univ. Press, 1985.

-----. *Speculum of the Other Woman*. trs. Gillian C. Gill, Ithaca, NY: Cornell Univ. Press, 1985.

-----. "When Our Lips Speak Together", trs. Carolyn Burke, *Signs*, 6/1 (1980), 69-79.

Jacobus, Mary. "A Difference of View", in Jacobus. Ed. *Women's Writing and Writing About Women*, 10-21.

-----. Ed. *Women's Writing and Writing About Women*. London: Jacobs Croom Helm, 1979.

Jameson, F. *The Political Unconcious: Narrative as a Socially Symbolic Act*. Ithaca: Cornell UP, 1981.

Janeway, Elisabeth. *Man's World, Woman's Place: A Study in Social Mythology*. NY: Dell, 1971.

-----. "Who Is Sylvia?: On the Loss of Sexual Paradigms", *Signs*, 5/4 (1980), 573-89.

Jardine, Alice. *Gynesis: Configurations of Women and Modernity*. Ithaca, NY: Cornell Univ. Press, 1985.

-----. "Opaque Texts and Transparent Contexts: The Political Difference of Julia Kristeva". in Miller, Ed. *The Poetics of Gender*, 96-115.

----- and Paul Smith, Eds. *Men in Feminism*. N.Y., London: Methuen, 1987.

Jehlen, Myra. "Archimedes and the Paradox of Feminist Criticism", *Signs*, 6/4 (1981), 575-601.

-----. *American Incarnation*. Cambridge, MA: Harvard Univ. Press, 1986.

Johnston, Eleanor. "The Quest of *The Diviners*", *Mosaic*, 11/3 (1976), 107-117.

Jung, C.G. *Archetypes and the Collective Unconscious*. Princeton, NJ: Bollingen Press, 1969.

-----. *The Development of Personality*. trs. R.F.C. Hull. N.Y.: Pantheon Books, 1954.

Kaplan, Sydney Janet. "Literary Criticism". *Signs*, 4/3 (1979), 514-527.

Kerber, Linda K. and Jane de Hart Mathews. *Women's America: Refocusing the Past*. N.Y.: Oxford Univ. Press, 1982.

Kermode, Frank. *The Sense of an Ending: Studies in the Theory of Fiction*. London: Oxford Univ. Press, 1967.

King, Ynestra. "The Eco-feminist Imperative", in Caldecott and Leland, Eds. *Reclaim the Earth: Women Speak Out for Life on Earth*, 6-14.

-----. "Toward an Ecological Feminism" in Rothschild, Ed. *Machina ex Dea*, 118-129.

Kolodny, Annette. "Dancing Through the Minefield: Some Observations on the Theory, Practice and Politics of a Feminist Literary Criticism," *Feminist Studies*, 6 (1980); rpt. in Showalter, Ed. *The New Feminist Criticism*, 144-167.

-----. "A Map for Rereading: Gender and the Interpretation of Literary Texts", in Showalter, Ed. *The New Femininst Criticism*, 46-62.

-----. *The Lay of the Land: Metaphor as Experience and History in American Life and Letters*. Chapel Hill: Univ of N. Carolina Press, 1975.

-----. *The Land Before Her: Fantasy and Experience of the American Frontiers, 1630-1860*. Chapel Hill: Univ. of N. Carolina Press, 1984.

-----. "Some Notes on Defining a 'Feminist Literary Criticism'", in Brown and Olson, Eds. *Feminist Criticism*, 37-58.

Kress, G. and R. Hodge. *Language as Ideology*. London, Boston: Routledge & Kegan Paul, 1979.

Kristeva, Julia. *About Chinese Women*. trs. Anita Barrows. N.Y.: Marion Boyars, 1977.

-----. *Desire in Language: A Semiotic Approach to Literature and Art*. trs. Léon Roudiez, Alice Jardine, and Thomas Gora. N.Y.: Columbia Univ. Press, 1982.

-----. "From Symbol to Sign", in Moi, Ed. *The Kristeva Reader*, 62-73.

-----. "The System and the Speaking Subject", in Moi, Ed. *The Kristeva Reader*, 24-33.

-----. "A New Type of Intellectual: The Dissident", in Moi, Ed. *The Kristeva Reader*, 292-300.

-----. "Women's Time", trs. Alice Jardine and Henry Blake, *Signs*, 7/1 (1981), 13-35; rpt. in Moi, Ed. *The Kristeva Reader*, 187-213.

-----."Word, Dialogue and Novel", in Moi, Ed. *The Kristeva Reader*, 34-61.

Krupnik, Mark, Ed. *Displacement: Derrida and After*. Bloomington: Indiana Univ. Press, 1983.

Kuna, Franz and Heinz Tschachler, Eds. *Dialog der Texte: Literatur und Landeskunde*. Tübingen: Gunter Narr, 1986.

Lakoff, Robin. *Language and Women's Place*. N.Y.: Harper & Row, 1974.

Laurence, Margaret. *The Diviners*. Toronto: Bantam Books, 1974.

Leiss, William. *The Domination of Nature*. Boston: Beacon, 1974.

Lenz, Elinor and Barbara Meyerhoff. *The Feminization of America*. Los Angeles: Jeremy P. Tarcher, 1985.

Lorber, Judith, Rose Laub Coser, Alice S. Rossi, and Nancy Chodorow. "On *The Reproduction of Mothering*: A Methodological Debate", *Signs*, 6/3 (1981), 482-514.

Marder, Herbert. *Feminism and Art: A Study of Virginia Woolf*. Chicago: Univ. of Chicago Press, 1968.

Marks, Elaine. "Women and Literature in France." Review Essay, *Signs*, 3/4 (1978), 832-842.

-----. and Isabelle de Courtivron, eds. *New French Feminisms: An Anthology*. Brighton, UK: Harvester Press, 1981.

Marx, Leo. *The Machine in the Garden: Technology and the Pastoral Ideal in America*. N.Y.: Oxford Univ. Press, 1964.

McCall, Dorothy Kaufmann. "Simone de Beauvoir, *The Second Sex*, and Jean Paul Sartre", *Signs*, 5/2 (1979), 209-223.

McConnell-Ginet, Sally. "Difference and Language: A Linguist's Perspective". in Eisenstein and Jardine, Eds. *The Future of Difference*, 156-165.

Merchant, Carolyn. *The Death of Nature: Women, Ecology, and the Scientific Revolution.* San Francisco: Harper & Row, 1980.

Miles, Rosalind. *The Fiction of Sex: Themes and Function of Sex Difference in the Modern Novel.* London: Vision Press, 1974.

Miller, Nancy K. "Arachnologies: The Woman, the Text and the Critic", in Miller, Ed. *The Poetics of Gender*, 270-289.

-----. "Emphasis Added: Plots and Plausibilities in Women's Fiction", *PMLA*, 96 (1981), 36-49.

-----, Ed. *The Poetics of Gender.* N.Y.: Columbia Univ. Press, 1986.

-----. "Writing (from) the Feminine: George Sand and the Novel of Female Pastoral". in Heilbrun and Higgonet, Eds. *The Representation of Women in Literature*, 124-151.

Millett, Kate. *Sexual Politics.* N.Y.: Avon, 1969.

Mitchell, Juliet. *Psychoanalysis and Feminism.* Harmondsworth: Penguin, 1974.

Moers, Ellen. *Literary Women.* London: The Women's Press, 1978.

Moi, Toril, Ed. *The Kristeva Reader.* N.Y.: Columbia Univ. Press, 1986.

-----. *Sexual/Textual Politics: Feminist Literary Theory.* London: Methuen, 1985.

Morgan, Ellen. "Humanbecoming: Form & Focus in the Neo-Feminist Novel", in Cornillon, Ed. *Images of Women in Fiction*, 183-205.

Nadeau, Robert. *Readings from the New Book on Nature: Physics and Metaphysics in the Modern Novel*. Amherst: Univ. of Massachusetts Press, 1981.

Nash, Roderick. *Wilderness and the American Mind*, 3rd ed. New Haven: Yale Univ. Press, 1982.

Naylor, Gloria. *The Women of Brewster Place*. N.Y.: Viking Press, 1982; Hammondsworth: Penguin, 1982.

Norwood, Vera L. "The Nature of Knowing: Rachel Carson and the American Environment", *Signs*, 12/4 (1987), 740-760.

Nye, Andrea. "Women Clothed With the Sun: Julia Kristeva and the Escape from/to Language" , *Signs*, 12/4 (1987), 664-686.

Olsen, Tillie. *Silences*. N.Y.: Delacourt, 1978.

Ortner, Sherry B. "Is Female to Male as Nature is to Culture?" in Rosaldo and Lamphere, Eds. *Woman, Culture, and Society*, 67-87.

Penfield, Joyce, Ed. *Women and Language in Transition*. Albany: State Univ. of New York Press, 1987.

Piercy, Marge. *Woman on the Edge of Time*. London: The Women's Press, 1976.

Pratt, Annis. *Archetypal Patterns in Women's Fiction*. Bloomington: Indiana Univ. Press, 1981.

-----. "The New Feminist Criticism", in Brown and Olsen, Eds. *Feminist Criticism*, 11-20.

-----. "The New Feminist Criticisms: Exploring the History of the New Space". in Roberts, Ed. *Beyond Intellectual Sexism: A New Woman, A New Reality*, 175-187.

-----. "Women and Nature in Modern Fiction", *Contemporary Literature* 13/4 (Fall 1972), 476-490.

Pratt, Linda Ray. "The Abuse of Eve by the New World Adam". in Cornillon, Ed. *Images of Women in Fiction*, 155-171.

Reed, Evelyn. *Woman's Evolution: From Matriarchal Clan to Patriarchal Family*. N.Y.: Pathfinder, 1975.

Reuther, Rosemary. *New Woman/New Earth: Sexist Ideologies & Human Liberation*. N.Y.: Seabury Press, 1975.

Rey, Jean-Michel. "Freud's Writing on Writing". *Yale French Studies*, 55/56 (1977), 301-328.

Rich, Adrienne. "Compulsory Heterosexuality and Lesbian Existence", *Signs*, 5/4 (1980); rpt. in Abel and Abel, Eds. *The Signs Reader*, 139-168.

-----. *Of Woman Born: Motherhood as Experience and Institution*. N.Y.: W. W. Norton, 1977.

-----. *On Lies, Secrets and Silence*. N.Y.: Norton, 1979.

Ricou, Laurence R. "Empty as Nightmare: Man and Landscape in Recent Canadian Fiction". *Mosaic*, 6/2 (1973), 145-154.

-----. *Vertical Man/Horizontal World: Man and Landscape in Canadian Prairie Fiction*. Vancouver: Univ. of British Columbia Press, 1973.

Rigney, Barbara H. *Madness and Sexual Politics in the Feminist Novel*. Madison: Univ. of Wisconsin Press, 1978.

Riley, Dick. Ed. *Critical Encounters: Writers and Themes in Science Fiction*. N.Y.: Ungar, 1972.

Roberts, Joan I. Ed. *Beyond Intellectual Sexism: A New Woman, A New Reality*. N.Y.: David McKay, 1976.

Robinson, Marilynne. *Housekeeping.* Toronto: Bantam Books, 1980.

Robinson, Sally. "The 'Anti-logos Weapon': Multiplicity in Women's Texts", *Contemporary Literature*, 29/1 (1988), 105-124.

Rockwell, Joan. *Fact in Fiction: The Use of Literature in the Systematic Study of Society.* London: Routledge & Kegan Paul, 1974.

Roller, Judi M. *The Politics of the Feminist Novel.* N.Y.: Greenwood Press, 1986.

Rosaldo, Michelle, Z. "The Use and Abuse of Anthropology: Reflections on Feminism and Cross-cultural Understanding", *Signs*, 5/3 (1980), 389-417.

-----."Woman, Culture and Society: A Theoretical Overview", in Rosaldo and Lamphere, Eds. *Woman, Culture and Society*, 17-42.

----- and Louise Lamphere, Eds. *Woman, Culture, and Society.* Stanford: Stanford Univ. Press, 1974.

Rosenzweig, Paul Jonathan. *The Wilderness in American Fiction: A Psychoanalytical Study of a Central American Myth.* Ann Arbor: Univ. of Michigan Press, 1972.

Ross, Catherine Sheldrick. "Female Rites of Passages in *Klee Wyck, Surfacing,* and *The Diviners*", *Atlantis*, 4 (1978), 87-94.

Ross, Gary. "The Divided Self", *Canadian Literature*, 71 (1976), 39-47.

Rothschild, Joan, Ed. *Machina ex Dea: Feminist Perspectives on Technology.* N.Y.: Pergamon Press, 1983.

Rubenstein, Roberta. "*Surfacing*: Margaret Atwood's Journey to the Interior", *Modern Fiction Studies*, 22 (1979), 387-399.

Ruthven, K.K. *Feminist Literary Studies: An Introduction.* Cambridge, UK: Cambridge Univ. Press, 1984.

Saftien, Volker. *Möglichkeiten des Naturlebens im zeitgenössische amerikanischen Roman.* Göppingen: Verlag Alfred Kümmerle, 1973.

Sargent, Lydia. Ed. *Women and Revolution: The Unhappy Marriage of Marxism and Feminism.* Boston: South End Press, 1981.

Scholes, Robert. *Fabulation and Metafiction.* Urbana: Univ. of Illinois Press, 1979.

-----. *Semiotics and Interpretation.* New Haven: Yale Univ. Press, 1982.

-----. *Structuralism in Literature.* New Haven: Yale Univ. Press, 1974.

Schultz, Elisabeth A. "The Insistence Upon Community in the Contemporary Afro-American Novel", *College English,* 41/2 (October, 1979), 170-184.

Schweickart, Patricino. "What If ... Science and Technology in Feminist Utopias" in Rothschild, Ed. *Machina ex Dea,* 198-212.

Shaktini, Namascar. "Displacing the Phallic Subject: Wittig's Lesbian Writing", *Signs,* 8/1 (1982), 29-44.

Showalter, Elaine. "Feminist Criticism in the Wilderness", *Critical Inquiry,* 8/2 (Winter 1981), 179-205.

-----. *A Literature of Their Own: British Women Novelists from Brontë to Lessing.* London: Virago, 1982.

-----, Ed. *The New Feminist Criticism: Essays on Women, Literature and Theory.* N.Y.: Pantheon Books, 1985; London: Virago, 1986.

-----. "Piecing and Writing", in Miller, Ed. *The Poetics of Gender,* 222-245.

-----. "Towards a Feminist Poetics", in Showalter, Ed. *The New Feminist Criticism,* 125-143.

Singer, Jane. *Androgyny: Toward a New Theory of Sexuality*. London: Routledge & Kegan Paul, 1978.

Slotkin, Richard. *Regeneration Through Violence: The Mythology of the American Frontier, 1600-1860*. Middletown, CT: Wesleyan Univ. Press, 1973.

Spacks, Patricia Meyer. *The Female Imagination*. N.Y.: Alfred A. Knopf, 1975.

Spender, Dale. *Man-Made Language*. London: Routledge & Kegan Paul, 1983.

----, Ed. *Feminist Theorists: Three Centuries of Women's Intellectual Tradition*. London: The Women's Press, 1983.

Spivak, Gayatri Chakravorty. "Displacement and the Discourse of Woman". in Krupnik, Ed. *Displacement*, 169-195.

-----. "Translator's Preface". in Derrida, *Of Grammatology*, ix-lxxxvii.

Stanton, Domna. "Difference on Trial: A Critique of the Maternal Metaphor in Cixous, Irigaray, and Kristeva". in Miller, Ed. *The Poetics of Gender*, 157-179.

-----. "Language and Revolution: The Franco-American Dis-Connection". in Eisenstein and Jardine, Eds. *The Future of Difference*, 73-87.

Starhawk. *Dreaming the Dark: Magic, Sex & Politics*. Boston: Beacon, 1982.

Stubbs, Michael. *Discourse Analysis: The Sociolinguistic Analysis of Natural Language*. London: Basil Blackwell, 1983.

Sullivan, Rosemary. *"Surfacing* and *Deliverance"*. *Canadian Literature*, 67 (1976), 6-20.

Thomas, Clara. "The Wild Garden and the Manawaka World", *Modern Fiction Studies*, 22 (1979), 401-411.

Thomson, Clive. "Mikhail Bakhtin and Contemporary Anglo-American Feminist Theory", *Critical Studies: A Journal of Critical Theory, Literature & Culture*, 1/2 (1989), 141-161.

Todd, Janet. Ed. *Gender and Literary Voice.* N.Y.: Holmes & Meier, 1980.

Toth, Emily. *Regionalism and the Female Imagination: A Collection of Essays.* N.Y.: Human Sciences Press, 1985.

Trilling, Diana. "The Liberated Heroine", *Partisan Review*, 45 (1978), 519-528.

Tronto, Joan C. "Beyond Gender Difference to a Theory of Care", *Signs*, 12/4 (1987), 664-663.

Truchlar, Leo, Ed. *Für eine offene Literaturwissenschaft: Erkundungen und Erprobungen am Beispiel US-amerikanischer Texte.* Salzburg: Verlag Wolfgang Neugebauer, 1986.

Trudgill, P. *Sociolinguistics: An Introduction.* Harmondsworth: Penguin, 1974.

Van Dijk, T.A. *Text and Context: Explorations in the Semantics and Pragmatics of Discourse.* London: Longman, 1980.

Walker, Alice. *The Color Purple.* N.Y.: Washington Square Press, 1982.

-----. "In Search of Our Mothers' Gardens". in Webber and Grumman, Eds. *Woman as Writer*, 193-201.

Washbourn, Penelope. *Becoming Woman: The Quest for Wholeness in Female Experience.* N.Y.: Harper and Row, 1977.

Watt, Ian. *The Rise of the Novel.* Berkeley: Univ. of California Press, 1959.

Webber, Jeanette L. and Joan Grumman. *Woman as Writer.* Boston: Houghton Mifflin, 1978.

Willis, Barbara. "Black Women Writers: Taking a Critical Perspective". Greene and Kahn, Eds. *Making a Difference,* 211-238.

Wittig, Monique. "The Mark of Gender". in Miller, Ed. *The Poetics of Gender,* 64-73.

Woolf, Virginia. *A Room of One's Own.* London: Granada, 1977.

Worster, Donald. *Nature's Economy: The Roots of Ecology.* San Francisco: Sierra Club Books, 1977.

Zima, Peter V. *Ideologie und Theorie: Eine Diskurskritik.* Tübingen: Francke, 1989.

-----, Ed. *Textsemiotik als Ideologiekritik.* Frankfurt/M.: Suhrkamp, 1977.

Zimmerman, Bonnie. "What Has Never Been: An Overview of Lesbian Feminist Literary Criticism", *Feminist Studies,* 7/3 (1981); rpt. in Showalter, Ed. *The New Feminist Criticisms,* 200-224.

About the Author

MAUREEN DEVINE (B.S., University of Texas; M.A., Utah State University; Ph.D., University of Klagenfurt) is a lecturer in the Department of English and American Studies at the University of Klagenfurt, where her primary responsibilities are in twentieth century American literature, American women's literature and feminist theory, and in the culture studies program. She has taught at Ohio University in its summer program in American culture, is active in both the Austrian and German Associations of American Studies and has been a board member of the Austrian association. She participated in the research group on feminist documentaries in the research project, "The American Documentary Film in Research and Teaching in American Studies Programs in Germany" at the University of Tübingen, 1988-91. An active member of the group "Feminist Academics" at the University of Klagenfurt, she has published several articles in professional journals and books, serves as head of the publishing board of *Script*, the feminist literary journal of the Alpine-Adriatic region, and co-edited a book on American feminist writing, *Women in Search of Literary Space* (Gunter Narr, 1991).